Backpacking Virginia

JOHNNY MOLLOY

Backpacking Virginia

The Definitive Guide to 40 Can't-Miss Trips from Cumberland Gap to the Atlantic Ocean

THE UNIVERSITY OF
NORTH CAROLINA PRESS
CHAPEL HILL

A Southern Gateways Guide

Designed by Heidi Perov
Set in Caecilia and Gotham by Rebecca Evans
Manufactured in the United States of America

The University of North Carolina Press has been a member of the Green Press Initiative since 2003.

Cover photo: Backpacking on the Appalachian Trail in Southwest Virginia, by Joel Carillet. iStock photo 498921256

Unless otherwise noted, all photos are by the author

Library of Congress Cataloging-in-Publication Data
Names: Molloy, Johnny, 1961– author.
Title: Backpacking Virginia : the definitive guide to 40 can't-miss trips from Cumberland Gap to the Atlantic Ocean / by Johnny Molloy.
Other titles: Southern gateways guide.
Description: Chapel Hill : University of North Carolina Press, [2019] | Series: A Southern gateways guide | Includes index.
Identifiers: LCCN 2018046929 | ISBN 9781469651583 (pbk : alk. paper) | ISBN 9781469651590 (ebook)
Subjects: LCSH: Backpacking—Virginia—Guidebooks. | Trails—Virginia—Guidebooks. | Virginia—Guidebooks. | LCGFT: Guidebooks.
Classification: LCC GV199.42.V8 M658 2019 | DDC 796.5109755—dc23 LC record available at https://lccn.loc.gov/2018046929

Thanks to all the trail blazers, trail maintainers, backpacking clubs, and all the folks who keep the pathways coursing through the Old Dominion, so backpackers like us can enjoy them.

Backpack Summary Chart

	Backpack	Distance (miles)	Difficulty
	Coastal Virginia		
1	Prince William Forest	2.2	Easy
2	Caledon State Park	5.6	Easy
3	Belle Isle State Park	3.8	Easy
4	False Cape State Park	11.8–17.6	Moderate to difficult
	Northern Virginia and Shenandoah National Park		
5	Sky Meadows State Park	5.9	Moderate
6	Big Schloss	26.6	Difficult
7	Elizabeth Furnace	21.7	Difficult
8	Duncan Knob	13.6	Moderate
9	Jeremys Run	14.0	Moderate
10	Thornton River	13.0	Moderate
11	Hazel Mountain	16.8	Moderate
12	Hughes River	14.3	Moderate to difficult
13	Rapidan River	18.6	Difficult
14	Bearfence Mountain	12.0	Moderate to difficult
15	Big Run	14.5	Moderate to difficult
16	Blackrock	20.7	Difficult
17	Moormans River	18.3	Moderate to difficult
18	Laurel Fork Backcountry	14.0	Moderate
19	Shenandoah Mountain	40.5	Difficult
20	Ramseys Draft Wilderness	21.4	Moderate to difficult

Highlights
Designated campsites, convenience, Chopawamsic Creek
Big trees, riverside camping, beach
Brewer's Point campsite, wildlife
Barrier island camping, Atlantic Ocean, Back Bay
Overlooks, Appalachian Trail, developed backcountry campsites
Big Schloss view, White Rock view, streams, Sugar Knob Cabin
Signal Knob views, Little Passage Creek gorge, Elizabeth Furnace
Views from Strickler Knob and Duncan Knob, multiple campsites
Pools of Jeremys Run, solitude on Neighbor Mountain
Piney River Falls, pioneer history, streams
Hazel Falls and Cave, views, streamside camps
Cascades along Hughes River, Corbin Cabin
Waterfalls, Rapidan Camp, views
Bearfence Mountain views, wildflowers along Conway River
Pools of Big Run
Views aplenty, solitude in places, ample camping opportunities
Big Branch Falls, pools on North Fork Moormans River
Beaver ponds, spruce woods, Laurel Fork
North River gorge, overlooks, Ramseys Draft Wilderness, North River headwaters
Ramseys Draft, views aplenty

Backpack Summary Chart (cont.)

	Backpack	Distance (*miles*)	Difficulty
	Heart of Virginia		
21	Saint Marys Wilderness	10.6	Moderate
22	Torry Ridge Loop	19.4	Difficult
23	Three Ridges Wilderness	13.1	Difficult
24	Mount Pleasant National Scenic Area	12.1	Moderate
25	Lake Moomaw	6.2	Moderate
26	Hoop Hole	13.9	Moderate to difficult
27	James River Face Wilderness	26.8	Difficult
28	Apple Orchard Falls Loop	7.1	Moderate
29	Roanoke Triple Crown Circuit	35.1	Difficult
30	Mountain Lake Wilderness	9.0–11.0	Moderate
31	Locust Knob	8.9	Moderate
32	Rock Castle Gorge Circuit	10.7	Difficult
	Southwest Virginia		
33	Garden Mountain Wilderness	33.5	Difficult
34	Little Dry Run Wilderness	19.4	Difficult
35	Mount Rogers High Country Circuit	26.2	Difficult
36	Rowland Creek Falls Loop	12.6	Moderate
37	Virginia Creeper Loop	13.8	Moderate
38	Chief Benge Scout Trail	19.1	Moderate
39	Pine Mountain Trail	16.7	Moderate to difficult
40	Cumberland Gap National Historical Park	20.0	Moderate

Highlights
Saint Marys Falls, other falls, historic ore-processing remains
White Rock Falls, views, Sherando Lake Recreation Area
Wilderness, views, waterfalls, abundance of campsites
Views galore, shorter loop possibilities
Lake views, lakeside camping
Falls and geology on Hipes Branch and Stony Run
Wilderness, views, James River hiker bridge, Devils Marbleyard
Apple Orchard Falls, views, Cornelius Creek Cascades
Views from McAfee Knob, Tinker Cliffs, and Dragons Tooth
High country, multiple views, spruce
Rhododendron thickets, solitude
Rock formations, panoramas, deep gorge, settler history
Views, wildernesses, waterside and mountaintop campsites
Little Dry Run Wilderness
Views galore, spruce-fir forests, good campsites, wild ponies
Rowland Creek Falls, solitude, wildflowers
Historic rail trail, stream, trail shelter, partial views
High Knob Tower, Falls of Little Stony
Eagle Arch, High Rock, Mars Rock, rock shelters, trail shelters
Views, preserved mountain community, giant rockhouse

Contents

Heart of Virginia

Southwest Virginia

Sidebars

Backpacking Virginia

Introduction

Looking for great places to go backpacking? The state of Virginia is blessed with plentiful tracts of wild lands, places where new and experienced backpackers can find large parcels of terrain laced with trails and places to trek for days. These backpacking destinations present crashing waterfalls, dramatic overlooks, and historic highlights—and alluring campsites to pitch your tent in the backcountry, where you can relax before a calming campfire and escape from electronic chains that bind us to the daily grind.

A Virginia backpacking adventure can lead to destinations high and low, from the Atlantic shores of False Cape State Park to the historic highlands of Cumberland Gap National Park, and a wealth of land between. Virginia's unforgettable backpacking destinations lead through federally designated wildernesses and scenic areas and along the Appalachian Trail.

The Old Dominion is a backpacker's paradise, as evidenced by 500 miles of the Appalachian Trail running through it, more than any other state. The George Washington and Jefferson National Forests, plus Shenandoah National Park, preserve millions of acres containing thousands of miles of trails presenting a multitude of overnighting opportunities.

So where to start backpacking in Virginia? That is where this book comes into play. It contains 40 specific backpacking adventures covering 650 miles of trails, every mile of which I hiked. My backpacking resume also includes having backpacked over 2,500 nights in more than 40 states throughout the United States, with a significant number of those nights backpacked in Virginia. That experience, combined with writing over 70 outdoor-related guidebooks on backpacking, hiking, camping, and paddling, hopefully will give you confidence in this book, a guide to help you make the most of your time backpacking in Virginia.

My own journey started years ago with a first backpacking trip in Great Smoky Mountains National Park, an adventure that ultimately launched me into a career as an outdoor writer. As the backpacking trips continued, I learned the backcountry can teach you fantastic life lessons: persistence in the face of obstacles, patience when you have miles and miles to go, and acceptance of your circumstances when they are less than ideal. So can it be with you, whether you are new to backpacking or a veteran of the great outdoors.

To see vistas, waterfalls, and wildlife—to backpack Virginia—and be able share them with you has brought me to the realization that purchasers of *Backpacking Virginia* are banking their money and their free time that Johnny Molloy knows what he is talking about. This is serious business and I take it seriously!

One of the joys of my occupation is sharing my love of the outdoors with you. I want y'all to see, smell, hear, and feel what lies out there, in the back of beyond, while backpacking Virginia. As electronics further infiltrate every aspect of our lives, we are losing our connection with nature. Backpacking provides a means to get outside, to explore, to stimulate our mental, physical, and spiritual selves in the great outdoors.

You can hit the trail with friends and family, discover and share the natural wonders of Virginia. While backpacking Virginia you can soak in horizon-to-horizon vistas from rock outcrops, wander among massive old-growth trees, visit rumbling waterfalls, traipse through wildflower-filled hollows, trek amid regal pine woods, or wander beside wild coastlines and along brawling rivers.

This book includes different types of backpacks in varied settings with varying layers of difficulty. Most backpacking adventures detailed are two-night trips typical for the weekend backpacker, yet additional backpacks range from 2-mile, one-night family treks to multiday, 40-plus-mile adventures.

The backpacks feature not only fine trails and campsites but also scenic sights—waterfalls such as Apple Orchard Cascades and overlooks like McAfee Knob and waters like Lake Moomaw. Well-known "must do" destinations such as Three Ridges Wilderness and Mount Rogers High Country are included, but undiscovered gems like the Laurel Fork Backcountry, Caledon State Park, and Chief Benge Scout Trail increase your Virginia backpacking possibilities.

This book delivers "must know" information for Virginia backpackers: how to get to the trailhead, how far the backpack is, hike difficulty, when to go, what you are going to see along the way, and where you are within reason at any given moment of the hike. Each hike includes all of the above, along with an easy-to-scan map, a trail mileage chart, and a photo to help you build a mental picture of the area.

I hope this guide will inspire you to create your own adventures and make memories that will leave you and your loved ones wanting more, and to want to share the great outdoors with others. The reason I travel and explore the outdoors is simple: The world is a beautiful place! Life is for living. Do everything now. Don't wait. Go now. Backpacking in Virginia can be so exciting—you never know what is going to happen next, what is around the bend in the river, what is over the next ridge, or what the weather will bring. Backpacking Virginia will bring a wealth of adventures and memories to last a lifetime.

BACKPACKING IN VIRGINIA

When looking at a map of Virginia, aspiring Old Dominion backpackers will be struck by several things. First, the state extends from the highlands of the Appalachians easterly through the rolling Piedmont and onward to the coastal plain all the way to the Atlantic Ocean. This varied terrain ranges from 5,729 feet all the way down to sea level. *Backpacking Virginia* includes backpacking trips traveling through the highest and lowest points in the state. Thus, backpackers can adventure in the elevation extremes in the Old Dominion and in elevations between. These varied elevations harbor distinct ecosystems containing different flora and fauna, augmenting your outdoor experience.

Virginia's varied landscape is located on a wealth of public lands where you can enjoy backpacking—national parks, national forests, and national recreation areas, as well as state parks. Virginia features two major national parks that offer first-rate backpacking: Cumberland Gap National Historical Park and venerable Shenandoah National Park.

However, the majority of Virginia's public lands—and the majority of its backpacking destinations—lie within the George Washington and Jefferson National Forests. These two national forests manage 1,664,110 acres within Virginia, with over 2,200 miles of trails within their bounds. Twenty-three federally designated wildernesses lie within national forest boundaries, as do more than 2,300 miles of streams, over 40 species of trees, over 60 species of animals, and over 50 endangered plant species.

The diversity of terrain, habitat, and trails is reflected in the backpacking adventures you can undertake here in Virginia. From west to east, you can walk the Ridge Trail at Cumberland Gap and march through history, from the time of Daniel Boone to the Civil War to the early 1900s at the Hensley Settlement. Next, you find the Pine Mountain Trail, straddling the Virginia–Kentucky border next to the famed Breaks Interstate Park. The Chief Benge Scout Trail navigates a remote slice of southwest Virginia past overlooks, ponds, and streams where impressive waterfalls roar.

And then you reach Virginia's rooftop, Mount Rogers National Recreation Area. Hike the Mount Rogers High Country Circuit, where spruce-fir forests give way to highland meadows where wild ponies roam. At lower elevations, you can also trek along the Virginia Creeper Trail and through remote Little Dry Run Wilderness.

Backpackers will have plenty of opportunities to hike the Appalachian Trail (AT) in Virginia. Some circuit backpack trips use the AT to help to form loops, while one end-to-end backpacking adventure exclusively uses the segment of the AT where it wanders through the view-laden meadows of Chestnut Knob and then traverses two wilderness areas near Burkes Garden.

Most of the AT hikes are parts of loops, such as the Roanoke Triple Crown Circuit, where you can see the Tinker Cliffs, McAfee Knob, and the Dragons Tooth, all in one backpack. And don't forget the view-laden circuit at Mount Pleasant National Scenic Area or Three Ridges Wilderness. Speaking of wildernesses, a number of backpacks take place in these special, untamed areas, including Ramseys Draft Wilderness, Mountain Lake Wilderness and Saint Marys Wilderness.

Yet other Virginia icons are included among the backpacks here, including Massanutten Mountain and Lake Moomaw. Along the Massanutten Mountain Trail you can grab a view from an overlook used during the Civil War as well as traverse a rugged gorge and visit and historic iron-forging operation. At mountain-rimmed Lake Moomaw you can wind among steep-sided hollows to end up at a lakeside campsite with an inspiring view.

Several backpacks in this guide take place in Shenandoah National Park, stretching for 100 miles along the Blue Ridge. Traverse the rocky ridges and big wild streams of the southern part of the park. Hike through historic hollows and visit some of the park's high country in the central area. The northern part of the park contains Jeremys Run, one of the most scenic streams in the Old Dominion.

Yet there are places to backpack beyond the Blue Ridge. Destinations such as Prince William Forest Park near Washington, D.C., Caledon State Park, and Belle Isle State Park provide shorter but accessible backcountry experiences for residents of the eastern part of the state. And finally you have False Cape State Park, a maritime spit of land fronting the Atlantic Ocean on one side and a marshy bay on the other. This salty backcountry experience tops off the mosaic of backpacking opportunities in the Old Dominion.

Weather

Virginia experiences all four seasons in their entirety, and given the state's elevations—from over 5,700 feet to sea level—the Old Dominion might be experiencing them all simultaneously! Summer can be warm, with occasional downright hot spells in the eastern lowlands. The mountains will be cooler. Morning hikers can avoid heat and the common afternoon thunderstorms. A smartphone equipped with internet access allows hikers to monitor storms as they arise, but don't count on service in mountain hollows and remote national forest areas.

Hikers are drawn outdoors in increasing numbers when the first northerly fronts of fall sweep cool, clear air across the Old Dominion. Crisp mornings, great for vigorous backpacks, give way to warm afternoons, more conducive to relaxing around the campsite. Fall is drier than summer. Winter will bring frigid, subfreezing days, chilling rains, and snows, especially in the mountains. There are also fewer hours of daylight. However, a brisk hiking pace and smart time management will keep you warm and walking while the sun is still above the horizon. Each cold month has a few days of mild weather. Make the most of them.

Spring will be more variable. A warm day can be followed by a cold one. Extensive spring rains bring regrowth but also keep hikers indoors. But any avid backpacker will find more good hiking days than they will have time to hike in spring and every other season. A good way to plan your backpack is to check monthly averages of high and low temperatures and average rainfall for each month in Lynchburg, roughly in the center of the state. Elevation and specific location will lead to different exact temperatures. Below is a table showing each month's averages for Lynchburg. This will give you an estimate of what to expect each month.

Average Temperature and Precipitation by Month (Lynchburg, VA)

Month	Average High (°F)	Average Low (°F)	Precipitation (in.)
January	45	25	3.1
February	49	27	3.0
March	58	34	3.6
April	68	43	3.3
May	75	51	3.7
June	83	60	3.6
July	87	64	4.4
August	85	63	3.3
September	78	56	3.9
October	69	44	3.1
November	59	35	3.4
December	48	27	3.2

How to Use This Guidebook

This guidebook covers backpacking adventures throughout Virginia. The backpacks are divided into four primary regions: Coastal Virginia, Northern Virginia and Shenandoah National Park, Heart of Virginia, and Southwest Virginia. The following is a sample of what you find in the description of each Virginia backpack:

23 • THREE RIDGES WILDERNESS

The Backpack: *Enjoy this scenic, untamed—and popular—loop, combining the Appalachian Trail (AT) and the Mau Tar Trail. First, climb from the Blue Ridge Parkway along Meadow Mountain, then reach the Maupin Field area, with camping possibilities including a trail shelter. Begin the loop portion of the hike, ascending Bee Mountain. Pass numerous overlooks before making Harpers Creek and another trail shelter. After leaving the AT, reach the geologically rich gorge of Campbell Creek, with two waterfalls and a swimming hole in a rugged canyon. Close the loop by returning to Maupin Field area. A final backtrack leads you back to the trailhead.*

The description begins with a short overview of the backpack, to give you a flavor of the adventure. Each backpack also contains an information box. From the information box, we can see that the trip is a 13.1-mile balloon loop trek, and it is difficult, mainly due to changes in elevation and the trail being rocky. You can expect to spend 7.5 or so hours actually toting your pack. Along the way you will enjoy wilderness, views, and waterfalls, and there is an abundance of campsites from which to choose. Elevations along the trek will range from 1,760 feet to 3,960 feet, giving you an idea of elevation changes as well as climatological considerations due to elevation.

The scenery is a 5 on a scale of 1 to 5, with 5 being the best. So expect a beautiful trip. Solitude is a 1, so you should expect company along the hike. The family friendly scale is a 3, meaning it is somewhere in the middle as to being a family backpacking destination. The canine friendly rating is a 2, since the trail is rocky and other backpackers are likely to be encountered. No fees or permits are required to undertake

23 THREE RIDGES WILDERNESS

Distance & configuration: 13.1-mile balloon loop

Difficulty: Difficult due to elevation changes and rocky trail

Backpacking time: 7.5 hours

Outstanding features: Wilderness, views, waterfalls, abundance of campsites

Elevation: 1,760′ low point, 3,960′ high point

Scenery: 5

Solitude: 1

Family friendly: 3

Canine friendly: 2

Fees/permits: No fees or permits required

Best season: Weekdays any time of year

Maps: National Geographic #789 Lexington/Blue Ridge Mountains

For more info: George Washington National Forest, Glenwood-Pedlar Ranger District, 27 Ranger Lane, Natural Bridge Station, VA 24579, 540-291-2188, www.fs.fed.us/

Finding the trailhead: From exit 96 on I-64 near Waynesboro, take Mount Torry Road, VA 624, north for 1.5 miles, then keep left, south at Lyndhurst, where Mount Torry Road changes to VA 664. Stay with VA 664 for 11.3 miles to emerge onto the Blue Ridge Parkway at Reeds Gap. The trailhead parking area is on the east side of the Blue Ridge Parkway. **GPS trailhead coordinates:** N37° 54.085′, W78° 59.123′

this hike. Some backpacks do require a camping fee, such as those at Virginia state parks. Best season tells you the prime times to enjoy the backpack. In this instance, the best time is weekdays throughout the year, as weekends regularly see traffic.

A high-quality map is included with each hike description in this guide and should suffice. However, I have recommended other published maps to augment the book map. Next, I provide trailhead directions along with GPS trailhead coordinates you can plug into your device to help you get there. "For more info" tells you the governing body of the area backpacked, as well as pertinent phone numbers and websites should you want to endeavor further research on your own.

Also included is a general discussion of the backpack, including must-know tips for the trek, not-to-be-missed highlights, and what to expect while out there—the feeling, the vibe. Each hike description ends with "Mileages," a quick reference table of mileages and milestones along the way.

Some backpacks include a sidebar. The sidebars, usually accompanied by a lesson learned on the trail, offer tips and advice to help you become a better and more complete backpacker. Each sidebar is paired with a particular trip because the trip likely has a scenario where the sidebar applies.

Backpacking Checklist

There is a reason why “hike your own hike” is a popular phrase in backpacking circles. Items needed for a backpacking trip that are dear to me may not seem so essential to you. A way to determine what you (and your group) need is to go down this list, assemble the items, then get out there and hit the trail. After each trip, assess your gear. Did you bring everything you needed? Did you carry unnecessary items? Next, adjust your gear list for the next trip, continuing to refine your list.

First, consider physical ability, trip desires, and expectations: What are the physical abilities of you and your party? What length and duration of trip do you want? What are the group expectations? Are y’all each carrying your own food/gear or sharing gear?

Now, go from your feet to your head in clothing, then check the needs of your shelter, bedroom, bathroom, bedroom, and kitchen. Think of other miscellaneous gear possibilities. The key is to take everything you need and no more.

Shoes
Hiking shoes/boots
Camp shoes/sandals

Clothes
Socks
Long pants
Short pants
T-shirt
Long-sleeve button-up shirt with collar
Vest
Jacket/poncho
Bandanna
Hat/toboggan
Extra clothes as needed or desired

Backpack

Shelter
Tent, tarp, or under the stars

Bedroom
Closed-cell sleeping pad
Ultralight air mattress
Sleeping bag
Pillow

Bathroom
Toothbrush/paste/floss
Toilet paper
Lotion
Biodegradable soap
Pack towel

Kitchen
Food: food, spices
Water purification: filter, tablets, or boil
Cookware: cup, spoon, knife, pot, potholder, frying pan, spatula
Cooking sources: stove or fire/grill

Other Stuff
Trekking poles
Maps
Compass
Lighter
Fire starter
Medical kit
Cord—enough to hang food to keep it from bears
Headlamp, lantern, solar-powered light
Other items to consider: bug dope, trash bag, GPS, weather radio, aspirin, book, radio, camera, cards, vitamins, watch, sunscreen, lip balm, extra batteries, sunglasses, small towel, binoculars, wildlife identification books

Just remember, backpacking Virginia is about the experience, not the stuff you carry. Be prepared, but prepare to enjoy your time interacting with nature. My personal rule of thumb is to absolutely carry no more than 15 percent of my body weight, and closer to 10 percent if I can get away with it. Use this rule of thumb for yourself, no matter your weight. It will work for you and kids, too.

Finally, carve out some free time, get out there, then make some memories backpacking Virginia.

Best Trips by Category

For Beginners

1 Prince William Forest
3 Belle Isle State Park
5 Sky Meadows State Park
25 Lake Moomaw

For Families

21 Saint Marys Wilderness
31 Locust Knob
32 Rock Castle Gorge Circuit
35 Mount Rogers High Country Circuit
37 Virginia Creeper Loop

For Water Lovers

2 Caledon State Park
4 False Cape State Park
10 Thornton River
36 Rowland Creek Falls Loop

For Anglers

9 Jeremys Run
10 Thornton River
15 Big Run
18 Laurel Fork Backcountry

For Waterfall Lovers

13 Rapidan River
17 Moormans River
22 Torry Ridge Loop
28 Apple Orchard Falls Loop

For Views

14 Bearfence Mountain
23 Three Ridges Wilderness
30 Mountain Lake Wilderness
39 Pine Mountain Trail
40 Cumberland Gap National Historical Park

For Solitude

8 Duncan Knob
12 Hughes River
20 Ramseys Draft Wilderness
34 Little Dry Run Wilderness
38 Chief Benge Scout Trail

In Winter

7 Elizabeth Furnace
24 Mount Pleasant National Scenic Area
26 Hoop Hole
33 Garden Mountain Wilderness

Best Long Backpacks

6 Big Schloss
16 Blackrock
19 Shenandoah Mountain
27 James River Face Wilderness
29 Roanoke Triple Crown Circuit

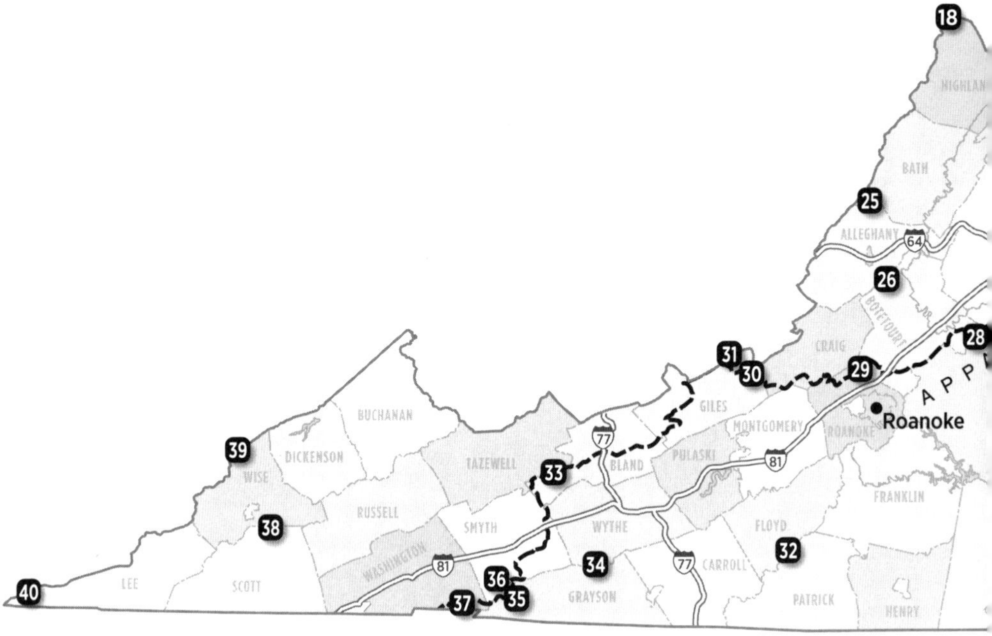

LOCATOR MAP

MAP KEY

1 Prince William Forest
2 Caledon State Park
3 Belle Isle State Park
4 False Cape State Park
5 Sky Meadows State Park
6 Big Schloss
7 Elizabeth Furnace
8 Duncan Knob
9 Jeremys Run
10 Thornton River
11 Hazel Mountain
12 Hughes River
13 Rapidan River
14 Bearfence Mountain
15 Big Run
16 Blackrock
17 Moormans River
18 Laurel Fork Backcountry
19 Shenandoah Mountain
20 Ramseys Draft Wilderness

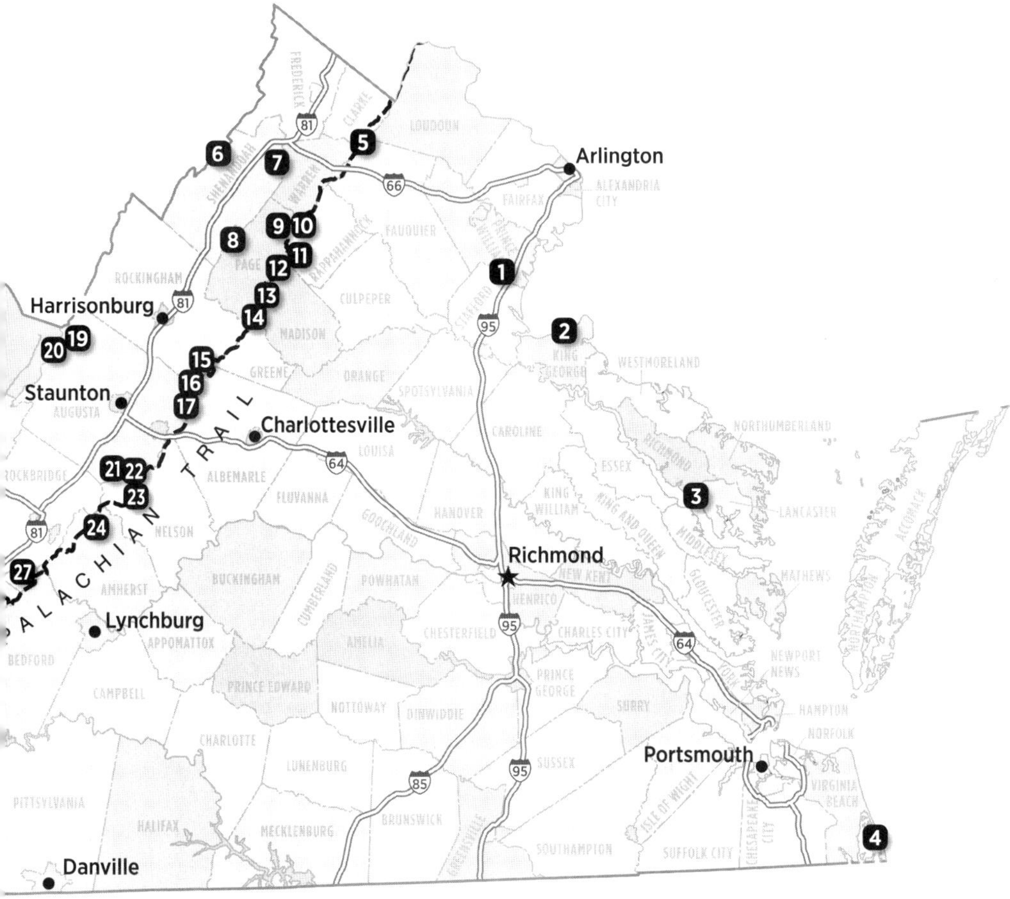

21 Saint Marys Wilderness
22 Torry Ridge Loop
23 Three Ridges Wilderness
24 Mount Pleasant National Scenic Area
25 Lake Moomaw
26 Hoop Hole
27 James River Face Wilderness
28 Apple Orchard Falls Loop
29 Roanoke Triple Crown Circuit
30 Mountain Lake Wilderness
31 Locust Knob
32 Rock Castle Gorge Circuit
33 Garden Mountain Wilderness
34 Little Dry Run Wilderness
35 Mount Rogers High Country Circuit
36 Rowland Creek Falls Loop
37 Virginia Creeper Loop
38 Chief Benge Scout Trail
39 Pine Mountain Trail
40 Cumberland Gap National Historical Park

Map Legend

- Directional arrows
- Interstates
- Major roads
- Minor roads
- Other roads
- National forests
- State lines
- Featured trails
- Alternate trails
- National trails
- Water bodies
- Intermittent lake
- Rivers/creeks
- Intermittent streams

- Appalachian Trail
- Boat launch
- Bridge
- Cabin
- Campsite
- Cemetery
- Dam
- Fee station
- Gate
- General point of interest
- Information
- Lookout tower
- Marsh area
- Overlook
- Parking area
- Picnic area
- Ranger station
- Rapids
- Scenic view
- Shelter
- Spring
- Trailhead
- Viewing platform
- Waterfall

Coastal Virginia

1 • PRINCE WILLIAM FOREST

The Backpack: *Located in the southern shadow of the D.C. metroplex, large Prince William Forest also includes a backcountry area with several designated campsites for those who want a quick overnight getaway. The sloping hills above Chopawamsic Creek on the southern edge of the park are the setting for this 2-mile loop along which the designated sites are stretched. Since the loop is short and the elevations are low, this is an ideal adventure for new backpackers as well as a good winter initiation trip.*

In the 1930s, with the United States deep into economic woes, President Franklin Delano Roosevelt instituted a taxpayer-sponsored work program known as the Civilian Conservation Corps (CCC). The program's goals were to reduce employment and teach job skills. Young men enrolled in the CCC were chosen to develop parks throughout the United States. Negligible farmland located on Quantico Creek and Chopawamsic Creek was purchased by the U.S. government to establish the Chopawamsic Recreational Demonstration Area. The CCC went to work, developing a "camp for low income, inner-city children and families to get away and experience the great outdoors."

Through the ensuing decades, metro D.C. has crept south, and now Prince William Forest Park has become an oasis of nature amid urban sprawl. Fortunately for us backpackers, the park has the Chopawamsic Backcountry, a slice of the preserve on Chopawamsic Creek, fast against the U.S. Marine Corps Reservation (more about that later).

The terrain is surprisingly hilly—expect some ups and downs as you seek out the eight backcountry campsites spread out along the 2-mile circuit, each located on a short spur trail of its own. The campsites have no amenities. A simple numbered post marks the site. You must reserve a specific spot when obtaining your backcountry permit, which can be a crapshoot if you've never been there. However, this guide details the sites, helping you choose the better ones. Since the hike is short, you can bring all your own water or get it from Chopawamsic Creek.

Expect to hear small-arms fire at any time of the day or night, since the Marine Corps is training just across Chopawamsic Creek. During my experiences here, I've only heard arms fire during the day. The park receives weekly updates on predicted small-arms fire times, so contact the park before your trip or when receiving your permit if you might find this bothersome.

1 PRINCE WILLIAM FOREST

Distance & configuration: 2.2-mile loop

Difficulty: Easy

Backpacking time: 1.5 hours

Outstanding features: Designated campsites, convenience, Chopawamsic Creek

Elevation: 145′ low point, 280′ high point

Scenery: 3

Solitude: 3

Family friendly: 5

Canine friendly: 5

Fees/permits: Backcountry camping permit required

Best season: Fall through spring; hot in summer

Maps: Chopawamsic Backcountry

For more info: Prince William Forest Park, 18100 Park Headquarters Road, Triangle, VA 22172, 703-221-7181, www.nps.gov/prwi

Finding the trailhead: From exit 150B on I-95, near Woodbridge, take VA 619, Joplin Road, west just a short distance and reach the entrance to Prince William Forest Park. Turn right onto the entrance road and follow it .4 mile to the park visitor center. You must get your backcountry permit there. After getting your permit and a key to the Chopawamsic Backcountry gate, backtrack to Joplin Road. Turn right, westbound on Joplin Road, and follow it 2.1 miles to turn left on Breckenridge Road, an easy-to-miss turn (at this left turn to Breckenridge Road, the right turn is Liming Road and an American Legion building stands at the corner). Follow Breckenridge Road south for .6 mile to the gated right turn to the Chopawamsic Backcountry parking. Open the gate, lock it behind you, and follow it to dead end at the trailhead. **GPS trailhead coordinates:** N38° 33.130′, W77° 23.544′

Leave the parking area southbound on a singletrack blazed trail in a mix of pine, oaks, and holly. Join the nose of a ridge and begin descending to reach the spur trail to Camp #1 at .3 mile. A spur leads right to the sloped, non-recommended spot. The main trail continues downhill, coming near Chopawamsic Creek after stepping over seasonal streams. At .6 mile, a spur leads steeply uphill to a level knob and Camp #2. The site is good and preferred when the mosquitoes are hopping along the creeks in summer.

Bridge a small creek at .7 mile, then reach the short spur to popular Camp #3 at .8 mile. The somewhat level, recommended camp is just above the flats of Chopawamsic Creek and provides access to the stream

1 Prince William Forest

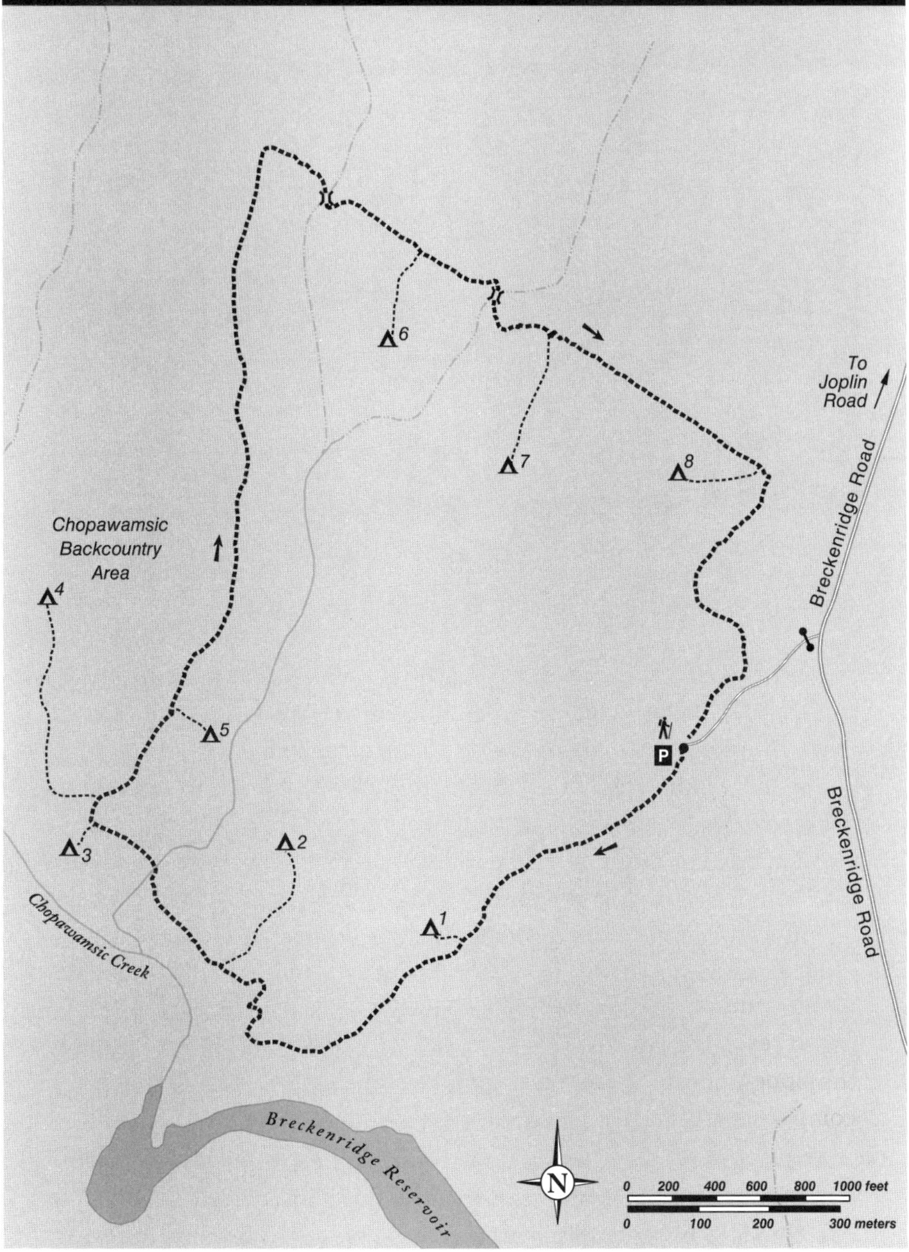

A backpacker treks the loop at Prince William Forest on an early spring day.

and nearby Breckenridge Reservoir. Just ahead, the long spur to Camp #4 leads uphill to a level spot, which is recommended.

The loop trail then climbs away from Chopawamsic Creek onto a ridge. Here, at .9 mile, is the short spur to Camp #5, a nice, level, recommended site. The main trail keeps along the ridge, enjoying a brief, level spell as it traces a long-abandoned, barely recognizable road. Then, at 1.4 miles, the path suddenly dives right into a steep hollow, crossing a small stream on a footbridge. A solid climb follows, reaching the spur to Camp #6 at 1.6 miles. The decent camp is located on a slight slope in pine-oak woods. Drop to a hollow and another hiker bridge, then climb to meet the spur to Camp #7 at 1.7 miles. The spur leads to a level, recommended site with good tent spots.

At 1.9 miles, reach the spur trail to Camp #8. It leads to a former homesite and roadbed, and the forest floor is a bit irregular. The main loop comes near the parking area access road, then reaches the parking area at 2.2 miles.

Practice Trail Etiquette

We often think of the great outdoors as a wild place, and it can be. However, even in the back of beyond, an expected amount of decorum should accompany backpackers. After all, we don't want to act like a bunch of heathens just because we are beyond the glare of an electric light.

Keep the following considerations in mind concerning proper behavior on the trail. Whether you're on a county, state, or national park trail, always remember that great care and resources have gone into creating these trails. Don't deface trail signs or trees. There's no need to let passersby know that you were here.

Hike on open trails only. Respect trail and road closures. There's usually a valid reason if a trail is closed—storm damage, mudslides, wildlife breeding area, etc. Obtain all permits and authorization as required. Leave only footprints. This means staying on the existing trail and not blazing any new trails. Mudholes can get wider and wider if walked around by everyone.

Have you ever reached an overlook only to find trash accompanying your view? Pack out what you pack in—and more. No one likes to see the trash someone else has left behind.

Never spook wildlife. An unannounced approach, a sudden movement, or a loud noise startles most animals. Surprised animals can be dangerous to you, to others, and to themselves. Give them plenty of space.

Honor leash laws. Many trails require keeping Fido on a 6-foot leash. Some pet owners believe leash laws don't apply to their pet. I cannot tell you how many times I have been jumped on by a dog with muddy feet while their owners were simultaneously yelling at the barking canine, creating a chaotic and unpleasant scene for everyone. Think of your fellow hikers before setting your dog free. Unleashed dogs will also chase wildlife and perhaps become lost.

Plan ahead. Know your equipment, your ability, and the area where you are hiking—then prepare accordingly. Be self-sufficient at all times; carry necessary supplies for changes in weather or other conditions. Most hiking accidents/rescues start with ill-prepared backpackers overestimating their abilities. They become tired or worried, then make poor decisions, turning a bad situation worse. In contrast, a well-executed trip is a satisfaction to you and to others.

Finally, be courteous to other hikers, bikers, and equestrians you encounter on the trails; this is especially important on multiuse trails such as the Virginia Creeper. Bikers should yield to hikers and equestrians. Hikers should yield to equestrians. If you encounter a horse, get well off the trail, be still, and talk in smooth tones.

A little etiquette at home—and on the trail—can go a long way to smooth out the rough patches in life.

Mileages

0.0 Leave Chopawamsic Backcountry parking on a singletrack path, southbound.
0.3 Right spur to Camp #1.
0.6 Right spur to Camp #2.
0.8 Left spur to Camp #3; left spur to Camp #4 just ahead.
0.9 Right spur to Camp #5.
1.4 Sharp right turn, descend.
1.6 Right spur to Camp #6.
1.7 Right spur to Camp #7.
1.9 Right spur to Camp #8.
2.2 Return to the trailhead, completing the backpack loop.

2 • CALEDON STATE PARK

The Backpack: *Hike to a camp on the banks of the Potomac River at a state park rich with natural beauty, including old-growth woods and wildflowers aplenty at this designated National Natural Landmark. The preserved former plantation is now home to winding trails underneath impressive trees that lead you to a designated waterside camp where a sandy beach enhances the environment and bald eagles majestically perch on shoreline treetops. This is a perfect trip for kids of all ages.*

Talk about a fun little trip! Caledon State Park is an underutilized Virginia backpacking getaway that rewards those who make their way to this designated National Natural Landmark noted for its old-growth oak and tulip trees. And the hiking here is a breeze to reach a designated backcountry campground, also accessed by paddlers. The camp is divided into 6 well-constructed sites just a little inland from a driftwood-covered beach on the Potomac River, near historic Stuart's Wharf. The state of Maryland lies across the waterway. Reservations are highly recommended and can be made by calling 800-933-7275.

Caledon Plantation was established in 1659 by John and Phillip Alexander, who also founded the city of Alexandria. Caledon Plantation passed down through the generations until it was donated to the state of Virginia in 1974. It was managed first as a state natural area, then became a full-fledged state park of 2,529 acres in 2012. The Smoot House at the park still stands, and you will see the brick structure at the trailhead. It is now the state park visitor center. Down near the backcountry

2 CALEDON STATE PARK

Distance & configuration: 5.6-mile there-and-back, loop possible

Difficulty: Easy

Backpacking time: 3 hours

Outstanding features: Big trees, riverside camping, beach

Elevation: 10′ low point, 160′ high point

Scenery: 4

Solitude: 3

Family friendly: 5

Canine friendly: 4

Fees/permits: Backcountry camping fee required

Best season: Fall through spring

Maps: Caledon State Park trail guide

For more info: Caledon State Park, 11617 Caledon Road, King George, VA 22485, 540-663-3861, 800-933-7275, www.dcr.virginia.gov/state-parks/

Finding the trailhead: From Fredericksburg, take VA 218 east for 23 miles. The state park will be on your left. Upon entering the park, head right for the visitor center and park there. **GPS trailhead coordinates:** N38° 20.030′, W77° 8.579′

campground, you can visit Stuart's Wharf, a former dock and loading area once used to ship locally grown tobacco.

However, many will argue that the bald eagles are the star of the show at Caledon State Park. The state park's shoreline is a no-motorized boat zone, enhancing opportunities for hikers and paddlers to see the majestic birds. I've seen eagles out here myself while strolling on the beach. Still other avian life can be observed, from osprey to herons.

Add to that the pleasure of walking through groves of big trees along the way on a series of doubletrack paths. The hike leaves the Smoot House/visitor center and follows the doubletrack Boyd's Hole Trail down a hill, then through the woods to turn right on the Hampstead Road Trail, also a gravel doubletrack. From here on out the hike is rolling and never steep or hard. While walking, look for the big trees never cut and other sizable oaks and tulip trees that have risen among once-tilled land.

Some of the biggest jack-in-the-pulpit wildflowers I have ever seen rise in flats in low marshy areas, where you'll find old ditches dug to drain the land for agriculture. These lowlands have now mostly become marsh, adding to the significance of the National Natural Landmark. You will also notice the trail travels directly along the park boundary;

2 Caledon State Park

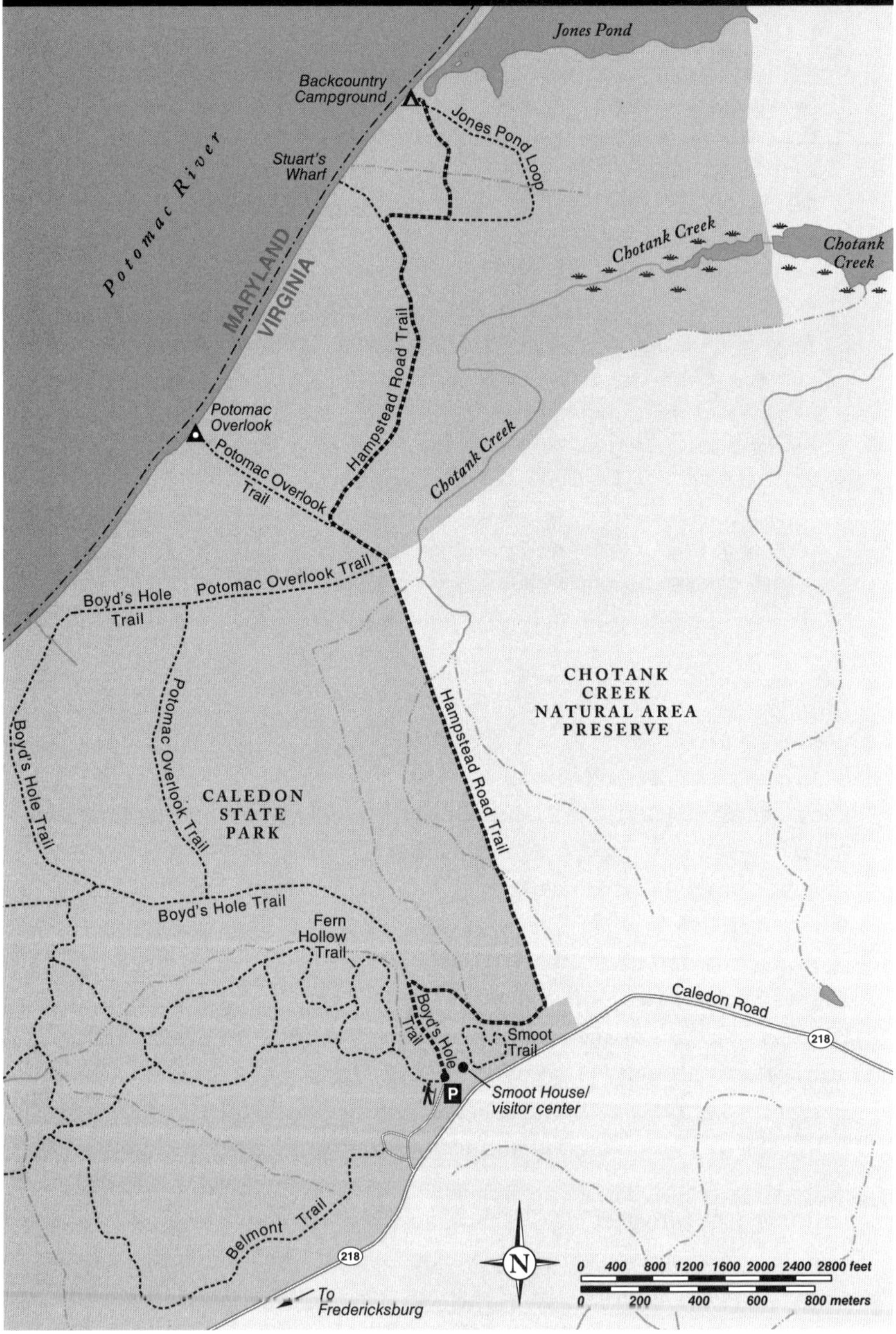

This part of the backpack takes a level course toward the Potomac River.

but worry not, for the land next door is part of the 1,100-acre Chotank Creek Natural Area Preserve, a privately owned tract that keeps the land in its native glory.

Ahead, you can detour to Potomac Overlook or save it for later. Make sure to head to Stuart's Wharf, then imagine the shipping of yesteryear along with the *Wawaset* disaster. In 1873 the steamboat *Wawaset* caught fire and landed near Stuart's Wharf. Half of the 100 passengers perished by either fire or water.

Finally, the hike reaches the hike-in/paddle-in campground. You will find the six campsites in a mix of sun and shade. Each has a tent pad, fire ring, picnic table and lantern post, perfect for families or newly initiated backpackers—or a respite for veteran backpackers. Note: You must bring your own drinking water. The camp has toilets. A covered gazebo provides a rainy-day refuge. The shore slopes down to the driftwood-littered beach. Take a walk or a swim in season.

In other areas, the shore is lined with bluffs. Make sure to call the park directly to reserve a site, then enjoy yourself here on the shores of the Potomac River at Caledon State Park. Finally, you can use the Potomac Overlook Trail and the Boyd's Hole Trail to make a loop on your way back to the trailhead.

Mileages

0.0 Leave the trailhead near the Smoot House visitor center. Keep straight, north, on the doubletrack Boyd's Hole Trail, passing through park maintenance area. The Smoot House is to your right.

0.2 Leave right on the doubletrack Hampstead Road Trail, amid rolling hills draped in oaks, sweetgum, and tulip trees.

0.4 Pass near but do not intersect the Smoot Trail, a series of garden paths.

0.6 Turn left, north, on a long straightaway lined with impressive trees. Chotank Creek Natural Area Preserve lines the right side of the trail.

1.5 The Potomac Overlook Trail enters from the left. Keep straight on Hampstead Road Trail/Potomac Overlook Trail.

1.7 The Potomac Overlook Trail keeps straight, but you stay right, still on the Hampstead Road Trail. Pass an area bordered on one side with growing-over fields. Ahead, look for old drainage ditches from the agricultural days.

2.4 Keep right, joining the Jones Pond Loop, as a short spur keeps straight for Stuart's Wharf.

2.5 Turn left as Jones Pond Loop splits. Dip to cross a pond dam.

2.8 Reach the backcountry campground. Numbered campsites are scattered to your left. Ahead, the land dips to a beach landing for self-propelled craft. Backtrack.

5.6 Return to the trailhead, completing the backpack. Consider an alternate return route if you want to see more of the park.

3 • BELLE ISLE STATE PARK

The Backpack: *An excellent beginner's trip, a family adventure, or just a way to overnight along a tidal portion of the Rappahannock River, Belle Isle State Park offers a backcountry camping experience sure to please everyone. User-friendly level trails lead backpackers along Porpoise Creek and a wildlife-viewing blind. Trek past marshes before heading out a peninsula to reach Brewer's Point and a waterside backcountry campsite replete with tent pads, picnic tables, and a fire ring. Additional park trails allow an alternate park return.*

Belle Isle State Park presents an opportunity to enjoy backcountry camping along a tidal river. Belle Isle, along with some other Virginia state parks, has established paddle-in and hike-in backcountry campsites. Ensconced on the Northern Neck, in far eastern Virginia, Belle Isle State Park is a menagerie of water and land, of fields and woods, of marshes and meadows. It is rich with hiking, paddling, and camping opportunities, one of which is backpacking to the Brewer's Point backcountry campsite, nestled amid pines, cedars, and hardwoods and set fast against

3 BELLE ISLE STATE PARK

Distance & configuration: 3.8-mile there-and-back

Difficulty: Easy

Backpacking time: 2 hours

Outstanding features: Brewer's Point campsite, wildlife

Elevation: 10′ low point, 24′ high point

Scenery: 4

Solitude: 2

Family friendly: 5

Canine friendly: 4

Fees/permits: Backcountry camping fee required

Best season: Fall through spring

Maps: Belle Isle State Park trail guide

For more info: Belle Isle State Park, 1632 Belle Isle Road, Lancaster, VA 22503, 804-462-5030, www.dcr.virginia.gov/state-parks/

Finding the trailhead: From the north side of Warsaw at the intersection of US 360 and VA 3, take VA 3 east for 14.5 miles, then turn right on River Road, VA 354 south. Follow it for 3 miles, then turn right on Belle Isle Road and follow it .7 mile to enter the state park. Stop and get your permit at the visitor center before embarking. **GPS trailhead coordinates:** N37° 46.422′, W76° 35.590′

3 Belle Isle State Park

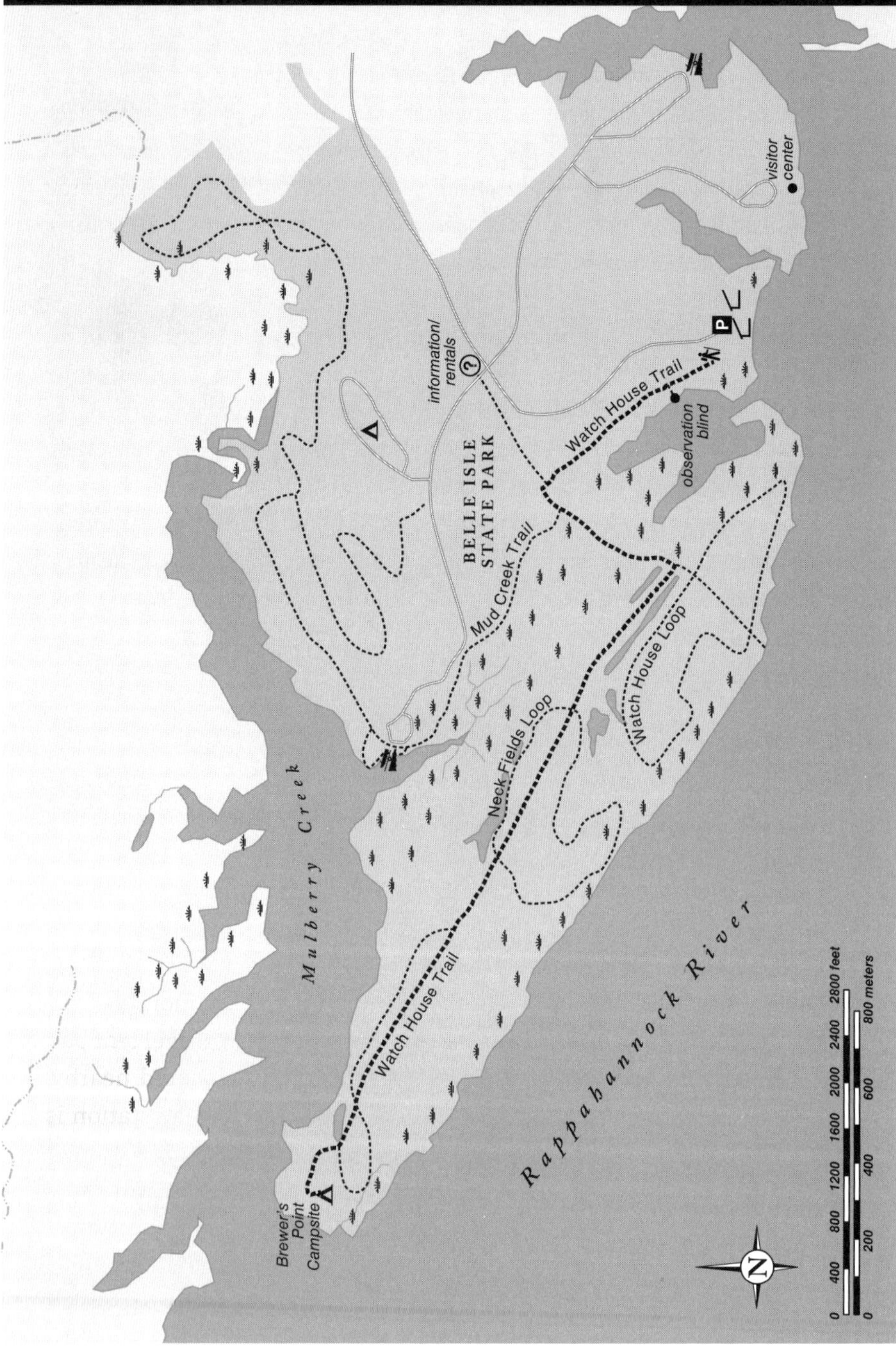

Arriving at the riverside backcountry campsite.

the confluence of Deep Creek and the Rappahannock River, both wide, tidal waterways. Call the park to reserve a site.

The hike from the trailhead to the campsite is just under 2 miles, making it doable by just about anyone, even very young or old backwoods backpacking aspirants. Furthermore, the Brewer's Point backcountry campsite can also be reached by canoe or kayak, in case you wanted someone to float a little extra gear or food from the park's canoe launch (by the way, canoes and kayaks can be rented overnight at the park). Brewer's Point is alluring. A small beach is located near the camp, which has four individual sites. The camp is centered by a common fire ring and picnic tables, along with fireside benches. A raised gravel tent pad is provided for each camping party. A vault toilet is located nearby. Drinking water is not provided—bring your own. A self-pay station is located at the Brewer's Point campsite. However, I'd just go to the ranger station or visitor center, register, and pay there. That way they'll know about your car being left there overnight. I suspect the pay station is primarily for boat-in campers launching from outside the park.

The trail system at Belle Isle State Park is comprehensively signed and meticulously maintained—you'd have to be blindfolded to get lost here—all the better for novice backpackers. Remember, even the most

Backpacking Philosophies Differ

Backpacking enthusiasts run the gamut in their philosophy and methodology. On one end are the professed backpacking purists. They generally have the best gear and are always on the lookout for the latest in high-tech offerings by the outdoor outfitting industry. And they are willing to pay for it.

Their fare often consists of costly freeze-dried food. Gore-Tex fabric and name-brand labels are prominently displayed on their clothing. Cards, reading, a radio, or any other diversionary pleasure not directly related to the mechanics of backpacking are disdained. Always prepared and ready to help the ill-prepared, they rarely get in over their heads, saving taxpayer dollars and ranger headaches from having to rescue them.

At the other end of the spectrum are the make-do backpackers. They probably borrowed half the equipment on their back and will not hesitate to tote a cast-iron skillet to fry some bacon at the campsite. They can be spotted on the trail invariably wearing too-tight jeans and combat boots. They would not be caught dead with a trail map in their hands.

At camp, make-do hikers try to think of ways to use that big knife in that leather case attached to their belt. An oversized cheap tent invariably pops up wherever they are. They are learning, and some will eventually move across and find their own place on the spectrum.

Two other subcategories exist: the minimalists and the gearheads. Minimalists become overly obsessed with weight, paring down their gear to such a degree that much enjoyment is lost from their wilderness experience, which has become a sheer survival test.

I once stayed with some women at a backcountry shelter who drank hot water for breakfast; they felt the weight of coffee did not justify its extravagance. Others become so concerned with pack weight that they will cut off the end of their toothbrush to save one-tenth of an ounce. However, when they tell about how much weight they save while around the campfire, they are in hog heaven!

The gearhead has it all, literally, and it is in his pack. Around the fire, you grumble about losing a tiny screw from your fishing reel; ten minutes later, he proudly returns with the exact size screw you needed. It is a good thing he has a hot water bottle because he is going to need it to soothe those back muscles that are cramping from carrying all that extra equipment on his back.

Pack weight has always been the source of spirited backpacker discussions. As a general guide, backpackers should carry no more than 15 percent of their body weight, always aiming for 10 percent. Nevertheless, wilderness adventuring has no commandments. Each person literally carries his or her own weight—and lives with his or her choices.

While out there, I relish the opportunities to see how others conduct business on the trails. With an open mind, I usually learn something, even if it is what not to do. To think my way is the only way merely restricts my growth as a backpacker.

So the next time you see somebody backpacking down the trail, they are not merely putting one foot in front of the other. There is likely a philosophy in there somewhere.

grizzled backpacking veteran was once a novice. The journey from novice to experienced backpacker is a rewarding one worth undertaking. The trek starts at a picnic shelter overlooking the Rappahannock River, a good spot to organize gear, pack, and have lunch before setting out—and to enjoy the views. You then join the Porpoise Creek Trail, traveling the margin between woods bordering Porpoise Creek—an inlet along the Rappahannock River—and sown fields that recall the time when what has become Belle Isle State Park was a working farm. Certain fields are still tilled to this day at the park, providing contrast to the maritime forests of cedar and oak. Don't miss the spur to the wildlife-viewing blind near the trail's beginning. Here you can look for the rich avian life for which the park is known—shorebirds such as blue herons, raptors such as osprey, and an assortment of songbirds from cardinals to mockingbirds.

Join the Watch House Trail and skirt between tree-bordered estuaries, delivering watery views toward island shores. It isn't long before you turn and pick up the Neck Fields Trail. Here, hikers border a mix of fields and woods, heading northwest along a peninsula, culminating at Brewer's Point and a small beach bordered by a grassy area. Boating campers using the campsites use this small beach. A short path leads into pines and oaks. Here the campsite stands. A central fire ring is bordered by four campsites, each with a picnic table and tent pad. The sites are a tad close together but are in good shape. A vault toilet serves the camp. Remember: bring your own water. On your return hike, consider taking some of the trails that spur off the Neck Fields Trail.

Mileages

- 0.0 Join Porpoise Creek Trail near picnic shelters on Rappahannock River.
- 0.2 Pass wildlife blind to left overlooking Porpoise Creek.
- 0.4 Left on Watch House Trail.
- 0.7 Right on Neck Fields Trail, easy doubletrack path.
- 0.9 Pass first of two intersections with Neck Fields Loop Trail.
- 1.2 Pass second intersection with Neck Fields Loop Trail.
- 1.3 Pass first intersection with Brewer's Trail.
- 1.7 Pass second and third intersections with Brewer's Trail.
- 1.9 Reach Brewer's Point and grassy area, backcountry campsite just to left.
- 3.8 Return to the trailhead, completing the backpack.

4 • FALSE CAPE STATE PARK

The Backpack: *Make a memorable trip to Virginia's most unusual backcountry overnighting possibility at False Cape State Park, located along the Atlantic Ocean. Backpackers can walk along the Atlantic shoreline or take interior trails through Back Bay National Wildlife Refuge to the state park, passing along open waters and under live oaks and pines. There, twelve campsites grouped in four areas offer you chances to pitch your tent along the bay side or the Atlantic side of the peninsula. Note: This adventure takes a lot of planning, including reserving sites and making overnight parking arrangements. Invest the time to plan for a successful backpack.*

A backpacking trip at False Cape State Park can be one of the most rewarding overnight camping experiences in the state of Virginia. Here, you can pitch your tent in maritime woods with either the Atlantic Ocean or Back Bay within a short distance. In fact, the four campsite areas are often accessed by paddlers as well as backpackers. However,

4 FALSE CAPE STATE PARK

Distance & configuration: 11.8- to 17.6-mile there-and-back, depending on site

Difficulty: Moderate to difficult depending on route and distance

Backpacking time: 6–9 hours

Outstanding features: Barrier island camping, Atlantic Ocean, Back Bay

Elevation: sea level low point, 20′ high point

Scenery: 5

Solitude: 3

Family friendly: 4

Canine friendly: 1

Fees/permits: Backcountry camping fee required, parking fee required, refuge entrance fee required

Best season: Spring through fall

Maps: False Cape State Park trail guide

For more info: False Cape State Park, 4001 Sandpiper Road, Virginia Beach, VA 23456, 757-426-7128, www.dcr.virginia.gov/state-parks/

Finding the trailhead: From the intersection of Sandbridge Road and Sandpiper Road in the community of Sandbridge, take Sandpiper Road for 4 miles to turn left into Little Island City Park. This is where you leave your vehicle overnight. **GPS trailhead coordinates:** N36° 41.610′, W75° 55.496′

4 False Cape State Park

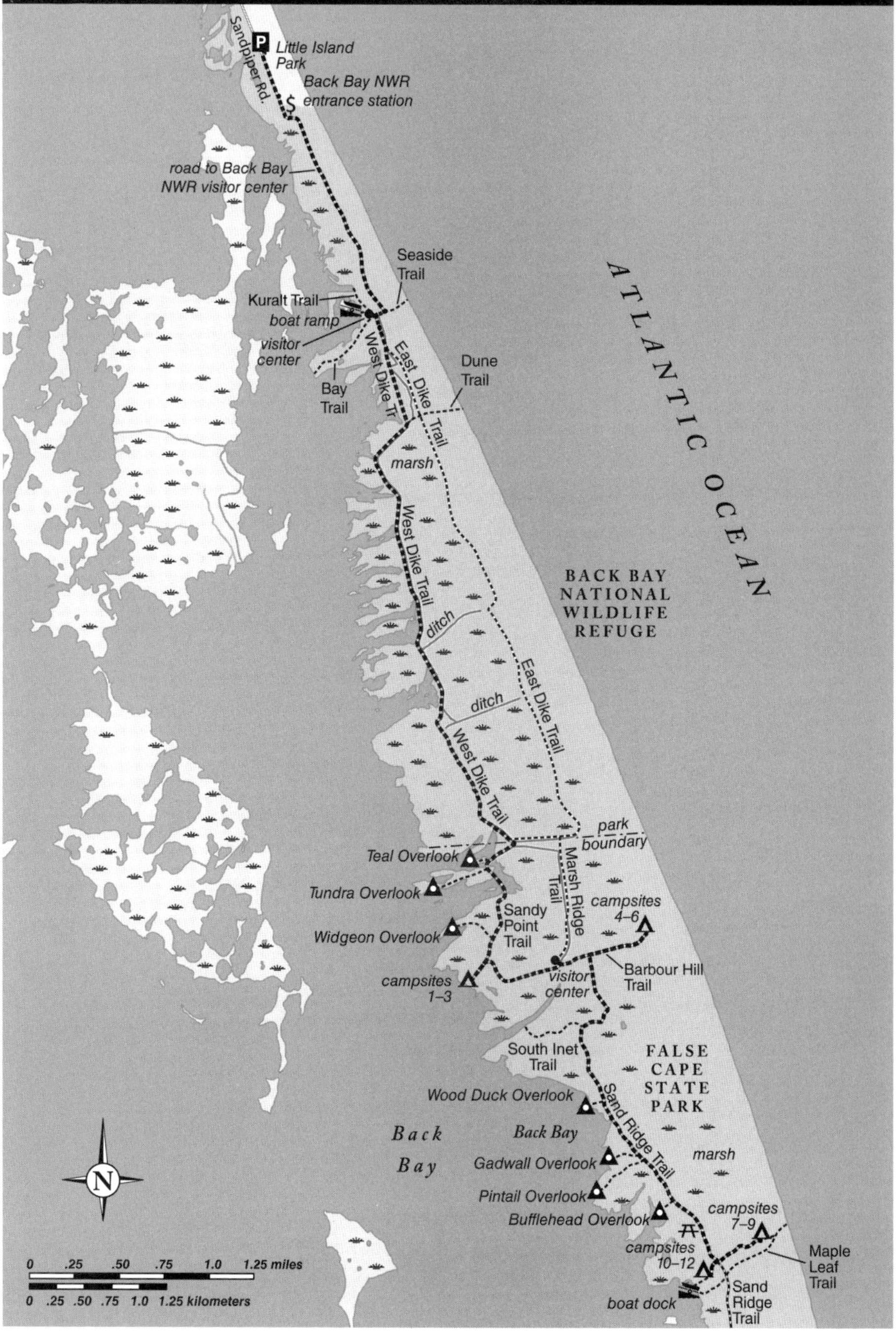

The Atlantic Ocean and the dunes astride it are what make backpacking at False Cape special.

whether you are backpacking or paddling to the campsites, preparation and planning are necessary.

The first order of business is to reserve your campsites for the dates you specify through reserveamerica.com. Then you arrange your overnight parking at Little Island City Park through either False Cape State Park or the city of Virginia Beach parks department, depending on the season. During holidays or the off-season, a False Cape State Park ranger may meet you at Little Island City Park to assist with your permit. And after all that, you will need to pay a fee to pass through Back Bay National Wildlife Refuge, which can be done in person.

Sounds like a hassle, huh? It is, but you will find backpacking at False Cape State Park worth the effort. After leaving Little Island City Park, you must first decide whether to walk the beach to False Cape or take the doubletrack trails through Back Bay refuge. I recommend taking the trails if possible on the way out and returning by the beach if you desire. (From November 1 through March 31 the trails through Back Bay National

Wildlife Refuge are closed, necessitating backpackers to access False Cape State Park by walking the beach only. The refuge trails are open the rest of the year. False Cape State Park trails are open year-round).

Make arrangements for your overnight parking at Little Island City Park. Parking is never available at Back Bay National Wildlife Refuge for overnight guests. Therefore, if hiking the interior trails, you start with a little road walk from Little Island City Park through the upper refuge to reach the refuge visitor center, with information and additional trails, plus a boat dock.

Then you strike forth, southbound on either the West Dike Trail or the East Dike Trail. The West Dike Trail is generally open in the spring, and the East Dike Trail in the fall, for wildlife management purposes. Both paths traverse atop exposed dikes with expansive views of open waters, marshes, and a few deeply wooded sections of live oak and pine. The variety of environments enhances the hike.

Backpackers join the Sandy Point Trail upon entering False Cape State Park, where the pathways are generally more wooded. It isn't long before you reach the first cluster of campsites—numbers 1–3. These camps are set just inland of Back Bay, amid tall pines and widespread live oaks. These sites, like all of the sites at False Cape State Park, have a tent pad, picnic table, and lantern post. No fire ring—campfires are not allowed at False Cape State Park. A pair of outhouses and drinking water are nearby, as is a small beach overlooking Back Bay (treat all water here).

The hike then leads you to the visitor center, where restrooms, souvenirs, and information are available. The next cluster of campsites, 4–6, is accessed by the nearby Barbour Hill Trail. Situated at the edge of the dunes facing the Atlantic Ocean, you can hear the crash of the sea from them. They are beneath wind-sculpted live oaks bordered by wooded dunes. A water spigot, small covered shelter, and outhouses are nearby. The Barbour Hill Trail continues beyond the camps to access the unspoiled beaches of the Atlantic Ocean.

The other two campsite clusters are farther down False Cape, accessed via the beautiful Sand Ridge Trail, cloaked in maritime woods. Spur trails lead to overlooks of Back Bay along the way. Then you reach the spacious third cluster of campsites 10–12. These are situated on the edge of a field near Tripps Cove. The large sites are partly sunny and partly shady and have an additional covered shelter, gazebo, and outhouses. An old-fashioned pump well delivers untreated water. The spur trail continues beyond the camp to a boat dock on Tripps Cove.

The final campsite cluster, 7–9, is not far away, at False Cape Landing, on the edge of a dune line—big dunes. The three sites are bordered by wooded sand hills as the roar of the ocean echoes in the distance. These are fine camps and also have a covered shelter, outhouses, and a pump well. An undulating path takes you through the dunes to a sand shoreline and the crashing Atlantic.

Those four campsite clusters constitute your overnighting options, but day-hiking trail possibilities extend farther south to the North Carolina state line. The Sand Ridge Trail leads to historic sites such as a cemetery of former False Cape residents, the Wash Woods Church site, and the 1894 wreck of the *Clythia*.

A little advice: if you are going through the motions of backpacking here, make it at least two nights, in order to absorb this special swath of the Old Dominion and allow yourself time to explore. Consider staying at a couple of different campsites. Relax on the beach or find a favorite overlook of Back Bay. On your return trip, the beach route along the Atlantic Ocean is shorter—about 7 miles one way to Little Island City Park—but can be complicated by sun, wind, and wet/dry sand. However, it may be an experience you will not forget.

Mileages

0.0 Leave Little Island City Park after securing your overnight parking permit. Head south down extension of Sandpiper Road.

0.4 Pass Back Bay National Wildlife Refuge entrance station. Use self-pay station if not manned. Walk down the refuge road.

1.6 Road turns right as Seaside Trail comes in. The refuge visitor center is just ahead. Pass the visitor center, then join the refuge trail system on a doubletrack trail southbound.

1.9 The doubletrack splits. Stay right with the West Dike Trail.

2.4 Keep right on the West Dike Trail as the extension of the Dune Trail comes in on your left.

4.9 Intersect East Dike Trail at right turn to enter False Cape State Park. Enter False Cape State Park, joining the doubletrack Sandy Point Trail.

5.1 Pass spur trail to Teal Overlook, then the Tundra Overlook.

5.6 Pass spur to Widgeon Overlook and ranger residence.

5.7 Right turn leads .2 mile to campsite cluster 1–3. Sandy Point Trail keeps south, then turns west.

6.1 Reach park visitor center and the Marsh Ridge Trail. Keep straight on the Sandy Point Trail.

6.3 Join the Sand Ridge Trail, turning right. Campsites 4–6 are dead ahead .3 mile on the Barbour Hill Trail.

6.8 South Inlet Trail leaves right from Sand Ridge Trail.

7.2 Trail leaves live oaks for open bayside marsh, then soon re-enters woods after passing spur to Wood Duck Overlook.

7.6 Pass spur to Gadwall Overlook, then Pintail Overlook.

7.9 Pass spur to Bufflehead Overlook.

8.1 Shaded picnic tables on right.

8.5 Spur leads right to campsites 10–12 bordering open field. Other spur leaves left .2 mile to campsites 7–9 toward False Cape Landing. Sand Ridge Trail continues south to additional day-use trails.

17.0 Return to Little Island City Park after backtracking on trails.

Northern Virginia and Shenandoah National Park

5 • SKY MEADOWS STATE PARK

The Backpack: *Sky Meadows State Park, perched on the east side of the Blue Ridge, provides a surprisingly scenic and fun backpack, good for families or those who want to rough it in a little more organized fashion. Take a mix of historic and wooded trails through an old farm, garnering multiple views from grassy slopes before entering woods to meet the Appalachian Trail (AT). Join the famed footpath, then split off to reach a designated backcountry camping area along Gap Run, nicely developed with tent pads, picnic tables, and restrooms. The next day's loop return is easy. Stay an extra day to explore other trails or the park's other highlights.*

Sky Meadows State Park presents an opportunity for backpackers to enjoy the improved organizational aspects of a state park—superlatively marked trails, specific campsites, and backpacker parking—with the beauty of the Blue Ridge. The nearly 2,000-acre preserve, carved out of a scenic and historic farm, and one of the most northerly backpacking opportunities in the Old Dominion, has an extensive trail network linking to the AT. These paths traverse a blend of woods and meadows and

5 SKY MEADOWS STATE PARK

Distance & configuration: 5.9-mile balloon loop

Difficulty: Moderate

Backpacking time: 3.5 hours

Outstanding features: Overlooks, Appalachian Trail, developed backcountry campsites

Elevation: 702′ low point, 1,800′ high point

Scenery: 5

Solitude: 2

Family friendly: 4

Canine friendly: 3

Fees/permits: Backcountry camping fee required

Best season: Fall through spring

Maps: Sky Meadows State Park trail guide

For more info: Sky Meadows State Park, 11012 Edmonds Lane, Delaplane, VA 20144, 540-592-3556, www.dcr.virginia.gov/state-parks/

Finding the trailhead: From exit 23 on I-66 near Delaplane, take US 17 north for 6.3 miles, then turn left on Edmonds Lane. Follow it for .5 mile to reach the park entrance station and the overnight parking area to your right. **GPS trailhead coordinates:** N38° 59.171′, W77° 57.582′

5 Sky Meadows State Park

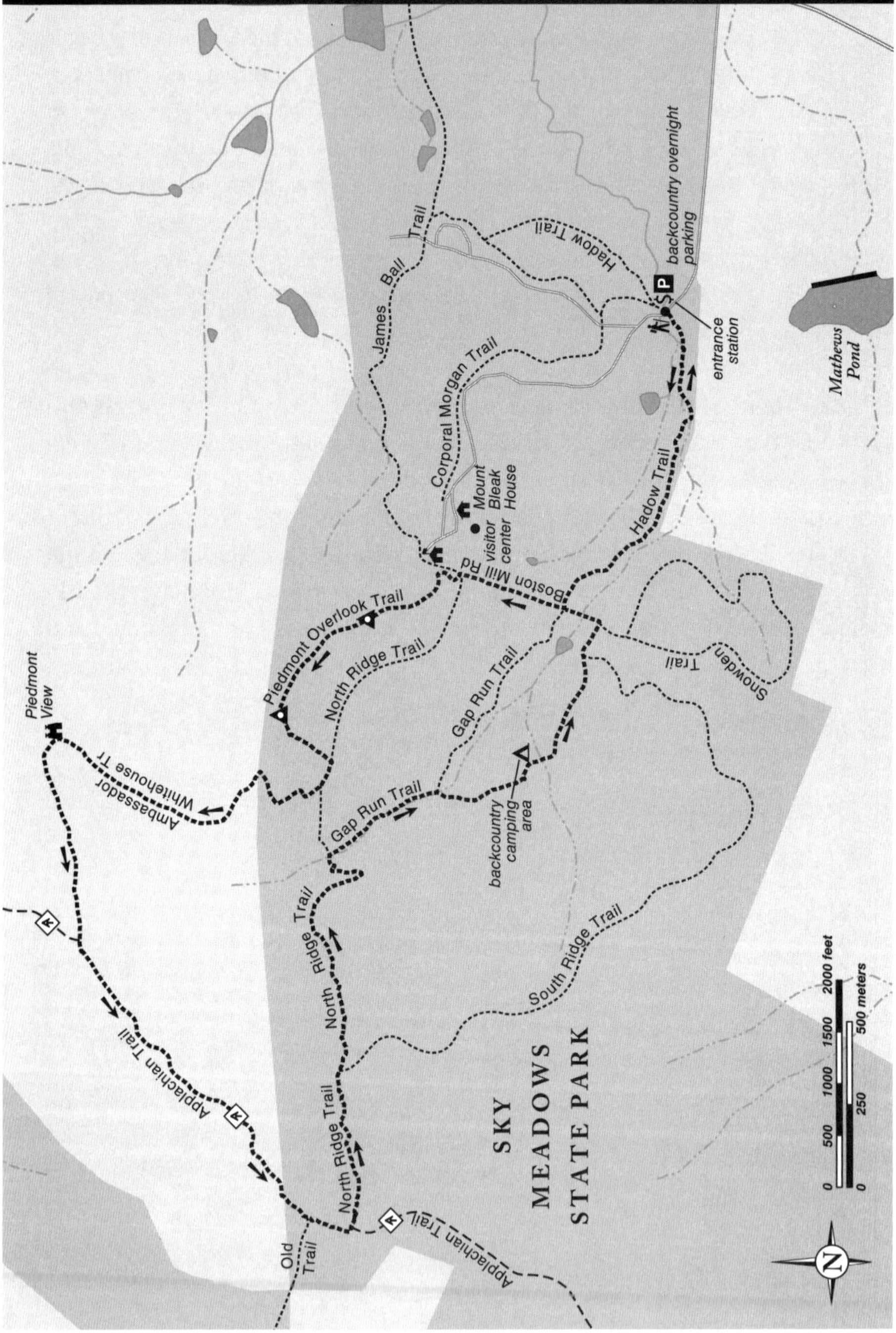

Even deer love the trails at Sky Meadows State Park.

travel atop ridges and along streams, along old stone fences, and upon tree-covered slopes, creating a mosaic of landscapes sure to please the most discriminating backpacker. Moreover, the views are something to behold: vast panoramas of hills and lowlands to the east affirm your notion that Sky Meadows in not your average state park of yesteryear.

This park started with a picturesque farm—cattle are still grazed here—where fields reveal a landscape that has been repurposed for both recreational participation and historical preservation. Standard park facilities are few here. On-site buildings are now used for park purposes, lending an agrarian yet majestic feel to the preserve. Deer find the mix of habitats a favorable situation.

And the backpacking is good as well, especially for families and newbies looking for a well-laid-out operation, yet with mountains, views, and good hiking. Sky Meadows has all that. After obtaining your backcountry campsite (reservations required) you'll leave the overnight parking area, traipsing along a tributary of Gap Run and passing hand-built stone fences, reminders of the past. Views are immediate in open areas, while woods crowd the path in places. The Hadow Trail leads to stone-fence-lined Boston Mill Road—now a park trail—then you head for the higher terrain on the aptly named Piedmont Overlook Trail. Ascend a meadow, looking back for vistas that improve by the step. The Ambassador Whitehouse Trail ups the ante, winding through field and wood, culminating in a stellar view just above adjacent conservation lands. By now, you will fully understand why the park was named Sky Meadows.

The loop meets the AT, and you turn southbound, gently ascending a rocky path to reach your high point of 1,800 feet. Then down you go on the North Ridge Trail, making your way to a camper-only spur trail along a tributary of Gap Run. Here, sixteen backcountry campsites are situated along the stream, with ample distance separating the leveled campsites on a slight slope. Each site has a fire ring, lantern post, picnic table, and tent pad—perfect for those who want their backcountry camping experience to equal the hiking experience on the 24 miles of foot trails here at Sky Meadows. It sure beats looking for a camp, then settling on a sloped, muddy spot with an abused fire ring. A pump well serves the camps, as do two outhouses.

Your exit from the camp is easy, just a jaunt to the lowlands followed by a short stint on Boston Mill Road, and then you are backtracking to the trailhead on the Hadow Trail.

Overall, this is a low-elevation backpack best suited for fall through spring. Sky Meadows would make a good initiation winter backpack, as the campsite is a mere 900 feet high. Finally, if you desire a short first day, simply reverse the loop and you've got it made.

Mileages

0.0 Join the Hadow Trail just north of the park entrance station. Head left, westerly, on the Hadow Trail underneath big oaks. Bisect a stone fence, then work up a stream.

0.7 Right on Boston Mill Road, flanked by more stone fences.

0.9 Left on singletrack Piedmont Overlook Trail. Ascend past old farm buildings.

1.0 Reach the first Piedmont Overlook, bench, fine views.

1.4 Second overlook with benches, spectacular view, enter woods.

1.5 Right on North Ridge Trail.

1.6 Right on Ambassador Whitehouse Trail just ahead.

1.7 Cross gas line clearing.

2.0 Enter broken woods and field.

2.2 Piedmont Memorial Overlook, also known as Paris View, outstanding panorama, conservation lands just below, picnic table and bench, curve west.

2.6 Left, southbound on Appalachian Trail, gently ascend a wide, easy path.
3.3 Old Trail (former AT route) leaves right.
3.4 Left on North Ridge Trail, descend rocky, irregular path.
3.8 South Ridge Trail leaves right.
4.3 Right on Gap Run Trail after crossing shallow stony creek.
4.5 Right on spur to backcountry campground. Begin passing numbered campsites ahead. Remember you must have reservation, except for AT thru-hikers. Pass pump well, outhouse and wood for sale. Pass a second outhouse.
4.9 Leave the camping area, pass second junction with South Ridge Trail and a pond.
5.1 Left on Boston Mill Road.
5.2 Right on Hadow Trail, backtrack.
5.9 Trailhead.

6 • BIG SCHLOSS

The Backpack: *This exciting adventure in the George Washington National Forest straddles the state line with West Virginia much of the way, even delving a bit into the Mountain State. The Mill Mountain Trail takes you up to Big Schloss, a massive outcrop with multiple stellar views—and a land bridge leading to the outermost outcrop. Pass highland camps before looping down to Wilson Cove. Rise back to the highlands and another panorama at White Rock. Pass by rentable Sugar Knob Cabin, then descend along gorgeous Little Stoney Creek, with waterside camps. Return to the highlands yet again, passing Big Schloss a second time before completing the backpack. Campsites low and high are spread throughout the loop, including some ridgetop camps near springs.*

This is a great trip. And it starts at a nifty little campground straddling the Virginia–West Virginia line, Wolf Gap, that you can stay in the night before you head into the backcountry. Trail conditions vary greatly along the way, from the busy, wide path to Big Schloss, to the lesser-used slender footpath going down Pond Run, to gravel Waites Run Road, to remote singletrack on upper Little Stoney Creek. Camping conditions vary as well. You can stay up high at campsites with or without water, in the deep hollow of Pond Run, along Waites Run Road, or up high near White Rock. Sugar Knob Cabin is open for rental from the Potomac Appalachian Trail Club, and fine streamside camps can be

6 BIG SCHLOSS

Distance & configuration: 26.6-mile balloon loop

Difficulty: Difficult due to almost 6,000 feet each of ascent and descent

Backpacking time: 14 hours

Outstanding features: Big Schloss view, White Rock view, streams, Sugar Knob Cabin

Elevation: 1,510′ low point, 3,280′ high point

Scenery: 5

Solitude: 4

Family friendly: 2

Canine friendly: 2

Fees/permits: No fees or permits required

Best season: Year-round; fall is great time

Maps: National Geographic #792 Massanutten and Great North Mountain, George Washington National Forest

For more info: George Washington National Forest, Lee Ranger District, 95 Railroad Avenue, Edinburg, VA 22824, 540-984-4101, 276-679-8370, www.fs.usda.gov/gwj

Finding the trailhead: From exit 283 on I-81 near Woodstock, take VA 42, Reservoir Road, west for 5.2 miles to turn right onto VA 768. Follow VA 768 west for .2 mile, then turn right onto VA 675 and follow it for 6.3 miles to Wolf Gap Recreation Area at the Virginia–West Virginia state line. The parking area is after the campground loop, and the Mill Mountain Trail starts near campsite #9. **GPS trailhead coordinates:** N38° 55.514′, W78° 41.341′

found along Little Stoney Creek. This allows you to make this anything from a one- to three-night adventure, all on your terms.

The circuit leaves Wolf Gap Recreation Area, with its primitive campground open year-round, near campsite #9. There is no water at the campground; bring your own if you overnight here and for the beginning of the backpack. The wide Mill Mountain Trail wastes no time climbing the west slope of Great North Mountain, making a switchback at .3 mile. At .7 mile, the path levels off atop the ridge. At .8 mile, pass a rock outcrop with a wonderful view to Massanutten Mountain and the Shenandoah Valley, with the heights of the Blue Ridge forming a backdrop. Traverse a narrow rock ridge with stunted tree cover in places. At 1.8 miles, reach the .3-mile Big Schloss Spur Trail. Head right up the spur, which soon opens onto a partly wooded outcrop with views in three directions. Ahead, reach a land bridge connecting outcrops. The views are even bigger at the end. You can see into West Virginia in the

6 Big Schloss

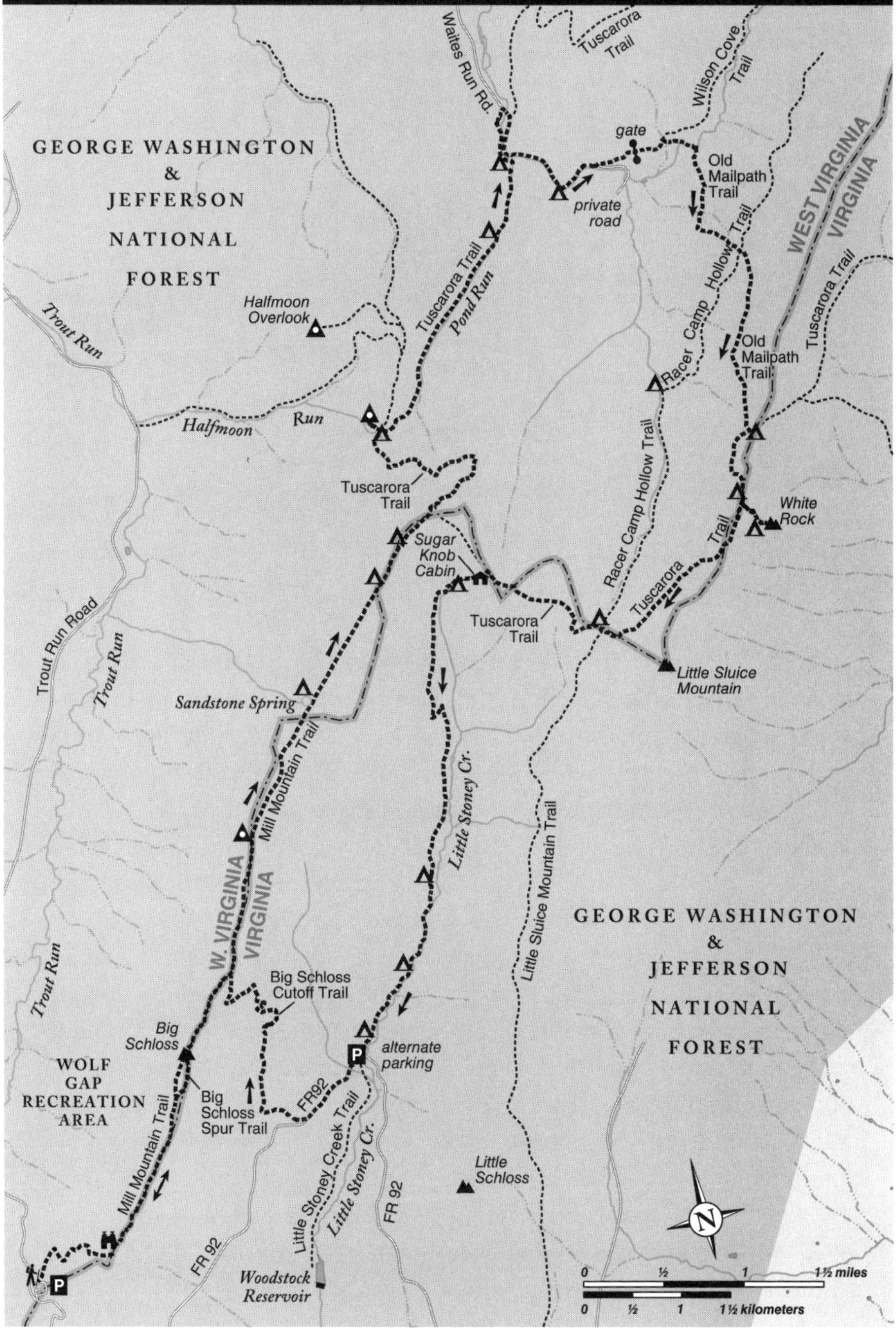

The author poses atop Big Schloss.

near and easterly to the Blue Ridge and south toward Wolf Gap. Multiple outcrops make exploration fun. Sloped and limited campsites are up here.

Backtrack to rejoin the now-much-less-used Mill Mountain Trail, rolling along the west side of Big Schloss. Outcrops and low brush allow additional views. At 3.3 miles, come to a trail intersection and an alluring but waterless campsite. Here, the Big Schloss Cutoff Trail—your return route—comes in from the right. Keep straight on the Mill Mountain Trail. At 4.2 miles, pass an overlook delivering westerly views.

Return to woods, then reach clear Sandstone Spring and a nearby campsite at 5.1 miles. This is your first trailside water opportunity. At 6.0 miles, pass a long-abandoned gate and lesser-used campsite to your right. Drift down from the high point, passing another camp at 6.3 miles. Intersect the Tuscarora Trail at 6.6 miles. Three official trails meet here. Keep straight, heading northeast, joining the Tuscarora Trail, ignoring the old jeep track to the far left. The Tuscarora Trail is a 252-mile track extending from Virginia into West Virginia and Maryland on to Pennsylvania and was originally designed as an alternate route for the Appalachian Trail, to which it connects on both ends.

The singletrack path winds around a knob, then joins a doubletrack before coming to water, a boardwalk, and then a trail intersection and nice campsite at 8.0 miles. Also, a spur trail goes left to a pine-bordered overlook with a face-on view of stony Halfmoon Mountain and the Trout Run valley below.

From this trail intersection, stay with the Tuscarora Trail (though a side trip to Halfmoon Mountain overlook isn't a bad idea), crossing another boardwalk, then descending a stony irregular trail through the tight Pond Run vale. Crisscross the stream a few times, passing a not-so-great campsite at 9.7 miles. Emerge near Waites Run and a waterside campsite at 10.2 miles (Waites Run Road is just across the creek). The Tuscarora keeps downstream along and above Waites Run to pop out on gravel Waites Run Road at 10.6 miles. Turn right here, bridging Waites Run. Just beyond the bridge the Tuscarora Trail splits left to traverse Great North Mountain.

The loop follows Waites Run Road, passing a few auto-accessible campsites. At 11.7 miles, a private road goes right to an inholding. We stay left, climbing FR 371. At 11.9 miles, reach a gate, open October through December. Continue on the forest road, descending. At 12.2 miles, turn right onto the signed Old Mailpath Trail. Pass a kiosk, then wander through mixed woods, crossing Cove Run at 12.4 miles (no campsites).

Trace the Old Mailpath Trail as the doubletrack wanders south. Step over a small stream at 12.9 miles, your last water for a few miles. Ascend to intersect the Racer Camp Hollow Trail in a clearing at 13.2 miles. A campsite with water a mile distant can be had by heading west on Racer Camp Hollow Trail. Our loop stays with the Old Mailpath Trail, still climbing a wooded doubletrack. At 14.5 miles, return to the Virginia state line, once again meeting the Tuscarora Trail. Head right, south along the crest of Little Sluice Mountain, still working uphill. Pass trailside campsites before coming to the spur to White Rock at 15.0 miles. This spur, marked with a rock cairn, descends left, winding past a campsite at 15.2 miles. Beyond there, the trail makes a final rise, then opens to a rock-and-pine panorama at 15.3 miles. Below, Woodstock Reservoir and the lowlands rise to Little Sluice Mountain.

Backtrack and rejoin the Tuscarora Trail. Mostly descend to meet the upper end of Racer Camp Hollow Trail and the Little Sluice Mountain Trail at 16.9 miles. A campsite and water can be found just down Racer Camp Hollow. Stay with the Tuscarora Trail, rolling on a doubletrack to reach another intersection at 17.8 miles. Here, head left on the Little Stoney Creek Trail, fully reentering the Old Dominion. Reach the Sugar Knob Cabin in .1 mile. This small stone structure must be rented prior to a trip from the Potomac Appalachian Trail Club. Keep downhill, passing a spring and sloped campsite at 18.1 miles.

Beyond here, the Little Stoney Creek Trail traverses a side slope, eventually switchbacking down to saddle alongside Little Stoney Creek at 19.2 miles. Come to a trailside campsite at 20.3 miles. Other camps can be found just down valley at 20.9 miles and 21.4 miles. Reach FR 92 and a parking area at 21.6 miles. Head right here on FR 92, tracing the gravel track to turn right onto the Big Schloss Cutoff Trail at 22.1 miles. This singletrack path makes a solid ascent among a very bouldery forest. At times you wind among stone monoliths. Switchbacks at 23.2 miles ease the uptick. Roll into an intersection and desirable campsite at 23.9 miles. From here, it is 2.7 miles back to the Wolf Gap Trailhead, providing you don't make the return trip up to Big Schloss.

Mileages

0.0 Wolf Gap.
0.8 View.
1.8 Spur trail .3 mile to Big Schloss.
3.3 Intersection with Big Schloss Cutoff Trail, campsite.
4.2 Westerly view.
5.1 Sandstone Spring, campsite.
6.0 Old forest gate, campsite.
6.3 Campsite.
6.6 Join Tuscarora Trail, stay northbound.
8.0 Water, boardwalk, trail intersection campsite, spur to nearby overlook.
9.7 Campsite in Pond Run hollow.
10.2 Campsite near Waites Run.
10.6 Right on gravel Waites Run Road.
11.7 Private road leads right; stay left.
11.9 Gate.
12.2 Right on Old Mailpath Trail.
13.2 Cross Racer Camp Hollow Trail; keep climbing.
14.5 Right on Tuscarora Trail, campsite to left, campsites ahead to right.
15.0 Spur leads right .3 mile to White Rock, views and campsite.
16.9 Intersection, campsite and water to right down upper Racer Camp Hollow.
17.8 Left on Little Stoney Creek Trail.

17.9 Pass Sugar Knob Cabin.
18.1 Spring, sloped campsite.
19.2 Come near Little Stoney Creek.
20.3 Campsite.
20.9 Campsite.
21.4 Campsite.
21.6 Right on gravel FR 92.
22.1 Right on Big Schloss Cutoff Trail.
23.9 Left on Mill Mountain Trail, campsite, backtrack.
26.6 Wolf Gap, complete backpack.

7 • ELIZABETH FURNACE

The Backpack: *This backpack on northernmost Massanutten Mountain makes a circuit through history. First, climb to Signal Knob, used by Civil War troops, and gaze upon Strasburg and the northern Shenandoah Valley. Drop to Little Passage Creek, where campsites can be had. Next, cross Passage Creek, climbing Massanutten Mountain. Traverse the narrow ridge, then descend to historic Elizabeth Furnace, where you can view the remains of this former forge. The backpack traverses a variety of terrain, from dry rocky ridges to boulder-strewn creeks to piney slopes. Though a mountain backpack, it is low elevation, and therefore a good late fall through early spring option. Summer can be hot.*

The northern end of Massanutten Mountain is the setting for this George Washington National Forest adventure. Using a well-developed trail system, the backpack traverses view-rich rocky ridges divided by Passage Creek and Little Passage Creek. Smart planners will factor in limited water in the uplands for hiking and camping. The low elevation makes it a less alluring summertime proposition. Additionally, since the backpack loop comes near the trailhead before pulling away, you can make a shorter 14-mile mini-loop or the full 21.7-mile circuit.

Campsites are situated throughout the loop, though water must be carried if you are camping along the ridgetops. Campsites with water can be found along Little Passage Creek. Overall, the loop is well marked, maintained, and signed, but the abundance of trail junctions will leave you wishing for the recommended map. Additionally, Elizabeth Furnace Campground makes an ideal night-before-the-trip camp and could even be incorporated into the backpack, since the loop comes near it; hot showers and water are available during the warm season.

7 ELIZABETH FURNACE

Distance & configuration: 21.7-mile loop

Difficulty: Difficult due to elevation changes

Outstanding features: Signal Knob views, Little Passage Creek gorge, Elizabeth Furnace

Elevation: 740′ low point, 2,270′ high point

Scenery: 4

Solitude: 3

Family friendly: 2

Canine friendly: 3

Fees/permits: No fees or permits required

Best season: Fall through spring

Maps: National Geographic #792 Massanutten and Great North Mountain, George Washington National Forest

For more info: George Washington National Forest, Lee Ranger District, 95 Railroad Avenue, Edinburg, VA 22824, 540-984-4101, 276-679-8370, www.fs.usda.gov/gwj

Finding the trailhead: From exit 6 on I-66 near Front Royal, take US 522 south/US 340 south for 1.5 miles, then turn right on VA 155 west. Follow VA 155 west for 5.1 miles to turn left on VA 678, Fort Valley Road. Follow VA 678 for 3.4 miles to turn right into the large parking area, a half-mile before the left turn to Elizabeth Furnace day-use area and picnic ground. The Massanutten Mountain Trail starts in the north end of the large parking area. **GPS trailhead coordinates:** N38° 56.102′, W78° 19.196′

A word about water: Many of the tributaries of Passage Creek you will cross on the mountain slopes are seasonal. They will likely be flowing late autumn through early summer in years of normal rainfall. However, during autumn and low-rainfall years, the streams will run dry. If you are not a gambler, get water when and where you can.

The backpack joins the rocky, singletrack Massanutten Mountain Trail, heading north for Signal Knob. The path turns up a draw, passing late-arriver camps before crossing a creekbed with a concrete springbox. Keep rising amid oaks and pines to reach an overlook and dry campsite at 1.5 miles. Gaze east across the Shenandoah Valley. The area remains rocky as you ascend more, passing the southward Fort Valley Overlook before zigzagging toward historic Signal Knob, used for observation by both the Confederacy and the Union. Look for stone fortifications from that era in the near and Strasburg and the lower Shenandoah Valley in the far.

7 Elizabeth Furnace

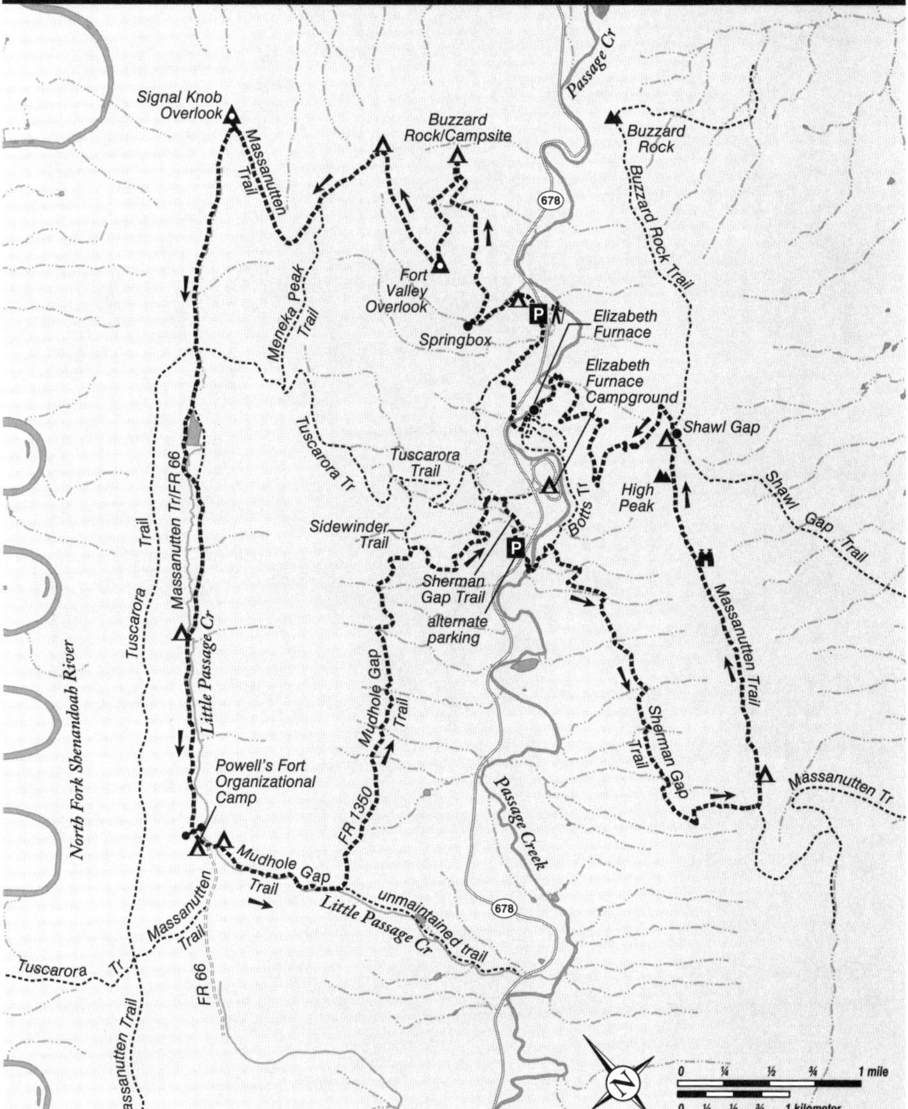

You will pass by this gnarled oak on the way to Signal Knob.

The Massanutten Mountain Trail joins doubletrack, gated FR 66 after visiting the spur to Signal Knob Overlook. Descend into the uppermost Little Passage Creek valley, passing the Tuscarora Trail. Ahead, the trail circles above the Strasburg Reservoir, passing illegal campsites. The Massanutten Mountain Trail then returns to the reservoir access road, continuing down the valley. Don't miss the left turn onto footpath and the Mudhole Gap Trail, leaving FR 66, just past relic buildings from the Powell's Fort Organizational Camp, built in the 1930s by the Civilian Conservation Corps. Cross Little Passage Creek five times in an uber-rocky, rugged gorge before splitting left away from the stream. Here, the Mudhole Gap Trail morphs into a gated forest road. Back in the lowlands, you join the singletrack Sherman Gap Trail, where you cross Fort Valley Road, then ford Passage Creek at a gravel shoal. From there, the Sherman Gap Trail angles along the side slope of Massanutten Mountain, winding in and out of hollows before making a final sharp ascent to the mountain crest. Here, once again pick up the Massanutten

The trails are rocky around Elizabeth Furnace.

Mountain Trail, passing an upland campsite overlooking the South Fork Shenandoah River. Roll along the rocky ridge, a study in geology. Views open across the valley to Shenandoah National Park.

The loop slips below High Peak, then reaches Shawl Gap, through which pig iron was once transported by mule from Elizabeth Furnace to the South Fork Shenandoah River and then loaded onto barges and floated to Harpers Ferry and fashioned into product. From Shawl Gap, you take a newer singletrack path, making switchbacks aplenty before returning to free-flowing Passage Creek, ultimately reaching Elizabeth Furnace. Consider taking the short, signed, interpretive loop at the 1800s industrial site.

The backpacking circuit continues to Elizabeth Furnace picnic and day-use area, then follows the road bridge from the picnic area, saving backpackers a second ford. Finally, cross Fort Valley Road, then return to the trailhead, completing the adventure.

Set Up Your Backpack Camp Like Home

Setting up a backcountry camp is like setting up your home. Think of your campsite as having a bedroom, kitchen, living room, and bathroom. Each area has its own distinctive characteristics that you will be emulating.

When setting up your sleeping quarters, whether they are in the open, under a tarp, or in a tent, try to find level ground that is not subject to water flow from uphill. Look on the ground where you plan to sleep. Do you see evidence of water running through that spot? If so, find another location. Also look for a layer of natural duff, such as leaves or pine needles, that indicates water not running through it—running water scours the ground. Duff pads your bedroom. Do not clear the ground before setting up your bedroom, but do look for sticks, rocks, and other obstructions that might interrupt your sleep, then remove them. Hammock campers simply need two conveniently located trees.

If you like to cook over a fire, as I do, your kitchen will be located near the fire ring. I will have my grill and stove—if I bring it—located in one general area. My food will be nearby while in camp, but if I leave, it will be hung up away from critters.

Backpackers expect a spartan living room. This may merely amount to a backpack leaning against a tree with a sleeping pad to sit on. That is one of the reasons I carry a closed-cell sleeping pad, because I can use it when sitting around the fire and don't have to worry about it popping as I do an air mattress.

Additional comforts will be found in your "camp furniture." Backpackers have to take what they can find in the natural surroundings for their camp furniture, though ultralight folding camp chairs are carried by backpackers these days. At already established sites, you will often find a combination of logs and rocks centered around the fire ring. Sometimes, logs are placed over rocks located at either end, creating a bench of sorts.

When looking for a campsite, consider the camp furniture, not only for yourself but also for your belongings. Satellite boulders and rocks can act as tables for your cook set and other gear you might prefer not to set on the ground.

The campsite bathroom should be well away from the other parts of camp. When using the bathroom, head away from camp and away from water, then find a concealed location. Dig a hole using a stick or the heel of your shoe, preferably 6 inches deep; do your business, burn your toilet paper, and then cover it up.

Backpackers should consider whether to set up a base camp or keep moving day to day. A base camp will free you from the chores of setting up and breaking down camp on a daily basis. This will avail you more free time and fewer camp chores. The advantage of moving camp on a daily basis is that you will be setting up in new surroundings every day. This allows for convenient sightseeing from each campsite.

If you are going on a long backpacking adventure, I suggest staying at one camp for two nights during the middle of the trip just to free yourself from the daily making/breaking camp ritual. So whether you stay one night or two, make your backpacking camp like home.

Mileages

0.0 Signal Knob parking area.

0.1 Late-arrival camp.

0.4 Springbox up from the trail at creek crossing.

1.5 Vista, dry campsite at Buzzard Rock.

2.2 Fort Valley Overlook.

2.8 Dry campsite.

3.3 Pass more campsites, then Meneka Peak Trail leaves left.

4.3 Spur to Signal Knob Overlook.

5.7 Intersect the Tuscarora Trail; ahead split right around Strasburg Reservoir.

6.5 Reservoir access doubletrack road.

7.4 Cross Little Passage Creek, campsite.

8.4 Pass around forest service gate.

8.6 Split left on Mudhole Gap Trail from FR 66 to cross Little Passage Creek and reach a campsite.

9.4 Mudhole Gap Trail splits left away from Little Passage Creek. Unmaintained trail continues downstream. Turn northeast, open onto a field, join gated FR 1350, the continuation of Mudhole Gap Trail.

11.7 Sidewinder Trail leaves left.

12.6 Blazed, official shortcut left to Tuscarora Trail; stay right on Mudhole Gap Trail/FR 1350.

12.8 Leave right just after passing forest road gate, joining single-track Sherman Gap Trail; wind through rocky, lowland woods, crossing a few streambeds.

13.2 Emerge at alternate parking area on Fort Valley Road. Cross road as Sherman Gap Trail comes to Passage Creek then reaches a gravelly ford.

13.6 Pass the intersection with the Botts Trail after turning down-stream along Passage Creek. Sherman Gap Trail winds along side of Massanutten Mountain.

15.3 Enter a boulder garden, passing an old building foundation. Begin a sharp climb.

16.2 Turn left on Massanutten Mountain Trail, northbound.

16.3 Pass campsite to right of trail with view of South Fork Shenandoah River.

17.1 Surmount high point on ridge.

17.6 Pass view into Shenandoah Valley. Descend below High Peak.
18.4 Shawl Gap, dry campsite. Stay left with Massanutten Mountain Trail, descending by numerous switchbacks, crisscrossing historic route from Elizabeth Furnace through Shawl Gap.
20.3 Come along Passage Creek, turn upstream.
20.6 Reach Elizabeth Furnace and its interpretive spur trail. Keep right, then enter Elizabeth Furnace picnic area. Reach picnic area access road and turn right, crossing Passage Creek via access road. Ahead, cross Fort Valley Road, then rejoin foot trail, leading right and uphill.
21.2 Stay right on Massanutten Mountain Trail at intersection.
21.7 Return to trailhead, completing the backpack.

8 • DUNCAN KNOB

The Backpack: *This backpack offers views and solitude on the southern end of Massanutten Mountain. Leave historic Camp Roosevelt Recreation Area on Massanutten Mountain Trail, exploring deeply wooded Duncan Hollow to reach the south end of Middle Mountain, where a spur trail leads over rocky terrain to a stunning view. Descend to Scothorn Gap, traversing uplands before climbing to Duncan Knob, where a boulder field presents another panorama. Head back to Duncan Hollow for a final backtrack. Campsites are present throughout the circuit. Elevation changes are not drastic, making this a viable novice or family hike.*

This backpack explores the southern end of Massanutten Mountain and adjacent ridges and valleys to cobble together a fairly easy circuit hike featuring two fantastic views. The Massanutten Mountain Trail, a 71-mile loop trail and one of Virginia's longer backpacking tracks, is the primary conduit. Camp Roosevelt Recreation Area, with a fine little campground and picnic area open May through October, is an ideal jumping-off point or night-before-the-backpack camp. This locale was the site of the first Civilian Conservation Corps camp in the entire United States. Although in a mountainous area, the lower elevations make this a preferred backpack when the chill winds are blowing. Note: Not all trail intersections are signed.

Start the adventure by leaving southwest from VA 675 on the Massanutten Mountain Trail, immediately entering pine-oak woods. Pass a late-arrival campsite, then go under a powerline at .1 mile. Bridge a wet-weather stream, then step over the primary stream of Duncan Hol-

8 DUNCAN KNOB

Distance & configuration: 13.6-mile balloon loop

Difficulty: Moderate

Backpacking time: 7 hours

Outstanding features: Views from Strickler Knob and Duncan Knob, multiple campsites

Elevation: 1,315′ low point, 2,720′ high point

Scenery: 4

Solitude: 4

Family friendly: 4

Canine friendly: 3

Fees/permits: No fees or permits required

Best season: Year-round, though summer could be warm

Maps: National Geographic #792 Massanutten and Great North Mountain, George Washington National Forest

For more info: George Washington National Forest, Lee Ranger District, 95 Railroad Avenue, Edinburg, VA 22824, 540-984-4101, 276-679-8370, www.fs.usda.gov/gwj

Finding the trailhead: From exit 279 on I-81 near Edinburg, take Stoney Creek Boulevard for .8 mile, then turn left onto Lee Highway/US 11 north and follow it for .6 mile, then turn right on VA 675 east. Stay with VA 675 for 9.2 miles, passing Camp Roosevelt Recreation Area on your left just before reaching the Massanutten Mountain Trail crossing the road. There are a couple of parking spots on VA 675, but you can also use the large lot accessed on your left just beyond the trail crossing. **GPS trailhead coordinates:** N38° 43.695′, W78° 31.026′

low at .8 mile. Find a campsite on the far side of the crossing. This part of the stream can run underground in late summer and fall.

Enjoy the natural, fire-managed forest with a clear little stream running through its heart. In places, the trail served as a firebreak, leaving differing age and composition of forest on each side of the path. At 2.1 miles, the path briefly steepens and the stream of Duncan Hollow flows well below. At 2.9 miles, a spur trail leads left to a creekside campsite. Step over a few spring branches, as well as the stream of Duncan Hollow, then come to a signed trail intersection at 3.3 miles. Here, a spur to a campsite and water leads left. The Gap Creek Trail—your return route—leads right.

Stay straight on the Massanutten Mountain Trail, rising through the upper hollow. Begin switchbacking up the side of Middle Mountain at 5.0 miles. Reach the bouldery crest of the mountain at 5.4 miles. Here, head left on the pink-blazed Strickler Knob Trail. This is a very stony,

8 Duncan Knob

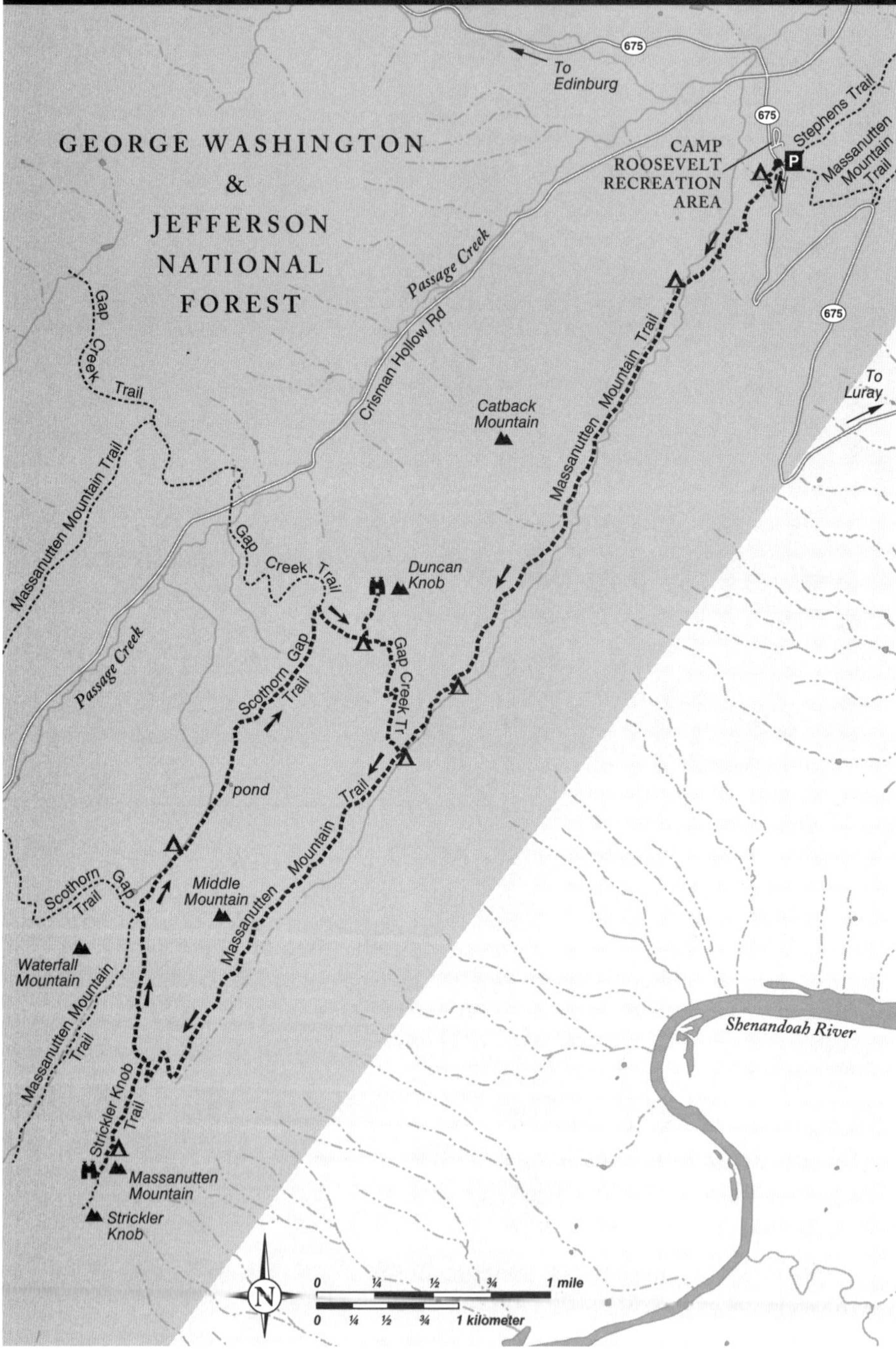

The view from Duncan Knob is a highlight of this backpack.

irregular track—keep an eye for blazes on trees and rock outcrops at your feet. Work southwesterly, passing an "almost view" to your right at 5.6 miles, then reach a waterless but sheltered campsite at 5.8 miles. Continuing on the path, you open to a spectacular view at 6.0 miles. Look down to see New Market Gap, Waterfall Mountain, Kerns Mountain, and beyond to West Virginia. The trail goes on to Strickler Knob but gets even rougher, almost a rock scramble in places.

Backtrack to the Massanutten Mountain Trail, then descend to reach a trail intersection and Scothorn Gap at 7.2 miles. Head right on Scothorn Gap Trail, entering the upper valley of a wet-weather tributary of Passage Creek. A seldom-used campsite can be found on the trail left at 7.5 miles. However, the nearby tributary can run dry in summer and fall. At 7.9 miles, pass a wildlife pond, then enter a forest of big hardwoods.

Then you meet the Gap Creek Trail at 8.9 miles. Head right here, climbing through hickories to reach a gap and big campsite at 9.1 miles. Whether you camp here or not, take the quarter-mile spur up to Duncan Knob. The path starts easy, then steepens before entering a huge boulder field. You might want to drop your pack. Clamber up the boulders, then fine panoramas open. Gaze southwest along the ridges of greater Massanutten Mountain, down into Passage Creek valley, and beyond. Backtrack from Duncan Knob.

Trip Planning Is an Important Component of Backpacking

I have a backpacking friend in northern Virginia. I was eager to backpack the Massanutten Mountain Trail, the 71-mile loop path circling Fort Valley. My northern Virginia friend advised me to pick a section of trail I wanted to hike, and he would accommodate the request, as he had already hiked the entire Massanutten Mountain Trail. I picked a 48-mile-or-so segment, from Moreland Gap to Habron Gap. This segment offered good views and campsites.

The two of us took off. That night around the campfire, I mentioned our nearly ideal backpacking progress, averaging 12 miles per day on this rocky ridge. This pace would lead us to our desired endpoint when the four-day trip was over.

That was when my buddy mentioned this was a three-day trip and he had to be at work the day after it was over. A simple misunderstanding of dates had led to this dilemma. So what once was a casual backpacking trip became a hike-athon.

We pushed hard those last two days, marking mileage, hiking hour after hour. It was painful to pass so much beauty without giving Massanutten Mountain the attention it deserved.

Don't let this happen to you.

Before you start an outdoor adventure, whether it is backpacking, canoe/kayak camping, or day hiking, get together with fellow members of your party to plan your trip. Go over the practicalities of the trip, such as who, what, where, when, and how. You also need to go over gear, especially gear to be shared by the group, such as tents, cooking items, and the like. Also go over the transportation and parking situations.

When getting a backcountry group together, consider the following things: group size, group dynamics, and trip expectations. The more people in a party, the more complicated things become.

For backpackers, I suggest keeping your group small, as this offers the best camping opportunities. Also, you may not want to mix your hard-partying college classmate with your fellow deacon at church. I prefer to keep backpacking groups no bigger than four people. Too many people requires too large of a campsite (not always easy to find) as well as the impact a single group can have on an area.

Trip expectations are very important. Everyone needs to be on the same wavelength as to what the trip will be like. This is very important. For example, does everyone want to hike hard all day long and spend very little time at camp? Or do they want to spend more time telling backpacking tales by the fire than actually backpacking? Is everyone willing to go for all five nights, or will someone want to leave early? Make sure everyone agrees about the length and style of the trip.

Also, make it clear up front about sharing expenses, chores, and other duties. This way there will be no unpleasant surprises when it comes time to collect money—or wood. Even after all parties come to agreement about the adventure, review the details one last time. That way you won't end up hiking too far in too short a period—like I did—because of a simple misunderstanding.

At 9.6 miles, continue down Gap Creek Trail. Switchback your way back down to Duncan Hollow, reaching a trail intersection at 10.3 miles. You have been here before. To close the loop, make a 3.3-mile backtrack to the trailhead.

Mileages

0.0 VA 675.
0.1 Late-arrival camp.
0.8 Creek crossing, campsite.
2.9 Campsite.
3.3 Trail junction; water and campsite to left.
5.4 Left on Strickler Knob Trail.
5.8 Campsite.
6.0 Rewarding view, backtrack.
7.2 Intersection; right on Scothorn Gap Trail.
7.5 Seldom-used campsite.
7.9 Intersection; right on Gap Creek Trail.
9.1 Gap and campsite; left .25 mile to Duncan Knob and views.
9.6 Descend on Gap Creek Trail.
10.3 Trail intersection and campsite, backtrack.
13.6 Return to trailhead, completing the backpack.

9 • JEREMYS RUN

The Backpack: *This Shenandoah National Park trip makes an excellent summertime backpack. Start your trip on the Appalachian Trail (AT), passing highland campsites before picking up the remote Neighbor Mountain Trail. Drop to gorgeous Jeremys Run, a stream featuring everywhere-you-look beauty as well as an abundance of campsites. Spend a day or two on Jeremys Run before returning to the trailhead. Be apprised that the hike up Jeremys Run entails fifteen creek crossings on a prolonged but gentle ascent.*

You can make this a one-, two-, or even three-night excursion. I have spent many a summer day—and night—laying up along Jeremys Run, enjoying the alluring stream and ample campsites strung along the watercourse. The high-country hiking is pleasant, too, whether you are cruising this relatively easy stretch of the AT or on secluded Neighbor Mountain Trail. The fifteen crossings of Jeremys Run make the trip best for summer and early fall, when the crossings are easy and getting wet

9 JEREMYS RUN

Distance & configuration: 14.0-mile loop

Difficulty: Moderate, does have 1,600-foot elevation change

Backpacking time: 7.5 hours

Outstanding features: Pools of Jeremys Run, solitude on Neighbor Mountain

Elevation: 1,060′ low point, 2,700′ high point

Scenery: 5

Solitude: 4

Family friendly: 3

Canine friendly: 3

Fees/permits: Park entrance fee and free backcountry permit required

Best season: Late spring through early fall

Maps: PATC Shenandoah National Park North District Map 9

For more info: Shenandoah National Park, 3655 U.S. Highway 211 East, Luray, VA 22835, 540-999-3500, www.nps.gov/shen

Finding the trailhead: From Thornton Gap, take Skyline Drive north for 7.4 miles to Elkwallow Picnic Ground at milepost 24.1. Drive to the low end of the picnic area and park. The spur trail to the AT leaves here. **GPS trailhead coordinates:** N38° 44.458′, W78° 18.725′

is no big deal. In fact, I bet you will be seeking the water, whether swimming in a cool hole or vying for the numerous brook trout that inhabit Jeremys Run. Avoid this trip in winter and cold weather.

The backpack leaves the lower end of Elkwallow Picnic Ground on a spur, quickly linking the AT. Head left, southbound, to descend past Elkwallow Spring just before meeting the Jeremys Run Trail at .2 mile. Stay left with the AT, crossing the outflow of Elkwallow Spring. Start a mile-long but modest uptick, which should be a breeze since you are fresh. Curve around a point of a ridge, then rise to the oak-and-mountain-laurel-covered ridgecrest. Look for Knob Mountain across the valley of Jeremys Run. The walking is glorious under a broken canopy of hickory and oak. Pass trailside campsites at 1.4 and 1.7 miles. Bring water from the trailhead if you are camping up here. By the way, no trailside water is available for the first 8.3 miles of the trip.

The Thornton River Trail leaves left at 2.4 miles. A gentle downgrade leads you through brush below Jeremys Run Overlook at 3.1 miles. There is no trail access to the Skyline Drive viewpoint. Start climbing again at 3.3 miles, to pass a spur trail leading left to an alternate parking area on Skyline Drive at 3.6 miles.

9 Jeremys Run

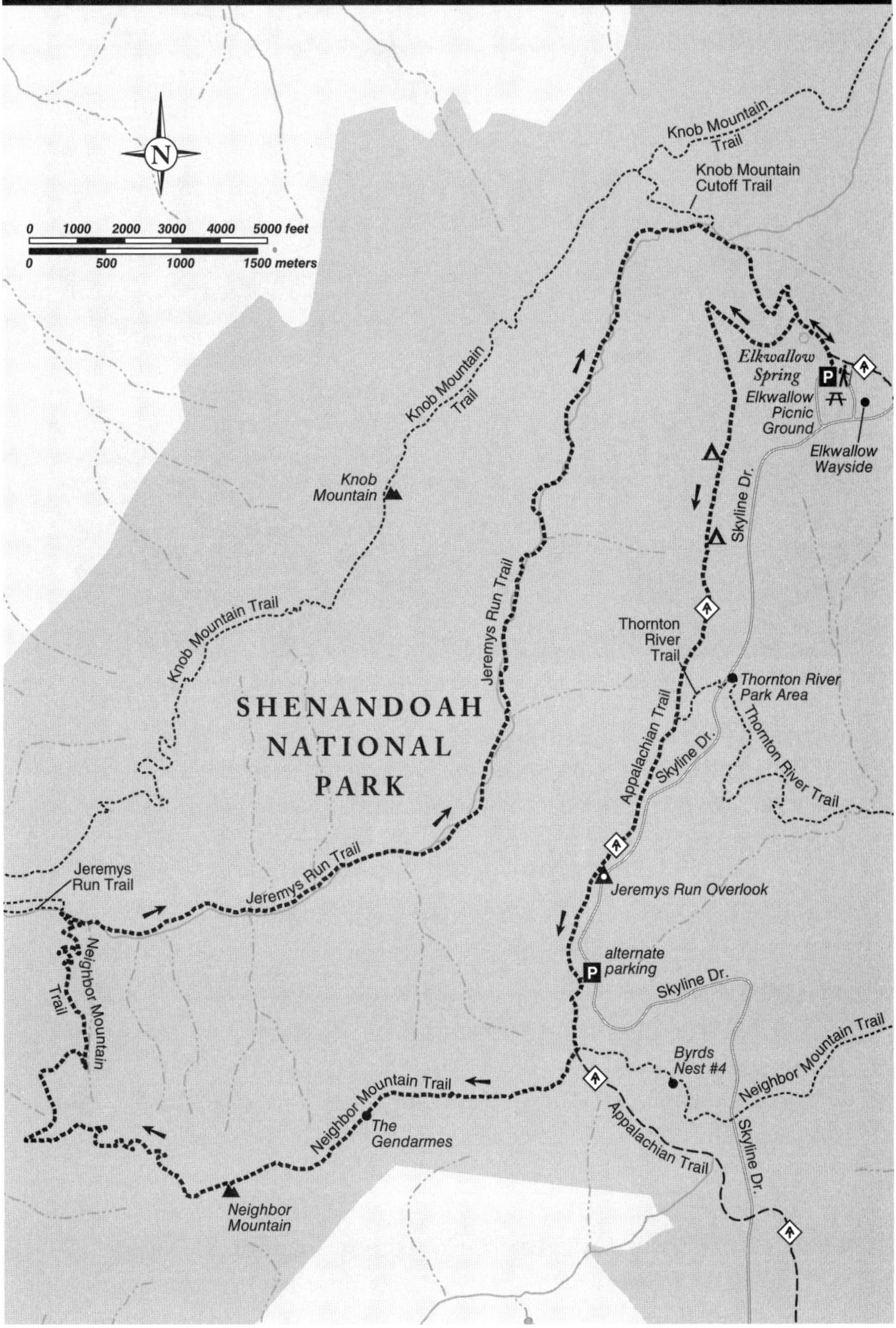

The cool, clear waters of Jeremys Run await the hot backpacker.

Work up Neighbor Mountain's western slope, intersecting the Neighbor Mountain Trail at 3.9 miles. Turn right on this lesser-used and underappreciated trail. Despite less use, it is well maintained, an advantage of backpacking in Shenandoah National Park versus Virginia's national forests, where lesser-used trails are generally in rougher shape. Solitude will be your companion for miles. Head westerly on a grassy track flanked by a gorgeous forest that spills away sharply on both sides of the ridge.

At 4.9 miles, come to a noticeable rock outcrop on your right known as The Gendarmes. If you climb onto the dark, upright rocks bordered with rounded boulders, the Shenandoah Valley will range to your right, while the Blue Ridge and its adjacent highlands will soar on the skyline to your left.

The already beautiful trail is enhanced with man-made stonework. At 5.7 miles, reach the marked crest of Neighbor Mountain, elevation 2,725 feet. No views are to be had, however. From here, begin your descent for Jeremys Run, leaving the crest of the Neighbor. Keep your brakes on, for the backpack descends over 1,600 feet in the next 2.5 miles. Switchbacks

Backpacking at Shenandoah National Park

Shenandoah National Park provides over 500 miles of trails threading through 200,000 acres of land, creating a host of backpacking opportunities. However, it is a national park, and backcountry camping is managed according to a rule system the park service has deemed best for Shenandoah. Therefore, it pays to know the rules before you go. Peruse the park's web pages on backpacking before leaving for your trip.

You must have a free backcountry camping permit. They can be obtained at visitor centers, at campgrounds, and by mail. Food, trash, and scented items must be stored so that wildlife cannot get them. You can hang food in a tree at least 10 feet above the ground and 4 feet out from a tree trunk, or store food within a park-approved, bear-resistant food storage canister. Backcountry campfires are not permitted. Bring a camp stove. Very limited areas of the park are closed to backcountry camping and are listed on the park website.

Upon selecting an area to camp, look for and try to camp on preexisting campsites out of sight of trails and roads. Campsites that have been created and established by prior visitor use are not posted, signed, or designated by the park. Camping may not exceed two nights in one campsite location or fourteen consecutive nights in the backcountry.

Specifically, no camping may occur

- within 10 yards of a stream or other natural water source;
- within 50 yards of standing building ruins, including stone foundations, chimneys, and log walls;
- within 50 yards of another camping party or "no camping" post or sign;
- within a quarter-mile of a paved road, park boundary, or park facilities, such as a campground, picnic area, visitor center, lodge, wayside, or restaurant;
- within 100 yards of a hut, cabin, or day-use shelter;
- within 20 yards of trails and unpaved roads.

Properly dispose of human waste. Maximum group size is limited to ten individuals. Carry all trash out of the backcountry and properly dispose of it. Pets must be leashed at all times and are not permitted on specific trails, also listed on the park website. The above list will help you get started on your Shenandoah backpacking adventure.

and quality trail ease the drop. Where the path faces south or west, squat pines give way to views of the Three Sisters in the near and the Shenandoah Valley in the yon.

At 7.4 miles, briefly pick up an old woods road along a rocky streambed. Keep dropping via switchbacks in pines. The forest thickens upon nearing Jeremys Run, its rapids urging you to finish the downgrade. At 8.3 miles, meet the stream and the Jeremys Run Trail. Campsites can be found down the Jeremys Run Trail, where the waterway forms deep pools at the base of noisy rapids complemented with sunning rocks. Campsites can also be found upstream along almost the whole length of the trail.

The backpacking circuit leaves right on the Jeremys Run Trail. Make the first of your fifteen stream crossings, then come to a cascade and swimming hole at 9.0 miles. Keep up the valley where sycamores shade trouty pools and sturdy bluffs rise above the stream. When this happens, the trail often crosses Jeremys Run. Most creek crossings are well upstream.

The trail rises, yet the hiking is splendid amid national-park-level scenery. At 13.0 miles, intersect the Knob Mountain Cutoff Trail. Stay right with the Jeremys Run Trail, climbing away from the stream to meet the AT at 13.8 miles. From here, backtrack to Elkwallow Picnic Ground, completing the backpack at 14.0 miles.

Mileages

0.0 Elkwallow Picnic Ground, milepost 24.1.
0.2 Jeremys Run Trail leaves right; stay left with AT.
1.4 Dry campsite.
1.7 Dry campsite.
2.4 Thornton River Trail leaves left.
3.1 Pass below Jeremys Run Overlook.
3.6 Spur to Skyline Drive.
3.9 Right on Neighbor Mountain Trail.
5.7 Signed Neighbor Mountain summit; descend.
8.3 Jeremys Run Trail; campsites in both directions.
9.0 Waterfall and swimming hole on right.
13.0 Knob Mountain Cutoff Trail leaves left.
13.8 Rejoin AT.
14.0 Elkwallow Picnic Ground.

10 • THORNTON RIVER

The Backpack: *This loop follows two of my favorite waterways at Shenandoah National Park. Along the way, enjoy pioneer history and waterfalls. Start by descending into the Thornton River, a fine trout stream replete with pioneer history, such as old homesites, farm implements, and other relics. From there, surmount Fork Mountain, dipping into lesser-visited Piney River. Pass two waterfalls while working your way back into the high country. Once on the Blue Ridge, join the Appalachian Trail (AT). Run the Blue Ridge back to the trailhead. The distance makes it an excellent novice or family backpack looking for a two-night trip. The best camping is along the streams, though camps and even a primitive rental cabin can be found up high.*

The Thornton River and Piney River seem to be on Shenandoah's list of overlooked places to visit. Don't make the same mistake, for you can come here to the park's North District, enjoy a highlight-rich loop, and see very few other hikers, much less backpackers. A night on the Thornton River and a night on the Piney River make a fun, easy two-night trip. Alternatively, you could extend your second day and camp up on the AT or even rent the primitive Range View Cabin from the Potomac Appalachian Trail Club.

From the trailhead, take the Thornton Hollow Trail, following a pioneer wagon track. At .9 mile, curve near a huge rectangular rock pile. At 1.0 miles, cross a tributary of the North Fork Thornton River. Rock walls line the track. At 1.1 miles, find the remains of a jalopy that rolled its last mile in the Thornton River valley. A homesite is nearby. Descend under a mantle of sycamores, white pines, and hardwoods. Stinging nettle can be troublesome here in late summer. Come alongside the North Fork Thornton River. Flats widen along the waterway.

At 1.4 miles, cross the tributary a second time. Find a campsite on trail right just after the crossing. Continue down Thornton Hollow. At 1.9 miles, the North Fork forms a noisy cascade while dashing through a rock chute. Pull away from the North Fork Thornton River as thickly wooded flats separate you from the river. Rock-hop the North Fork Thornton River at 2.3 miles. Sycamores rise overhead. Cross back over to the right bank at 2.5 miles. Look for campsites in the flat to your right, as well as signs of pre-park civilization. The woods where you camp were once open cornfields. Today, this can be difficult to imagine.

10 THORNTON RIVER

Distance & configuration: 13.0-mile loop

Difficulty: Moderate

Backpacking time: 7 hours

Outstanding features: Piney River Falls, pioneer history, streams

Elevation: 1,320′ low point, 3,005′ high point

Scenery: 4

Solitude: 4

Family friendly: 4

Canine friendly: 4

Fees/permits: Park entrance fee and free backcountry permit required

Best season: Spring through mid-fall

Maps: PATC Shenandoah National Park North District Map 9

For more info: Shenandoah National Park, 3655 U.S. Highway 211 East, Luray, VA 22835, 540-999-3500, www.nps.gov/shen

Finding the trailhead: From Luray, take US 211 east for 8.8 miles to Thornton Gap entrance of Shenandoah National Park. Here, join Skyline Drive northbound for 6.1 miles to the Thornton River Trail parking area, on the east side of Skyline Drive at milepost 25.4. The Thornton River Trail starts on the north side of the parking area. **GPS trailhead coordinates:** N38° 43.4388′, W78° 19.2003′

Cross the river again at 2.8 miles. Enter a small grassy area to meet the Hull School Trail at 2.9 miles. The Hull School once stood to the right of you as you face downriver. If you want more solitude, continue down the Thornton River Trail to look for campsites.

To continue the loop, join the Hull School Trail, northeast bound, and climb along a small stream. Step over the stream, winding upward to make a gap between Fork Mountain and Piney Ridge at 3.5 miles. Here, the Fork Mountain Trail heads left, while we stay with the Hull School Trail, descending among straight, gray trunks of tulip trees populating a mountain cove.

At 4.1 miles, reach the Piney Branch Trail (yes, it is called the Piney Branch Trail and travels along the Piney River). Campsites are in the vicinity. At this point, the Hull School Trail and Piney Branch Trail coincide for a bit as you turn left and immediately rock-hop the Piney River. This valley was once heavily settled also. Evidence abounds.

At 4.2 miles, the Hull School Trail splits off to the right, while our route stays up the Piney Branch Trail, passing a campsite just after a

10 Thornton River

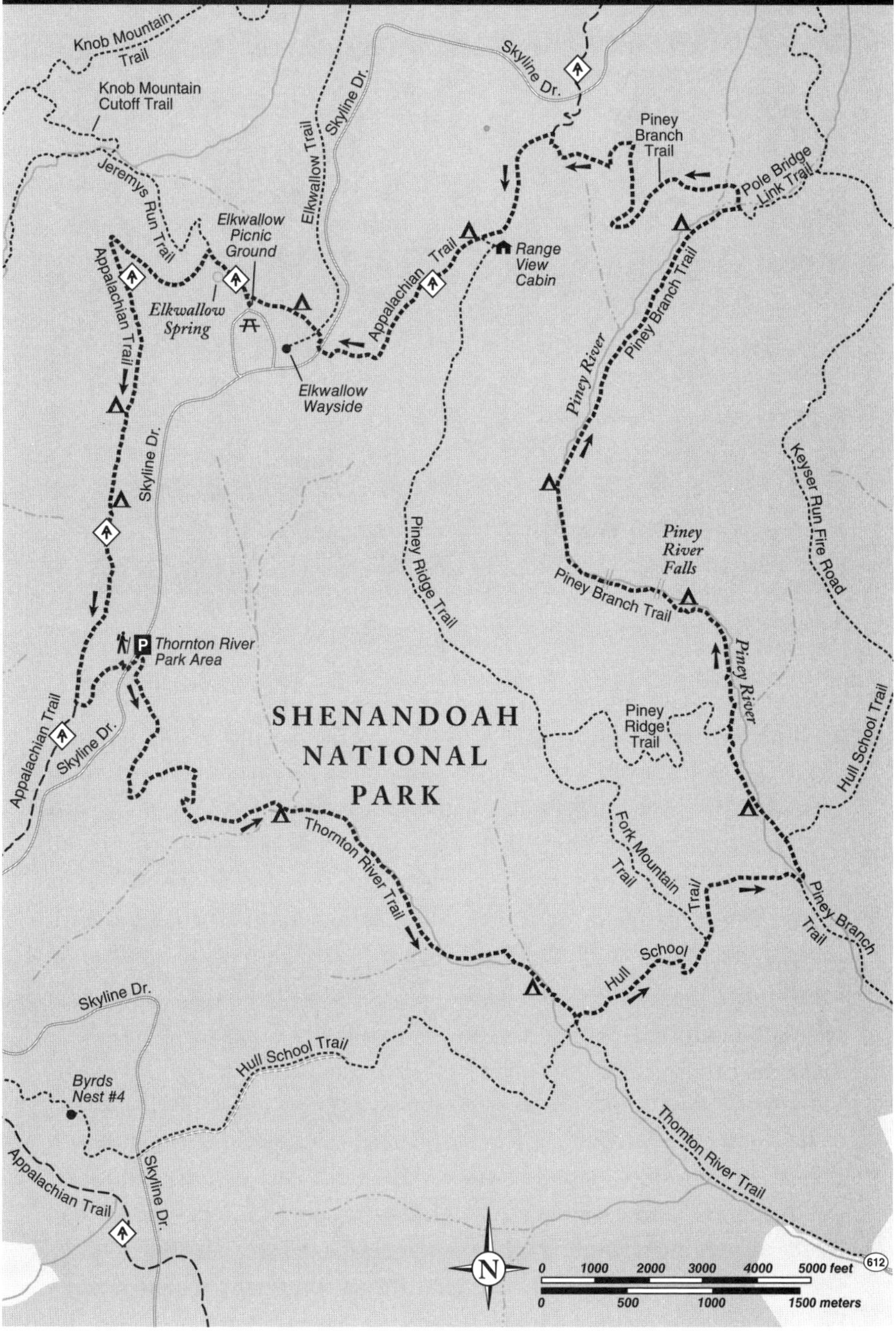

A backpacker makes one of many crossings of the Thornton River.

river crossing at 4.4 miles. Pass the Piney Ridge Trail at 4.7 miles. Keep up the Piney River, reaching a campsite at 5.2 miles just before the trail climbs away from the river. The stream gradient markedly sharpens. A couple of switchbacks lead up the mountainside.

Reach the spur to Piney River Falls at 5.4 miles. Take the side trail down to an open outcrop beside the watercourse as it slides and dashes 25 feet over an angled rock slope, along which you can walk before it dives into a plunge pool. The open rock slope makes a good break spot. Continuing uptrail, pass a ragged bluff at 5.6 miles to find a second fall. This one has a fainter access, dropping about 10 feet in two tiers amongst mossy boulders.

Cross over to the right-hand bank of Piney River at 5.8 miles. At 6.0 miles, look for a campsite in flats to the left. Climb past a transmission line, then join an old woods road heading left. Pass a spur leading far down to a flat and campsite. At 7.3 miles, reach an intersection. Head left here, staying with the Piney Branch Trail, crossing several tributaries that form the Piney River. Come to a grassy flat with a conspicuous boulder at 7.3 miles. This is a time-honored resting spot.

From there, make a few very gentle and very wide switchbacks before meeting the AT at 8.7 miles. Turn left on the AT, southbound, before coming to the Range View Cabin spur trail at 9.1 miles. A spring is down that way, too. The Range View Cabin is open for public rental through the Potomac Appalachian Trail Club. Find a campsite on the right just after resuming the AT.

Begin an extended downgrade on the AT, meeting Skyline Drive at 10.0 miles. Cross Skyline Drive and veer right, intersecting the Elkwallow Trail just ahead (to the left you can take the Elkwallow Trail to Elkwallow Wayside—ice cream, food, and drinks available during the warm season). Stay on the AT, descending amid a picturesque woodland carpeted in grass during the summer, passing a campsite at 10.2 miles.

Intersect the side trail to Elkwallow Picnic Ground at 10.3 miles. Resume the downgrade, still on the AT, before passing Elkwallow Spring and reaching Jeremys Run Trail at 10.5 miles. Make an acute left, staying on the AT.

The AT crosses the spring branch and begins an extended but gentle climb. Views of Knob Mountain open to your right. Round the point of the Blue Ridge at 11.0 miles. The ascent continues, then levels off at 11.5 miles.

Pass a campsite on this very pleasant stretch of the AT in Shenandoah National Park. Find a second campsite at 12.0 miles. The hiking remains easy to the junction with the Thornton River Trail at 12.7 miles. Turn left on the Thornton River Trail, quickly topping the Blue Ridge, then angling downslope using switchbacks to reach Skyline Drive at 13.0 miles. The Thornton River Trail parking area is a short distance to your left, across the scenic motor road.

Mileages

- 0.0 Thornton River parking area, milepost 25.4.
- 1.4 Cross tributary of North Fork Thornton River; campsite after crossing.
- 1.9 Cascade.
- 2.3 Cross Thornton River.
- 2.5 Cross Thornton River; campsites ahead.
- 2.8 Cross to left bank Thornton River.
- 2.9 Left on Hull School Trail.
- 3.5 Fork Mountain Trail leaves left.

4.1 Left on Piney Branch Trail/Hull School Trail; campsites in vicinity.
4.2 Hull School splits right; campsite ahead.
4.4 Cross Piney River; campsite.
4.7 Piney Ridge Trail leaves left.
5.2 Campsites; trail switchbacks uphill.
5.4 Spur to Piney River Falls; smaller fall .2 mile ahead.
5.8 Cross to right bank of Piney River; campsites ahead.
7.3 Trail intersection; stay left with Piney Branch Trail.
8.7 Left on AT.
9.1 Spur to Range View Cabin, spring, campsite ahead.
10.0 Cross Skyline Drive; Elkwallow Trail and campsite ahead.
10.3 Spur to Elkwallow Picnic Ground.
10.5 Intersect Jeremys Run Trail after passing Elkwallow Spring.
12.0 Campsite along AT.
12.5 Campsite.
12.7 Left on Thornton River Trail.
13.0 Skyline Drive, end of backpack.

11 • HAZEL MOUNTAIN

The Backpack: *This overnight adventure takes place in a large swath of interconnected trails—pre-park pioneer roads—in Shenandoah National Park. Leave Skyline Drive on Hazel Mountain Trail, dipping to view Hazel Falls and Cave. Pass views on White Rocks en route to the scenic Hazel River. From there, climb Sams Ridge, returning to the level lands of Hazel Mountain. Drop to the Hughes River. Circle back to the uplands via Hannah Run. Roll through formerly inhabited highlands, crossing the uppermost reaches of the Hazel River before backtracking to the trailhead. Campsites can be found low and high.*

The area of Shenandoah National Park through which this hike wanders is also known as Hazel Country, a locale of settled valleys and mountain plateaus where pre-park Virginians carved out lives. Thus, you can backpack in a mix of natural beauty and human history. The natural beauty shows in the mountain cascades, waterfalls, and pools as well as in vistas and rich woods punctuated with rock geological wonderment. The human history will be seen in rock walls and chimneys, now silent reminders of days gone by. Campsites are scattered throughout the loop, on ridgetops and rivers. I suggest camping one night along

11 HAZEL MOUNTAIN

Distance & configuration: 16.8-mile loop

Difficulty: Moderate, does have two short but steep sections

Backpacking time: 8 hours

Outstanding features: Hazel Falls and Cave, views, streamside camps

Elevation: 1,110′ low point, 2,850′ high point

Scenery: 4

Solitude: 4

Family friendly: 2

Canine friendly: 3

Fees/permits: Park entrance fee and free backcountry permit required

Best season: Spring through fall

Maps: PATC Shenandoah National Park Central District Map 10

For more info: Shenandoah National Park, 3655 U.S. Highway 211 East, Luray, VA 22835, 540-999-3500, www.nps.gov/shen

Finding the trailhead: From Luray, take US 211 east for 8.8 miles to Thornton Gap entrance of Shenandoah National Park. Head south on Skyline Drive for 2 miles to the Meadow Spring parking area, milepost 33.5, on your left. **GPS trailhead coordinates:** N38° 38.301′, W78° 18.825′

the Hazel River and the second night along the Hughes River, making a rewarding two-night circuit. Note: Trail intersections are frequent on this hike. Keep well apprised of your position.

Leave Skyline Drive on the Hazel Mountain Trail. Buck Hollow Trail immediately drops left. Pass the Buck Ridge Trail at .4 mile and stay with the Hazel Mountain Trail, tunneling through a dense canopy overhead. Soon the trail bears left, levels out, and crosses several small spring branches coursing off Buck Ridge. At 1.0 mile, come alongside the smallish Hazel River, then intersect the White Rocks Trail at 1.6 miles. Turn left on the White Rocks Trail, which ascends slightly in pine and chestnut oak as it attains the ridgetop.

At 2.0 miles, a spur trail leaves left to a level, shaded campsite. At 2.4 miles, intersect the signed spur to Hazel Falls and Cave. Campsites are in the vicinity. To reach the falls, drop steeply on a well-constructed path. Reach the river in .2 mile. Turn right, following the footpath through a geological wonderland of boulders, bluffs and cliffs, and Hazel Cave, about 10 feet deep, 24 feet wide, and 7 feet high. It lies at the base of a huge granite bluff. Nearby, Hazel Falls makes its slide about 25 feet down a narrow chute into a deep pool.

11 Hazel Mountain

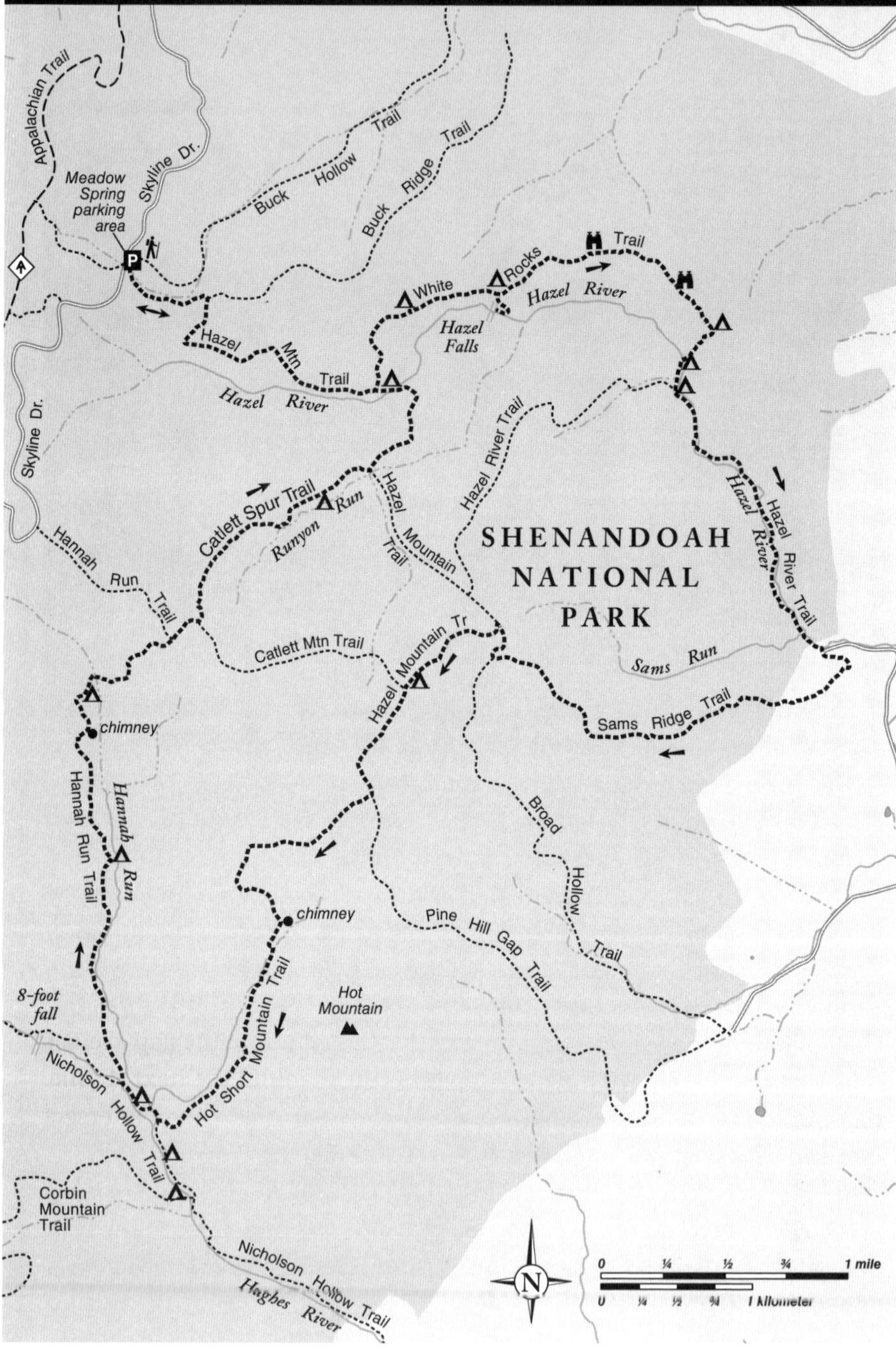

Hazel Falls spills into a rocky cathedral.

Return to the White Rocks Trail and turn right, easterly. The trail makes more down than up, rolling over the ridge of White Rocks, giving sporadic westerly views. At 3.1 miles, the White Rocks—to your left—exposes a pine-framed view of Skyline Drive, Buck Ridge, and the backside of Marys Rock. The trail alters character according to sun exposure. Where it is moist, tulip trees and northern red oak thrive; in drier areas, pine and laurel dominate. Watch for another outcrop to your left that avails eastward views at 3.6 miles.

The trail drops to a gap at 3.8 miles. Notice the triple-trunked oak tree here, shading a seldom-used campsite. Dive right from the gap to cross the Hazel River at 4.0 miles. Campsites can be found the next .4 mile. Pass through wooded flats, stepping over a small creek, then intersect the Hazel River Trail at mile 4.1. Turn left on the Hazel River Trail.

Continue down the attractive Hazel River valley, crossing the river four times in .7 mile. The sycamore-lined path crosses Sams Run, then intersects the Sams Ridge Trail at 5.6 miles. Get your climbing mojo on. Turn right on the Sams Ridge Trail and immediately begin rising, briefly leaving the park boundary on an easement. Look for sizable oak trees about.

The steep grade levels out briefly near a rock wall and resumes climbing until arriving at an old homesite on your left at 7.0 miles. Cross a spring branch. The walking is easy to the junction with the Broad Hollow Trail at 7.4 miles. Turn right at the junction. Both trails share the same treadway to meet the Hazel Mountain Trail at 7.6 miles. Turn left on the Hazel Mountain Trail, which heads a leisurely half-mile through crowded woods to pass a piney campsite on trail right just before meeting the Catlett Mountain Trail at 8.2 miles. Continue straight through the junction, staying on the Hazel Mountain Trail in pine woodland.

The Pine Hill Gap Trail enters from your left at 8.7 miles. Stay right here, picking up the Hot Short Mountain Trail. It skirts the south side of Catlett Mountain. Intermittent views open up to your left of Old Rag. Look for an old chimney on your left at mile 9.7, then drop to cross a small stream. The trail then turns away from the creek, traversing a bluff before descending to big flats with rock walls aplenty. Intersect the Nicholson Hollow Trail at 10.8 miles. Campsites can be found downstream along the Hughes River, as well as upstream.

The loop turns right, up the Nicholson Hollow Trail. Soon rock-hop Hannah Run, then turn right on the Hannah Run Trail at 11.1 miles. Traverse a rising flat with rock walls, rock piles, and even a chimney on your left. Pass a seldom-used campsite on trail right at 12.1 miles. The rocky trail veers away from Hannah Run and parallels the stream high above the run. Locate a mostly intact chimney and a few rusted-out washtubs marking a homesite at 12.6 miles. Pass a sloped campsite in pines just before descending back to Hannah Run. Step over the stream and begin a very tough .2-mile climb out of the watershed.

The walking is much easier for the remaining distance to a trail junction at 13.3 miles. Here, the Hannah Run Trail heads left for Skyline Drive, but we stay right on the Catlett Mountain Trail, going downhill for .1 mile, then come to a second junction. Turn left on the Catlett Spur Trail, still descending, off and on an old road among the headwaters of Runyons Run.

Pass a campsite and rock walls on your right at 14.4 miles, then make a near-level course before coming to the Hazel Mountain Trail at 14.6 miles. Turn left, back on the Hazel Mountain Trail, and round over a small ridge before dropping to meet the Hazel River near campsites at 15.1 miles. Come to the junction with the White Rocks Trail at 15.2 miles. Retrace your steps up the Hazel Mountain Trail to arrive at Skyline Drive at mile 16.8, completing the national park backpack.

Mileages

0.0 Meadow Spring parking area, milepost 33.5.
0.4 Buck Ridge Trail leaves left.
1.6 Left on White Rocks Trail.
2.0 Campsite left.
2.4 Spur right to Hazel Falls and Cave; campsites near intersection.
2.7 Hazel Falls and Cave; backtrack.
3.0 Resume White Rocks Trail; views ahead.
3.8 Gap, campsite; descend to Hazel River.
4.0 Cross Hazel River; campsites.
4.1 Left on Hazel River Trail; campsite.
5.6 Right on Sams Ridge Trail, steep climb.
7.4 Broad Hollow Trail.
7.6 Left on Hazel Mountain Trail.
8.2 Catlett Mountain Trail enters right; campsites.
8.7 Right on Hot Short Mountain Trail.
10.8 Right on Nicholson Hollow Trail; campsites.
11.1 Right on Hannah Run Trail.
12.1 Seldom-used campsite.
13.3 Right on Catlett Mountain Trail.
13.4 Left on Catlett Spur Trail.
14.4 Campsite, rock walls.
14.6 Left on Hazel Mountain Trail.
15.1 Cross upper Hazel River; campsites.
15.2 Intersection; stay left with Hazel Mountain Trail, backtracking.
16.8 Return to trailhead, completing the backpack.

12 • HUGHES RIVER

The Backpack: *This Shenandoah National Park backpack is along or near water most of its 14-mile distance. It starts high on Skyline Drive, then descends to the Hughes River, where you view historic Corbin Cabin. Follow the Hughes River past cascades before turning up Brokenback Run in the shadow of famed Old Rag Mountain. Climb farther into wild Corbin Hollow, eventually reaching the high country, only to drop along Indian Run, returning to the Hughes River. Hike the upper valley of the Hughes to its spring-fed origins. A brief stint on the Appalachian Trail (AT) takes you back to the trailhead. Campsites—though not always easy to spot—are spread all along the loop.*

12 HUGHES RIVER

Distance & configuration: 14.3-mile loop

Difficulty: Moderate to difficult

Backpacking time: 8 hours

Outstanding features: Cascades along Hughes River, Corbin Cabin

Elevation: 915′ low point, 3,170′ high point

Scenery: 4

Solitude: 3

Family friendly: 3

Canine friendly: 3

Fees/permits: Park entrance fee and free backcountry permit required

Best season: Spring through fall

Maps: PATC Shenandoah National Park Central District Map 10

For more info: Shenandoah National Park, 3655 U.S. Highway 211 East, Luray, VA 22835, 540-999-3500, www.nps.gov/shen

Finding the trailhead: From Luray, take US 211 east for 8.8 miles to Thornton Gap entrance of Shenandoah National Park. Head south on Skyline Drive for 6.6 miles to the Corbin Cabin Cutoff Trail trailhead, milepost 37.9, on the west side of Skyline Drive, with seven spaces. The trailhead is on a hilly curve and is easily missed. The Corbin Cabin Cutoff Trail starts across the road from the parking area. **GPS trailhead coordinates:** N38° 36.938′, W78° 21.030′

This route allows you to explore some of Shenandoah's preserved pioneer history, see some attractive waterways, and even spend the night in a cabin built and lived in by a pre-park resident named George Corbin. Furthermore, with a layover day, you can make a side trip to Old Rag, Virginia's contribution to great mountains of the world. Campsites are found at typical Shenandoah locations—in flats along streams and near trail intersections. Be apprised that despite the moderate difficulty rating of the backpack, it does entail over 2,000 feet variance between high and low points. Novices may treat this as a difficult hike. Also, backpackers can make this a short 4-mile loop, shortcutting the longer circuit hike at Corbin Cabin.

Start the full adventure by joining the Corbin Cabin Cutoff Trail, a pre-park path used by local residents, improved by the park service, as are many of the paths in the Hughes River valley, one of the most heavily settled areas in what became Shenandoah National Park. Approximately twenty families lived along the Hughes River when the park was established.

12 Hughes River

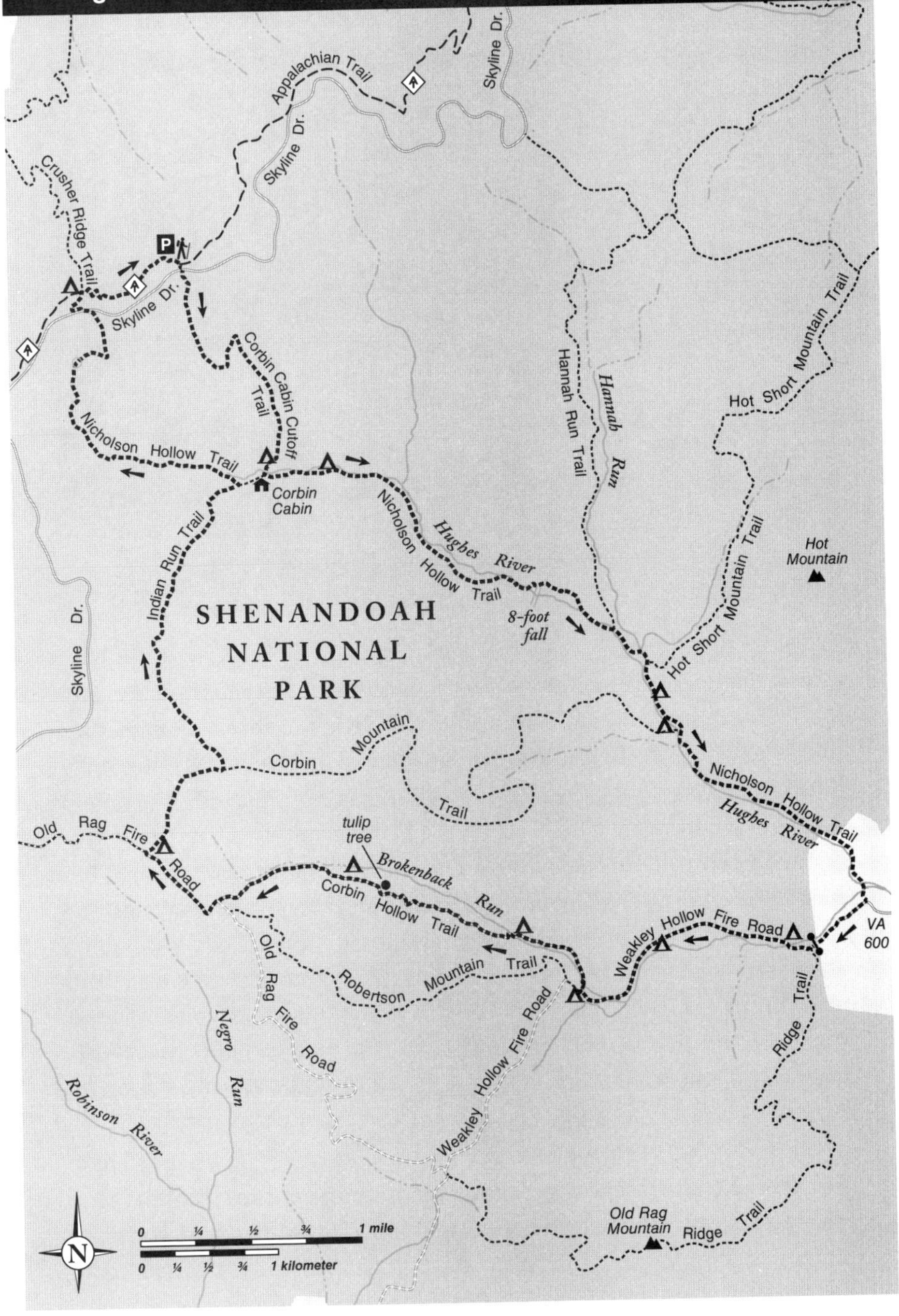

You can upgrade your overnighting options by spending the night in the historic Corbin Cabin.

Join a wooded ridgeline before the gradient sharpens to turn into a hollow at .5 mile. Saddle alongside a gurgling branch. Look for rock piles and walls, the first of plentiful pioneer evidence. At 1.2 miles, hike beside an exposed rock wall. Pass a spur leading right uphill to an old pioneer cemetery.

Pass a campsite to the left and a spur to a structure on the right before rock-hopping the Hughes River, entering the clearing around the Corbin Cabin at 1.5 miles (no camping immediately around the cabin). The cabin—listed on the National Register of Historic Places and rentable through the Potomac Appalachian Trail Club—received a restoration in 2017. You can rent the Corbin Cabin with prior planning. This is also where you can cut off the longer loop and go for the 4-mile circuit backpack, a good one-nighter.

Check out the century-plus old cabin, then head east, down the Nicholson Hollow Trail. Quickly pass a crumbled chimney. Trace the old wagon track past a campsite at 1.7 miles. The stream flows as rocky rapids and slows in dark pools under rich woods. By 2.6 miles, the trail and stream gradient steepen amid tall tulip trees. Stream pools increase, too.

At 2.9 miles, cross the Hughes River atop massive boulders lined up to aid passage. Keep down the left bank, passing a no-camping area near an 8-foot waterfall. Enter larger flats to step over Hannah Run, then meet the Hannah Run Trail at 3.5 miles. Stay with Nicholson Hollow Trail, looking for campsites to your left. Pass the Hot Short Mountain Trail at 3.7 miles. Additional piney campsites lie ahead on Nicholson Hollow Trail. At 4.1 miles, the Corbin Mountain Trail comes in on your right. Campsites are located across the Hughes River near this intersection.

Keep down the Hughes River, briefly leaving the old wagon track, to return to the river. At 4.4 miles, watch for a big stream pool with a campsite a little downtrail. At 5.1 miles, cross the park boundary. Follow an easement, rock-hopping the Hughes River, then come to a gate and access road at 5.3 miles. Head left on the road to quickly reach the Weakley Hollow Fire Road near Nethers. Turn right here, walking up a paved track. Pass around a gate at 5.8 miles, officially reentering Shenandoah National Park. Here, you may see hikers joining the Ridge Trail, the very popular hike to Old Rag.

We stay straight on the Weakley Hollow Fire Road, crossing a couple of tributaries before crossing Brokenback Run at 5.9 miles (there is a footbridge here). A poor campsite is on the right just after the crossing. A better site can be found in the flats below the fire road at 6.5 miles. Cross Brokenback Run on a road bridge at 6.8 miles, then come to a trail intersection and campsite at 7.0 miles. This would be a good area to camp if making a side trip to Old Rag. Allow a full extra day if heading to Old Rag.

The Hughes River Backpack joins the Corbin Hollow Trail here, rock-hopping Brokenback Run. The singletrack path is crowded with laurel and rocks exuding a deep woods aura. At 7.4 miles, cross Brokenback Run, passing a campsite. Climb away from the stream, looking for an old homesite ahead. Step over a wide spring branch at 8.0 miles. Swing above an old-growth tulip tree at 8.2 miles. Pass a sloped campsite at 8.5 miles and keep climbing.

At 9.0 miles, turn right onto Old Rag Fire Road. The walking is easy as you cruise upland woods on a doubletrack. At 9.5 miles, leave the fire road right, picking up the Corbin Mountain Trail. Pass a campsite, then cross a few spring branches before ascending a bit to turn left onto Indian Run Trail at 10.1 miles. Turn into the Indian Run streamshed, making a rocky descent with a dearth of campsites. At 11.7 miles, return

To Drink or Not to Drink: Water in the Backcountry

I drink untreated water. No I'm not talking about down Mexico way (I did that and got sick). I'm talking about drinking water in the backcountry in the United States. Locally, I mean springs and creeks flowing off the Appalachians of Virginia. I've drank from swamps down in Florida and wilderness rivers in New Mexico. I've drank from alpine lakes high in the California Sierras and iron-rich lakes in Minnesota.

Face it, while backpacking, we cannot bring all the water we will need to drink. That means we will have to obtain water from local sources. Backpackers are faced with the dilemma while in the back of beyond: Do I drink the water?

I am in the minority, but I drink the water directly from the source and don't treat it. To the chagrin of my backpacking compadres I haven't gotten sick. However, consider the following do-as-I-say-not-as-I-do advice: Treat your water. When I first got into backpacking, the group I begin going with didn't treat their water. As a novice, I did what they did and somehow became acclimated to drinking untreated water, a simple twist of aquatic fate you might say.

Another time, two of us were backpacking near Yellowstone's Heart Lake for several days. We drank the water directly from the area streams and lakes. My fellow backpacker got sick from the water and I didn't. The same thing happened while backpacking Michigan's Ottawa National Forest and Montana's Glacier National Park (all of the above filter their water now.)

So what can drinking bad water do? Microbes such as giardia and cryptosporidium get into your intestines and disrupt your life with excessive gas, diarrhea, and other unpleasantries. Giardiasis—the illness caused by giardia—won't ruin your average backpacking trip, as it takes 1 to 2 weeks for symptoms to appear. But once symptoms crop up, expect to be ill for 2 to 6 weeks. Weight loss and dehydration follow. A doctor's

to the Nicholson Hollow Trail. The Corbin Cabin is but .2 mile distant to the right, but we head left, to the upper reaches of the Hughes River.

At 13.0 miles, pass a trailside stone-lined spring. Climb into pine-oak-laurel woods, then emerge onto Skyline Drive at 13.5. here; turn left, walking along Skyline Drive for about 50 yards before returning to foot trail on the west side of the drive. Quickly reach an intersection. Stay right here, briefly joining the Crusher Ridge Trail to meet the AT at 13.6 miles. Campsites can be found to the left on the AT. Our loop heads right on the AT, northbound. Switchback downhill, then cruise below Skyline Drive, reaching the short spur to the Corbin Cabin Cutoff Trail parking area at 14.3 miles. Walk right just a few feet on the spur, completing the backpack.

gut-relieving prescription and plenty of fluids may help with the symptoms, which will eventually run their course, resulting in one painful weight-loss program.

Treating your water has become a lot easier these days, but let's harken back for a moment. The old method was to boil your water for at least a minute—there's nothing like hot water to sate a big thirst! It's not convenient either; you have to wait until after your water is boiled, which means you have to have made a fire or broken out a camp stove.

Then came the pump filters—you literally pump your water through a device that filters out the demon microorganisms. Pump filters were once bulky but are now smaller and commonly used. Many people use chemical water treatments.

Iodine was the choice of days gone by, but it has an awful taste and gives you iodine breath, which ain't good. Nowadays we have products like Aqua Mira, where you mix two drops of chemicals, making chlorine dioxide, and wait 30 minutes; then your water is fine. Again, the wait is a problem, but it is the lightest option. Buying a water bottle with a built-in filter is an easier choice. Simply fill your water bottle, then suck through a straw, which forces the water through a built-in small filter, which needs to be replaced often.

UV filters are another option, using ultraviolet rays to kill the bad things in the aqua. These products, such as Steripen, use batteries, which can die.

Simple filters such as the gravity-fed Sawyer are lightweight and cheap, and they last for years. They use special microbe-blocking membranes and operate using gravity—or squeeze pressure if you're in a hurry. The filters are used in undeveloped countries throughout the world.

No matter your method, treating your water is smart. Otherwise, you may spend your time being sick instead of backpacking.

Mileages

0.0 Corbin Cabin Cutoff Trail parking area, milepost 55.1.
1.4 Campsite.
1.5 Cross Hughes River, Corbin Cabin; left on Nicholson Hollow Trail.
1.7 Campsite.
2.9 Cross Hughes River; waterfall ahead.
3.5 Intersect Hannah Run Trail; campsite downtrail.
3.7 Intersect Hot Short Mountain Trail; piney campsites downtrail.
4.1 Intersect Corbin Mountain Trail; campsite across river.
4.4 Big pool; campsite downtrail.

5.1 Leave park, follow easement, cross Hughes River.
5.3 Left at gate, then right onto paved Weakley Hollow Road.
5.8 Reenter park; Ridge Trail leaves left; stay straight on Weakley Hollow Fire Road.
5.9 Rock-hop Brokenback Run; poor campsite beyond crossing.
6.5 Campsite in flats below trail.
6.8 Cross Brokenback Run on a road bridge.
7.0 Intersection, campsite, right on Corbin Hollow Trail.
7.4 Cross Brokenback Run; campsite.
8.2 Old-growth tulip tree.
8.5 Campsite on Brokenback Run.
9.0 Right on Old Rag Fire Road.
9.5 Right on Corbin Mountain Trail; campsite ahead.
10.1 Left on Indian Run Trail.
11.7 Left on Nicholson Hollow Trail.
13.0 Trailside spring.
13.5 Skyline Drive.
13.6 Right on AT.
14.3 Return to trailhead, completing the backpack.

13 • RAPIDAN RIVER

The Backpack: *This challenging, scenic, and highlight-heavy loop takes place at Shenandoah National Park and adjacent Virginia state lands. Start atop the Blue Ridge before descending to the Staunton River, rich with cascades and waterfalls, before turning up the Rapidan River, featuring deep pools and massive boulders. Stop by historic Rapidan Camp, mountain getaway of President Hoover, before climbing past Big Rock Falls to reach the Appalachian Trail (AT). Cruise the high country, soaking in a view or two before completing the backpack. Campsites can be found throughout the circuit.*

This backpack explores the highs and lows of Shenandoah National Park as well as adjacent Rapidan Wildlife Management Area (WMA). Though you may be camping in the WMA, it is best to get a Shenandoah National Park camping permit, since you are leaving your vehicle in the park overnight. Additionally, having a permit keeps open the option of camping in the park. Remember, campfires are not allow in the park but are allowed in the WMA. Also, know that part of the route through the

13 RAPIDAN RIVER

Distance & configuration: 18.6-mile loop

Difficulty: Difficult due to elevation changes

Backpacking time: 10.5 hours

Outstanding features: Waterfalls, Rapidan Camp, views

Elevation: 980′ low point, 3,805′ high point

Scenery: 5

Solitude: 3

Family friendly: 1

Canine friendly: 2

Fees/permits: Park entrance fee and free backcountry permit required

Best season: Late spring through late fall

Maps: PATC Shenandoah National Park Central District Map 10

For more info: Shenandoah National Park, 3655 U.S. Highway 211 East, Luray, VA 22835, 540-999-3500, www.nps.gov/shen

Finding the trailhead: From the intersection of US 340 and US 33 in Elkton, take US 33 east to Swift Run Gap entrance station of Shenandoah National Park. From there, drive north on Skyline Drive for 10.6 miles to Bootens Gap parking area, a small lot on the east side of Skyline Drive at milepost 55.1. **GPS trailhead coordinates:** N38° 28.102′, W78° 27.440′

WMA is on a road open to vehicles, though Rapidan Fire Road in the park is closed to public vehicles, except the portion accessing Rapidan WMA.

Join the AT from Bootens Gap, northbound, gently ascending toward Hazeltop. At .4 mile, turn right on the stony Laurel Prong Trail, descending past springs originating on Hazeltop. A sharp drop precedes your arrival at Laurel Gap at 1.4 miles. Dry campsites for late arrivers can be found in the vicinity. Keep straight, joining the short but steep Cat Knob Trail, winding upward among boulders. Top out, then drop a bit to meet the Jones Mountain Trail at 2.0 miles.

Here, you turn left on the Jones Mountain Trail, dipping into gorgeous maple-oak-laurel woodland, leveling out among ferns. You could make a remote camp here, minus water. Reach The Sag and a trail intersection at 2.9 miles. Head right on the Fork Mountain Fire Road, descending a wide, gravel doubletrack closed to public vehicles. At 3.7 miles, turn right onto the singletrack footpath Staunton River Trail. The hiking immediately becomes much tougher on a stony track paralleling the

13 Rapidan River

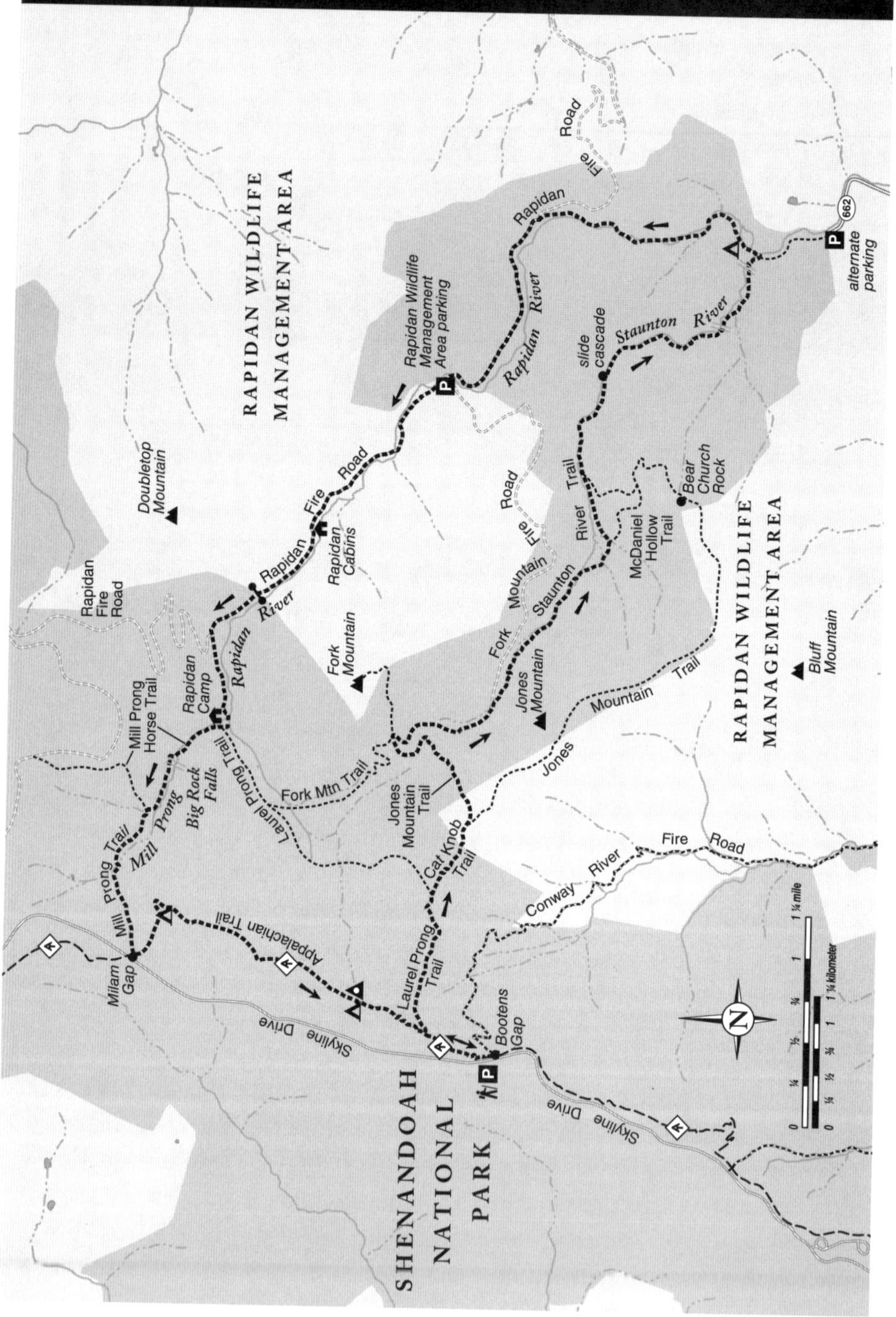

Soak in this Appalachian Trail view near Hazeltop.

quickly tumbling Staunton River, ensconced in yellow birch and other hardwoods.

The path alternately nears and turns away from the almost continuously cascading waterway in a steep-sided valley. Rock-hop over to the left bank at 4.7 miles. Pass a flat with piled chestnut boards at a place known as Hundley's Ford, then cross the Staunton again. The path eases and widens, tracing a woods road once used for training troops in World War II. The valley flattens—look for rock walls and other evidence of habitation.

Pass the McDaniel Hollow Trail near a massive boulder, then continue down the valley to reach the other end of the Jones Mountain Trail at 5.5 miles. This part of the valley was heavily settled. Pass a noteworthy 12-foot slide cascade at 6.2 miles and a 20-foot slender spiller snaking over naked rock into a plunge pool at 7.1 miles. Below here, the Staunton breaks up into channels, braiding around islands. At 7.6 miles, pass above another waterfall just upstream of a USGS water gauge. This one drops about 20 feet over a stone face.

At 7.7 miles, turn left on the Graves Mill Trail, bisecting a flat then rock-hopping the Staunton River at its confluence with the bigger Rapidan River. Campsites are ahead. The walking is easy on the wide trail. Rock-hop the Rapidan River at 8.8 miles. Uptrail, pass miles of big pools and bigger boulders, luring hikers to the water. The trail and river gradients increase. Meet the Rapidan Fire Road at 9.4 miles. Join a gravel doubletrack open to auto traffic, so visitors can access Rapidan WMA.

Continue upriver. Cross the bridge over the Rapidan at 11.0 miles, entering Rapidan WMA. Roadside campsites become numerous ahead. Pass the Rapidan WMA parking area. At 12.3 miles, come near the historic Rapidan Cabins, an outlier of Herbert Hoover's camp. These cabins can be rented through rapidancamps.org. At 12.9 miles, leave Rapidan WMA and easy roadside campsites, reentering Shenandoah National Park. The walking remains easy, however. At 13.3 miles, Rapidan Fire Road leaves right; you stay left toward Rapidan Camp, the Hoover retreat. No camping is allowed from here until a half-mile beyond Rapidan Camp.

At 13.8 miles, split left, crossing Mill Prong on a footbridge to reach Rapidan Camp. Explore the buildings and extensive interpretive information concerning what was also known as Camp Hoover, the first presidential retreat, occupied during President Hoover's term, 1929–33. It is worth your time. From here, join the relatively narrow Mill Prong Horse Trail, ascending from the camp in lush woods. At 14.3 miles, cross Mill Prong at Big Rock Falls, an 18-foot spiller sliding over a big rock. Continue a steeper uptick, leaving the no-camping zone.

At 14.8 miles, stay left with the Mill Prong Trail while the Mill Prong Horse Trail heads right. Campsites are in the vicinity. Ahead, cross a shallow section of Mill Prong, then rise through brushy woods to meet the AT at 15.8 miles, near Milam Gap. Head left, southbound on Shenandoah's backbone trail. Pass a dry campsite at 16.3 miles. Enjoy a long, straight, and level stretch on a narrowing ridge.

At 17.7 miles, a spur trail leads right to an overlook and sloped campsite. Gaze westerly into the Shenandoah Valley and beyond to West Virginia. Ahead, gently rise, reaching 3,800 feet in elevation before drifting down to meet the Laurel Prong Trail at 18.2 miles. From here, it is but a .4-mile backtrack to Bootens Gap and the end of the Virginia backpacking adventure.

Mileages

0.0 Bootens Gap parking area, milepost 55.1 Skyline Drive.
0.4 Right on Laurel Prong Trail.
1.4 Laurel Gap, campsites in vicinity; join Cat Knob Trail.
2.0 Left on Jones Mountain Trail.
2.9 Reach The Sag; right on Fork Mountain Fire Road.
3.7 Right on Staunton River Trail.
4.7 Reach two crossings and piled chestnut boards at Hundley's Ford.
5.5 Pass other end of Jones Mountain Trail, falls ahead.
7.7 Left on Graves Mill Trail; campsites ahead.
9.4 Left on Rapidan Fire Road.
11.0 Enter Rapidan WMA; roadside campsites.
12.3 Pass rentable Rapidan Cabins.
13.8 Historic Rapidan Camp; join Mill Prong Horse Trail.
14.3 Big Rock Falls.
14.8 Left on Mill Prong Trail; campsites in vicinity.
15.8 Left on AT, southbound.
16.3 Campsite.
17.7 Overlook and sloped campsite.
18.2 Pass Laurel Prong Trail.
18.6 Bootens Gap, end backpack.

14 • BEARFENCE MOUNTAIN

The Backpack: *This adventure is challenging and rewarding as it winds through Shenandoah National Park and adjacent Rapidan Wildlife Management Area (WMA). Leave Skyline Drive, tracing the Conway River from its highland origins. From the lower Conway, climb the remote Slaughter Trail, reaching the upper Devils Ditch before meeting the Appalachian Trail (AT). Pass a trail shelter before climbing Bearfence Mountain, where 360-degree views await. From there, the AT leads you back to the point of origin. Campsites are found mostly along the Conway River.*

This backpack descends from the crest of the Blue Ridge to follow picturesque Conway River, leaving Shenandoah National Park and entering state of Virginia–managed Rapidan Wildlife Management Area, where campsites can be easily found. Fires are allowed in the WMA. No fires

14 BEARFENCE MOUNTAIN

Distance & configuration: 12.0-mile loop

Difficulty: Moderate to difficult due to one steep section

Backpacking time: 7.5 hours

Outstanding features: Bearfence Mountain views, wildflowers along Conway River

Elevation: 1,250′ low point, 3,540′ high point

Scenery: 5

Solitude: 3

Family friendly: 2

Canine friendly: 3

Fees/permits: Park entrance fee and free backcountry permit required

Best season: Spring through late fall; avoid winter

Maps: PATC Shenandoah National Park Central District Map 10

For more info: Shenandoah National Park, 3655 U.S. Highway 211 East, Luray, VA 22835, 540-999-3500, www.nps.gov/shen

Finding the trailhead: From the intersection of US 340 and US 33 in Elkton, take US 33 east to Swift Run Gap entrance station of Shenandoah National Park. From there, drive north on Skyline Drive for 10.6 miles to Bootens Gap parking area, a small lot on the east side of Skyline Drive at milepost 55.1. **GPS trailhead coordinates:** N38° 28.102′, W78° 27.440′

are allowed in Shenandoah National Park. Backpackers can turn this loop into a laidback two-night trip. Nearby Lewis Mountain Campground makes a good night-before-the-backpack camping option or alternately could be incorporated into the backpack with an under-one-mile detour off the described loop.

Join the Conway River Fire Road, leaving the Bootens Gap Trailhead on a wide, grassy track, sometimes overgrown in mid- to late summer. The hiking is easy as you make two switchbacks before catching sight of the upper Conway River at 0.7 mile. In late summer and fall this part of the river can run dry. The hardwood forest rises correspondingly as you descend into the valley. At 1.4 miles, walk around a gate, entering Rapidan WMA. Campsites are more frequent in the WMA. Join a rough doubletrack after crossing a stream at 1.6 miles. Reach an unnamed stream at 2.6 miles, where a wet-weather, springtime waterfall spills about 25 feet. Look upstream about 50 yards from the trail crossing. The fire road then follows this tributary downstream to reach a fork in the road at 2.8 miles. The left fork leads to a grassy opening. Stay on the right fork, crossing Bootens Run at 3.3 miles. Just ahead you will

14 Bearfence Mountain

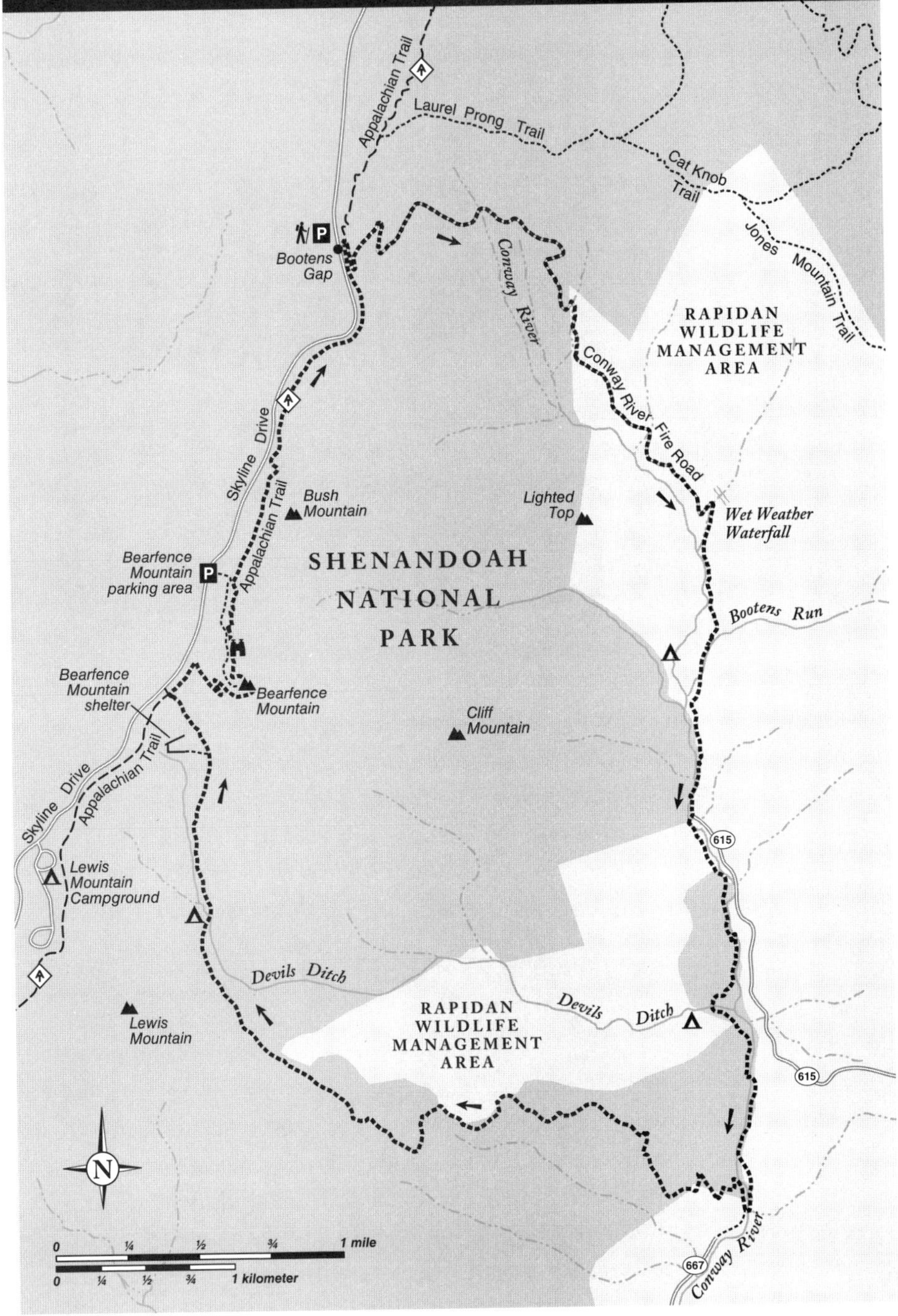

Bearfence Mountain presents some of the best panoramas in the Old Dominion.

saddle alongside the Conway River. This rocky, trouty, and bold stream makes a scenic boundary between the national park and the WMA at this point. Campsites are found in this area.

Come to a signature concrete Shenandoah National Park trail signpost at 3.8 miles. Here, VA 615 leads left. Leave right on the Conway River Trail. Reaching the first crossing of the Conway River, reenter the national park. When the water is low, such as summer and fall, it is a matter of a simple rock-hop. However, expect to ford during winter and early spring.

From here on out, the jeep traffic is gone. Enjoy the Conway River, alternately showing off its pools and rapids, as well as a vast array of wildflowers in spring, all under a rich tree canopy. At 4.4 miles, come to a former homestead, with its level ground and rock piles. At 4.8 miles, cross the Devils Ditch. You are briefly back in the Rapidan WMA, and a path leads right up to a piney campsite. At 5.0 miles, come to a challenging ford of the Conway River. It is littered with big boulders and can be fairly deep if the water is up. Beyond the ford, the path leads uphill among pines, then descends back to the Conway. Reach the third and final river crossing—a likely ford—at 5.5 miles. A deep pool near the crossing makes a fine hot-weather swimming hole and fishing spot. The Conway is a haven for brook trout, with special regulations. From here, VA 667 is just .3 mile downriver (very limited parking).

Across the ford, reach the Slaughter Trail intersection. Join the Slaughter Trail and begin heading upstream along the Conway River, now to your right. View rock walls and planted bushes of an old riverside homesite. The Slaughter Trail leaves the river, climbing steeply up a spur ridge leading toward Lewis Mountain. You will be in Shenandoah National Park for the remainder of the backpack.

At 5.7 miles, the trail switchbacks left and becomes even steeper, to level off at 6.5 miles, making an 850-foot ascent in 1 mile! The Slaughter Trail then cuts through a gap and climbs a bit more before reaching the crumbling chimney and foundation of a homesite at 6.6 miles. However, the homesite's spring is still flowing, beyond the chimney.

Keep ascending on the Slaughter Trail, nearing blazed boundary trees. Pass the ruins of an outbuilding on your left and a split-rail fence on your right. Find another spring at 7.3 miles. The trail mercifully levels out at 7.7 miles, just a little below 3,000 feet in elevation. Cruise the east slope of Lewis Mountain.

Irregularly lose some of that hard-earned elevation, dropping to the upper mountain-laurel-laden Devils Ditch at 8.6 miles. Look for a campsite just before crossing the stream. Enjoy easy hiking as you parallel the Devils Ditch to reach an intersection at 9.4 miles. To the left, a doubletrack leads to Bearfence Mountain trail shelter, a three-sided stone hut. The Slaughter Trail goes but .1 mile farther to meet the AT at 9.5 miles.

Turn right, northbound, on the well-trammeled AT, ascending through low pines and mountain laurel as you work up the southwest side of Bearfence Mountain (a left turn takes you a little under a mile to Lewis Mountain Campground). Work into rocky terrain. At 10.1 miles, intersect the Bearfence Mountain Loop Trail. Turn right, leaving the AT, to join the loop trail. At 10.2 miles, take a short spur left to an outcrop. Soak in panoramas of Skyline Drive, Massanutten Mountain, and Shenandoah Valley below.

Just ahead, turn right onto the signed Bearfence Mountain Rock Scramble. The scramble is doable with a full backpack but is closed to pets. Frequent blue blazes take you amid outcrops and boulders leading to incredible views stretching 360 degrees, one of Shenandoah's best panoramas. Clamber to upthrust rocks with additional vistas. Wow!

The scramble morphs to standard trail, returning to the AT at 10.6 miles. Rejoin the AT southbound, skirting Bush Mountain beneath in oak woods before coming near Skyline Drive. It isn't long before you return to Bootens Gap parking area, finishing the backpack at 12.0 miles.

Mileages

0.0 Bootens Gap parking area, milepost 55.1.
1.4 Gate into Rapidan WMA.
2.6 Waterfall about 40 yards up a side stream.
3.3 Cross Bootens Run; campsites ahead.
3.8 Cross Conway River.
4.8 Cross Devils Ditch; campsite up side trail beyond crossing.
5.0 Cross Conway River.
5.5 Cross Conway River, pick up Slaughter Trail.
6.6 Homesite.
8.6 Campsite just prior to crossing upper Devils Ditch.
9.4 Left spur to Bearfence Mountain shelter.
9.5 Right on AT.
10.1 Right on Bearfence Mountain Loop Trail.
10.2 View, then right at Bearfence Mountain Rock Scramble.
10.4 Panorama stretching in all directions.
10.6 Right on AT.
12.0 Bootens Gap, end backpack.

15 • BIG RUN

The Backpack: *The circuit trip takes you into Shenandoah National park's largest watershed: Big Run. Descend from the Blue Ridge and drop along the watercourse, passing numerous campsites, following the stream for miles. Return to remote uplands, passing Rockytop and other spots with vistas before looping back on a portion of the Appalachian Trail (AT). The preferred camping is along Big Run. Spend a day or three along the stream, fishing, swimming, and relaxing, then make a break back to the trailhead, though waterless campsites can be found along the ridges.*

The backpack departs Big Run Overlook, where you can look down upon the Big Run watershed before picking up the singletrack Big Run Loop Trail as it winds under a canopy of strong oaks, stronger hickory, and gnarly mountain laurel. Boulders are strewn about the trailside vegeta-

15 BIG RUN

Distance & configuration: 14.5-mile loop

Difficulty: Moderate to difficult

Backpacking time: 8 hours

Outstanding features: Pools of Big Run

Elevation: 1,260′ low point, 2,870′ high point

Scenery: 5

Solitude: 2

Family friendly: 3

Canine friendly: 3

Fees/permits: Park entrance fee and free backcountry permit required

Best season: Spring through late fall

Maps: PATC Shenandoah National Park South District Map 11

For more info: Shenandoah National Park, 3655 U.S. Highway 211 East, Luray, VA 22835, 540-999-3500, www.nps.gov/shen

Finding the trailhead: From exit 99 on I-64 between Waynesboro and Charlottesville, head north into Shenandoah National Park and Rockfish Gap entrance station. From there, drive north on Skyline Drive for 23.6 miles to Big Run Overlook, on the west side of Skyline Drive at milepost 81.2. The Big Run Trail begins on the south side of the overlook. **GPS trailhead coordinates:** N38° 15.222′, W78° 41.053′

tion as you switchback toward Big Run. At 1.2 miles, the path crosses an intermittent stream that can feature a small cascade in winter and spring.

The path next joins a piney ridge, cuts through a gap, then resumes its course for Big Run, which you reach at 2.2 miles. Note the overhanging rock shelter to the left of the trail just before reaching Big Run. Step over the stream, entering a cool cove hardwood forest of tulip trees, black birch, and sugar maple.

Reach a concrete-post-marked intersection here. Turn right onto the Big Run Portal Trail. A flat off to your right once housed a trail shelter before the area became part of the Shenandoah Wilderness. The shelter was removed, and now the flat sports a "No camping" sign.

The trail gradient moderates as you descend along Big Run, crossing it numerous times, passing campsites aplenty before coming to the Patterson Ridge Trail at 4.4 miles. Stay on the Big Run Portal Trail under a green tunnel, rock-hopping Rocky Mountain Run, then make another intersection at 4.6 miles. Here, the Rocky Mountain Run Trail rises right toward the Blue Ridge, offering streamside scenery and more campsites. Stay with the Big Run Portal Trail, descending through wooded

15 Big Run

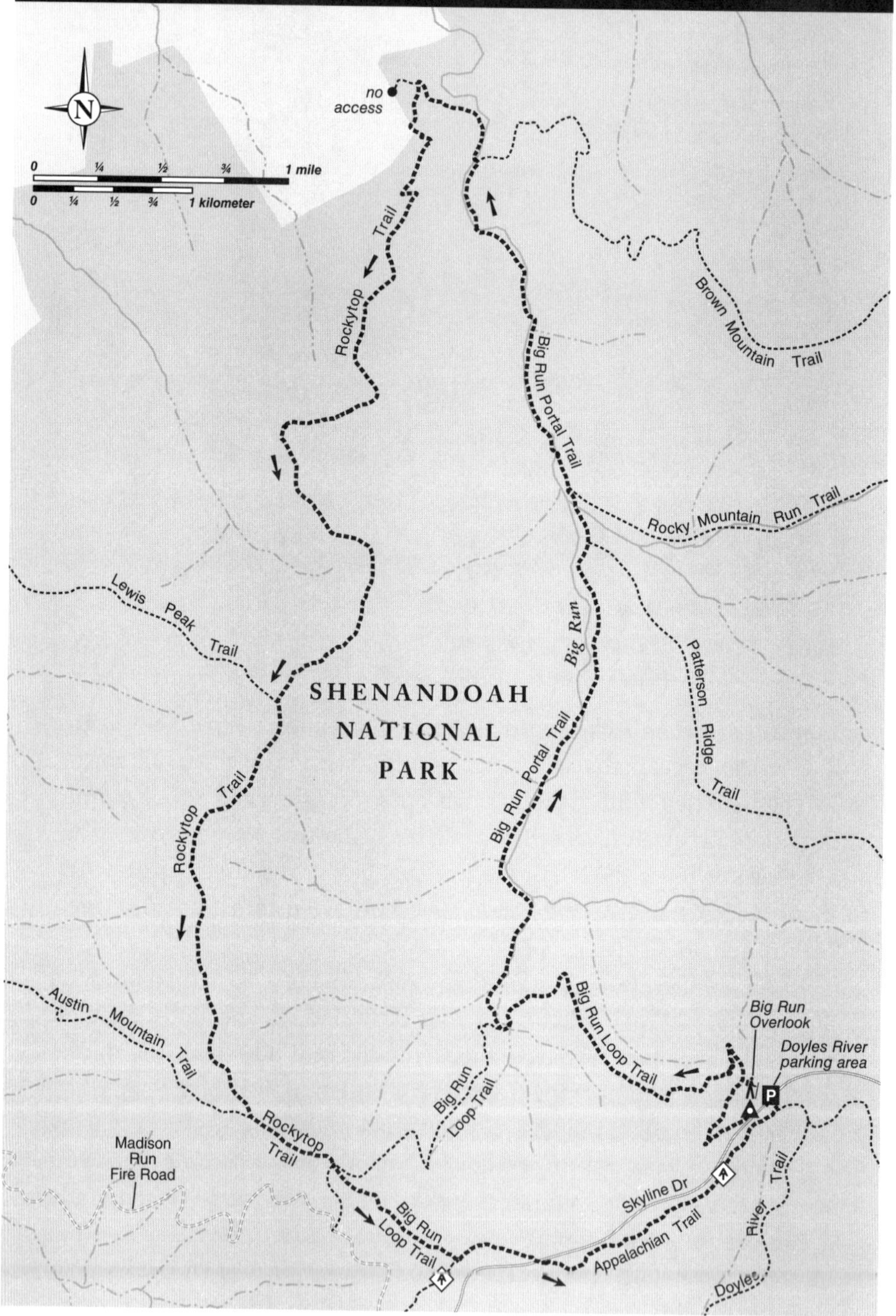
N
0
¼
½
¾
1 mile
0
¼
½
¾
1 kilometer
no access
Rockytop Trail
Big Run Portal Trail
Brown Mountain Trail
Rocky Mountain Run Trail
Lewis Peak Trail
Big Run
SHENANDOAH NATIONAL PARK
Patterson Ridge Trail
Rockytop Trail
Big Run Portal Trail
Austin Mountain Trail
Big Run Loop Trail
Big Run Overlook
Doyles River parking area
P
Big Run Loop Trail
Rockytop Trail
Madison Run Fire Road
Big Run Loop Trail
Skyline Dr
Appalachian Trail
Doyles River Trail

Looking out on the Shenandoah Valley from the truly rocky Rockytop Trail.

flats, many with walnut trees overtaking former fields and homesites. In this area, Big Run often splits into braids, some of which may run dry in summer and fall. These stream braids separate wooded islands. Campsites are frequent. Look for spur trails leading from the Big Run Portal Trail to flats.

Stream crossings are frequent as well. In times of high flow, these crossings can be challenging; use good sense. In summer, you will likely see more rock than water, allowing dry-shod crossings at normal water levels. Alders and sycamores overhang the crystalline waterway, bordered in grasses in places, too. Canyon walls rise above the woods both near and far from Big Run as you cut deeper into the watershed.

Come to a trail intersection and big metal bridge spanning Big Run at 6.1 miles. Here, the Brown Mountain Trail climbs right, but we stay with the Big Run Trail. Walk onto the bridge and soak in views up and downstream. Continue down the valley in hickory-oak woods to a

About Backpacking Footwear

Steele, my oldest brother, and I were hiking the Ozark Trail deep in the Missouri Ozarks. The late spring weather had taken a turn for the worse, dumping 4 inches of rain on us and raising area streams to scary heights. We waited a whole day and night for the waterways to drop, stranded between potential trail exits. This was not a big problem, as we were on day one of a three-day backpack trip.

The next day we came to Whites Creek, a brown flowing fury. My impatience clouded my sanity and we hiked forward, trying to ford the swollen stream. I pushed through and made it. Steele did, too, minus a sandal. His left sandal was torn off his foot. Once across, we inventoried our situation and beelined toward the nearest road, Steele hiking with two pairs of socks in lieu of his lost sandal. Wrong shoes, wrong place.

Another time I was embarking on a four-night backpack in Georgia's Cohutta Wilderness. The early fall skies promised a good trip. Hiking pal John Cox and I took the Hickory Creek Trail, aiming for the Conasauga River and trout that were waiting. I hadn't made a quarter-mile in my brand-new boots when my heels started heating up. Uh, oh.

A mile farther, I was limping and asking for Band-Aids from John. We cut the day short, camping on a small creek. By the time we reached the Conasauga River the next day, my heels resembled hamburger meat. I was relegated to barefoot camp tender while John quarried for trout. Three days later, I hobbled to the nearest trailhead while John got the car and picked me up. Right shoes, bad fit. Plus, I didn't take the time to break them in.

I should've listened to David Ramsay, longtime manager at an outdoor retailer. He states, "It doesn't matter if the shoe size number is 75. What matters is that the shoe actually fits

reach a gap and trail intersection near the park boundary at 6.6 miles. The boundary is only .2 mile distant yet does not offer public access.

Join the Rockytop Trail, climbing away from Big Run. Occasional switchbacks ease the uptick. Ascend through shrubby oaks and pines mixed with rocks and sand. The low-slung flora delivers nearly continuous views of the fields, forests, and farms of the Shenandoah Valley. Blueberry bushes rise at your feet. At 8.4 miles, the path levels off, but the fun is not over as you circle around the west side of Rockytop. Here, open rock slopes interposed in the forest deliver first-rate views. Here, the Shenandoah Valley stretches below while the southern tip of Massanutten Mountain forms a backdrop.

your feet." I believed I was a size 12 shoe and that was that. My obstinacy cost me.

When dropping a significant amount of hard-earned dough on boots, consider having them fitted by professionals at outdoor stores. Fit is more important than brand name or shoe type or numerical shoe size.

When choosing backpacking footwear, consider the typical terrain through which you hike. Are the trails rough and rocky? Are they steep or are they smooth and widely graded? Today's backpackers can get away with low-top hiking shoes if the trails are moderate and their pack is light. However, if you don't have strong ankles as I do, go with shoes that give ankle support. If the trail is rough, consider additional support, using boots with a metal shank in them and a more rugged sole.

Backpackers have a dilemma when considering footwear. They desire boots that will support a fully loaded backpack while hiking as well as a comfortable shoe in which they can hang around the campsite. Big, heavy boots aren't so fun at the campsite, unless it's winter, when you need them for warmth. Having two pairs of shoes on your person during a backpacking trip adds weight, though camp shoes get lighter all the time. Crocs are popular camp shoes. I can't stand them myself, for stylistic reasons, instead going for lightweight flops as a camp shoe.

If you are going to do a lot of hiking or going on a very long trip, I strongly recommend having good trail shoes with ankle support and a lug sole. And if you find a brand that works for you, stick with that brand.

When backpacking, you literally carry your own weight, so you live with your decisions, for better or worse. Remember, a successful backpack trip starts from the ground up—with your shoes.

Continue rolling through pine-oak and rock woodlands, along with mountain laurel. Solitude is yours in these parts. A lack of water makes it unfavorable for camping, however. At 9.9 miles, the little-used Lewis Peak Trail leaves right. It is 1.1 miles to a worth-the-side-trip vista from Lewis Peak. There's camping here, too—no water however.

Stay with the Rockytop Trail, heading south while passing over a couple of small knobs. Summer wildflowers will color the understory in season. Views of Skyline Drive open to your east. At 11.8 miles, meet the Austin Mountain Trail as it comes in from Madison Run. Stay left, still on the Rockytop Trail, to reach a grassy gap and four-way trail intersection at 12.2 miles. Here, keep straight, rejoining the Big Run

Loop Trail as it gently climbs a grassy track. Surmount the Blue Ridge before dropping to meet the AT at 12.9 miles.

Turn left here, northbound on the master path of the Old Dominion, in brushy forest full of vines, fire cherry, and tulip trees. Bisect boulders to cross Skyline Drive at 13.2 miles. Flip over the east side of the Blue Ridge, hiking astride stone bluffs. The AT emerges onto the Doyles River Overlook at 13.5 miles. This view on Skyline Drive opens easterly into the Doyles River watershed, bordered by Little Flat Mountain and Cedar Mountain. Stay with the AT on the north side of the overlook. The walking remains easy on the east slope below Skyline Drive. Continue on the AT north to reach a trail intersection at 14.4 miles. Here, turn left and walk a short way to reach the Doyles River parking area just off Skyline Drive. From this parking area, turn south along Skyline Drive a short piece to reach Big Run Overlook, completing the hike.

Mileages

0.0 Big Run Overlook, milepost 81.2.
2.2 Cross tributary of Big Run.
2.3 Join Big Run Portal Trail; campsites aplenty for next several miles.
4.4 Patterson Ridge Trail comes in on right.
4.6 Rocky Mountain Run Trail leaves right.
6.1 Metal bridge over Big Run.
6.6 Left on Rockytop Trail, end of nearby water; ascend past views.
8.4 Trail levels off.
9.9 Lewis Peak Trail leaves right.
11.8 Austin Mountain Trail enters.
12.2 Rejoin Big Run Loop Trail.
12.9 Left on AT.
13.2 Cross Skyline Drive.
13.5 Cross Doyles River Overlook.
14.4 Intersection; quick left to Doyles River parking area.
14.5 Big Run Overlook.

16 • BLACKROCK

The Backpack: *The rewards are as big as the climbs on this Shenandoah National Park backpack. Enjoy national-park-level scenery, views galore, and good camping options. Start on the Appalachian Trail (AT), then join rocky Austin Mountain Trail, with views, before dropping to Madison Run, a cool mountain stream. Ascend past Furnace Mountain with more panoramas before climbing to Trayfoot Mountain. Walk a remote part of the Trayfoot before dropping to Paine Run, another attractive rill. Here, a foot-friendly path leads past historic Blackrock Spring. Ascend more, back on the AT, topping out at Blackrock, where you can oversee the entirety of your journeyed lands before finishing the circuit.*

If you like mountaintop views and camping on streams, this two- to three-night loop is for you. Often you can see where you were—and where you are going. The scenery will please the eye, and campsites can be found both high and low, though the ridgetop camps—like almost all of Shenandoah National Park—are waterless. Bring your own. The difficulty of this backpack lies in the two major climbs: from Madison Run up to Trayfoot Mountain, about 2,000 feet, and the second climb

16 BLACKROCK

Distance & configuration: 20.7-mile loop

Difficulty: Difficult due to elevation changes

Backpacking time: 11 hours

Outstanding features: Views aplenty, solitude in places, ample camping opportunities

Elevation: 1,360′ low point, 3,374′ high point

Scenery: 5

Solitude: 3

Family friendly: 1

Canine friendly: 2

Fees/permits: Park entrance fee and free backcountry permit required

Best season: Spring through late fall

Maps: PATC Shenandoah National Park South District Map 11

For more info: Shenandoah National Park, 3655 U.S. Highway 211 East, Luray, VA 22835, 540-999-3500, www.nps.gov/shen

Finding the trailhead: From exit 99 on I-64 between Waynesboro and Charlottesville, head north into Shenandoah National Park and Rockfish Gap entrance station. From there, drive north on Skyline Drive for 20.5 miles to Jones Run parking area, mile 84.1, on your right. **GPS trailhead coordinates:** N38° 13.7979′, W78° 43.5670′

16 Blackrock

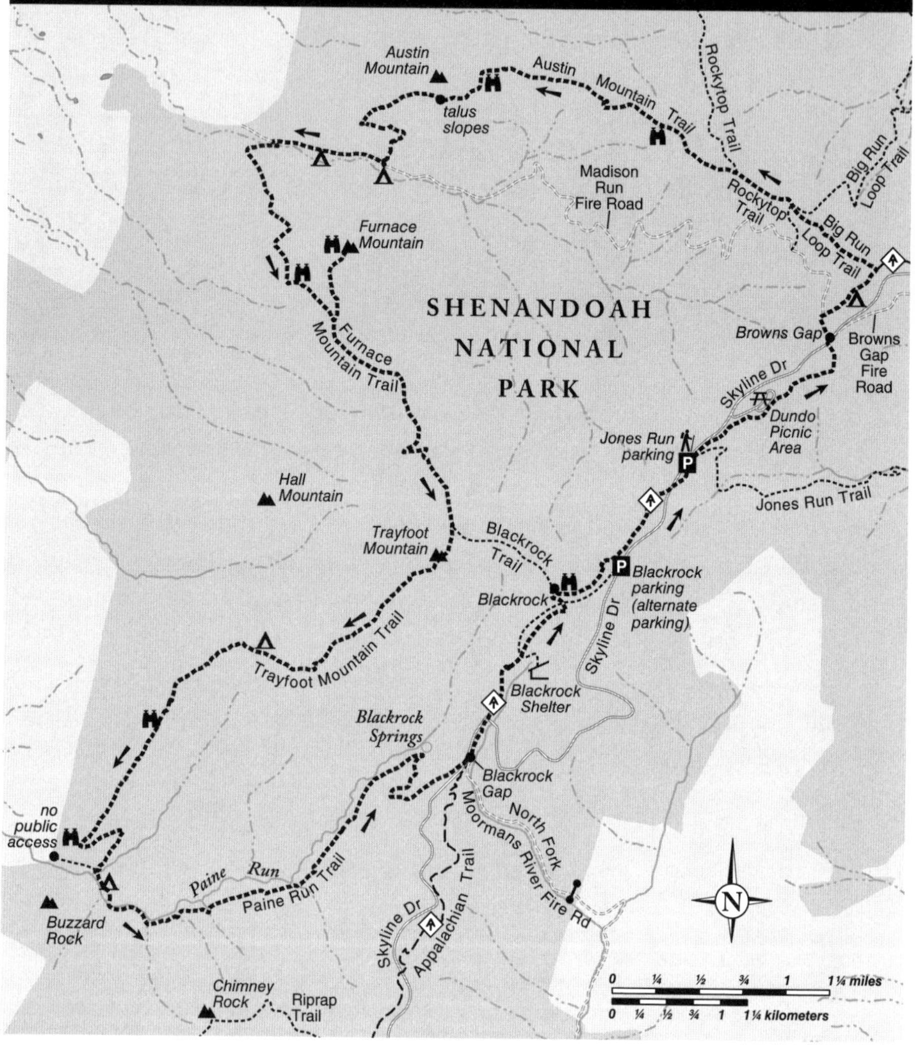

from Paine Run to Blackrock, about 1,700 feet. However, making just one climb per day, spending the night on the streams, makes it doable by most aspiring backpackers.

The hike leaves Jones Run parking area, northbound on the AT. It soon swings by Dundo picnic area, with water spigots and restrooms—no camping allowed. Descend into Browns Gap at 1.3 miles. Stay with the AT, soon passing a badly sloped campsite at 1.6 miles. Reach a trail junction at 1.8 miles. Turn left on the Big Run Loop Trail, ascend brushy

Peering into Paine Run valley from Blackrock.

woods, then descend, passing a couple of small late-arrival campsites (bring water) before reaching a trail junction. Keep straight, now on the Rockytop Trail, running a ridgeline to then bear left on the stony Austin Mountain Trail at 2.9 miles. Hike in solitude among pines, azaleas, and blueberries. At 3.4 miles, look across Madison Run for the stony slopes of Blackrock Summit. Undulate along Austin Mountain, then grab another view at 4.6 miles. Look west for the Shenandoah Valley and southeast for Dundo Overlook on Skyline Drive. Open onto the first of a series of talus slopes, at 5.0 miles, with still more views. Furnace Mountain rises across Madison Run. Ahead, additional rock outcrops present bonus panoramas as you descend. At 5.5 miles, make a sharp switchback to the left, rapidly dropping. Cross a wet-weather draw before meeting Madison Run Fire Road at 6.1 miles. Recommended campsites can be found around this intersection and down the fire road.

From here, the backpack continues down Madison Run Fire Road to join Furnace Mountain Trail at 6.7 miles. Here, you rock-hop Madison Run, turn downstream, then climb the western slope of Furnace Mountain, enjoying sporadic vistas of Shenandoah Valley. Intersect the spur to the outcrop on Furnace Mountain at 8.3 miles.

Make the half-mile one-way side trip to the outcrop of Furnace Mountain (this side trip is added to the total hike mileage). Peer across at Austin Mountain, where you were, and Madison Run below. From Furnace Mountain, hike the ridge through pines and mountain laurel, then amid partly vegetated talus slopes to reach the Trayfoot Mountain Trail at 10.9 miles.

Climb the old roadbed of the Trayfoot Mountain Trail, topping out at 11.1 miles, elevation 3,374 feet. Begin a long, mostly downhill trek along the ridgecrest. The first part of Trayfoot Mountain meanders through hardwoods, passing a dry campsite at 12.5 miles. The lower trail becomes rockier, more piney, and more scenic, with views such as that you find at 13.4 miles. Chimney Rock stands out across Paine Run.

Continue the scenic downgrade. Reach a sharp left turn at 14.2 miles. An outcrop here allows a stellar panorama across the hollow at Buzzard Rock and the Shenandoah Valley beyond. Drop into Lefthand Hollow, then switchback to reach Paine Run at 14.8 miles. Turn left here on the Paine Run Trail. Popular campsites can be found upstream in the flat between Lefthand Hollow and Paine Run.

Rock-hop Paine Run at 15.0 miles. Paine Run is an exceptionally attractive stream. Enter pine–mountain laurel woodland, climbing moderately, then begin a pattern as the trail crosses feeder streams and then returns to the main valley. As Paine Run Hollow narrows, the forest slowly changes character from open pine to lush hardwood. At 17.4 miles, the trail makes a sharp switchback to the right. Look for a footpath to your left. This leads to historic Blackrock Springs and a resort site that operated in one form or another for over a century. A few fallen trees may block the way, but work around them to discover building foundations, flat spots, and springs.

Return to the Paine Run Trail, climbing onto a dry ridge and coming to Blackrock Gap at 18.3 miles. Cross Skyline Drive and join the AT, northbound, soon recrossing Skyline Drive. Ascend past the side trail to the Blackrock hut at 19.0 miles. The stone shelter does have a spring.

Continue climbing, then stay with the AT as it circles around open Blackrock Summit at 19.5 miles. Spot the terrain you have covered at the view to top all views: Austin Mountain, Furnace Mountain, Trayfoot Mountain, Madison Run, and Paine Run. Continue north on the AT, descending past a parking area for Blackrock. Cross Skyline Drive yet again, then reach Jones Run parking area, completing the backpack at 20.7 miles.

Mileages

0.0 Jones Run parking, northbound on AT.
1.3 Browns Gap.
1.6 Badly sloped campsite.
1.8 Left on Big Run Loop Trail; campsites ahead on left.
2.4 Intersection; straight on Rockytop Trail.
2.9 Left on Austin Mountain Trail, solitude, views ahead.
5.0 Talus slopes, views.
6.1 Madison Run Fire Road; campsites in vicinity and downstream.
6.7 Left on Furnace Mountain Trail; climb.
8.3 Spur left to Furnace Mountain overlook; backtrack.
9.3 Resume Furnace Mountain Trail.
10.9 Right on Trayfoot Mountain Trail, soon reach high point.
12.5 Dry campsite.
13.4 View of Chimney Rock.
14.8 Left on Paine Run Trail; campsites ahead.
17.4 Pass spur left to Blackrock Springs at right-hand curve.
18.3 Blackrock Gap, left, northbound on AT.
19.0 Spur right to Blackrock hut, spring.
19.5 Blackrock Summit, incredible views.
20.7 Jones Run parking, complete backpack.

17 • MOORMANS RIVER

The Backpack: *This Shenandoah National Park adventure combines the Appalachian Trail (AT) and the two forks of the Moormans River to fashion a two- to three-day loop that highlights a waterfall, cascades, pools, and piney highlands. Campsites can be found along the streams and up top on the AT. In late spring and summer, bring a fishing rod and bathing suit.*

This loop takes you along the crest of the Blue Ridge into the upper Moormans River watershed and back around to the high country. Ply the AT and savor some views before entering the North Fork Moormans River valley and its big pools. Visit Big Branch Falls before heading to South Fork Moormans River valley, where more cascades await. The final part of the circuit cruises the high country on the park's rocky spine. Be apprised that this trip entails several crossings of the above rivers, making it best for the warm season. Also, the area near the Char-

17 MOORMANS RIVER

Distance & configuration: 18.3-mile loop

Difficulty: Moderate to difficult

Backpacking time: 10 hours

Outstanding features: Big Branch Falls, pools on North Fork Moormans River

Elevation: 1,030′ low point, 3,100′ high point

Scenery: 4

Solitude: 3

Family friendly: 2

Canine friendly: 3

Fees/permits: Park entrance fee and free backcountry permit required

Best season: Mid-spring through late fall

Maps: PATC Shenandoah National Park South District Map 11

For more info: Shenandoah National Park, 3655 U.S. Highway 211 East, Luray, VA 22835, 540-999-3500, www.nps.gov/shen

Finding the trailhead: From exit 99 on I-64 between Waynesboro and Charlottesville, head north into Shenandoah National Park and Rockfish Gap entrance station. From there, drive north on Skyline Drive for 14.6 miles to Riprap parking area, mile 90.0, on your left. **GPS trailhead coordinates:** N38° 10.662′, W78° 45.907′

lottesville Reservoir (aka Sugar Hollow Reservoir) can be busy. Finally, a recommended trip could have you overnighting first on the South Fork, then the North Fork. If you want to spend a third night out, stay atop the Blue Ridge on the AT. However, bring your water to camp on the AT.

Start your loop at the Riprap parking area. Take the Riprap Trail a few feet to meet the AT. Hike north on the AT through low-slung woods to an intersection at .4 mile. Campsites are in the vicinity for late arrivers.

The Riprap Trail leaves left. Stay with the AT, where you can view Pasture Fence Mountain to your right and the Moormans River far below. Descend to cross Skyline Drive at 1.1 miles. The AT circles around the east side of a knob. Come near Skyline Drive in a gap, then undulate along the ridgecrest to finally descend among rocky woods, making Blackrock Gap at 2.9 miles. Turn right here, following the gated and yellow-blazed North Fork Moormans River Fire Road. Shortly cross a feeder stream of the river that the trail begins to parallel, passing around a gate at 4.0 miles. Temporarily leave the park and reach a junction at 4.3 miles. Turn right and cross North Fork Moormans River on rocks, staying with the main doubletrack. Stay right at a second junction after passing ramshackle hunt camps. Cross the river ahead at 4.8 miles.

17 Moormans River

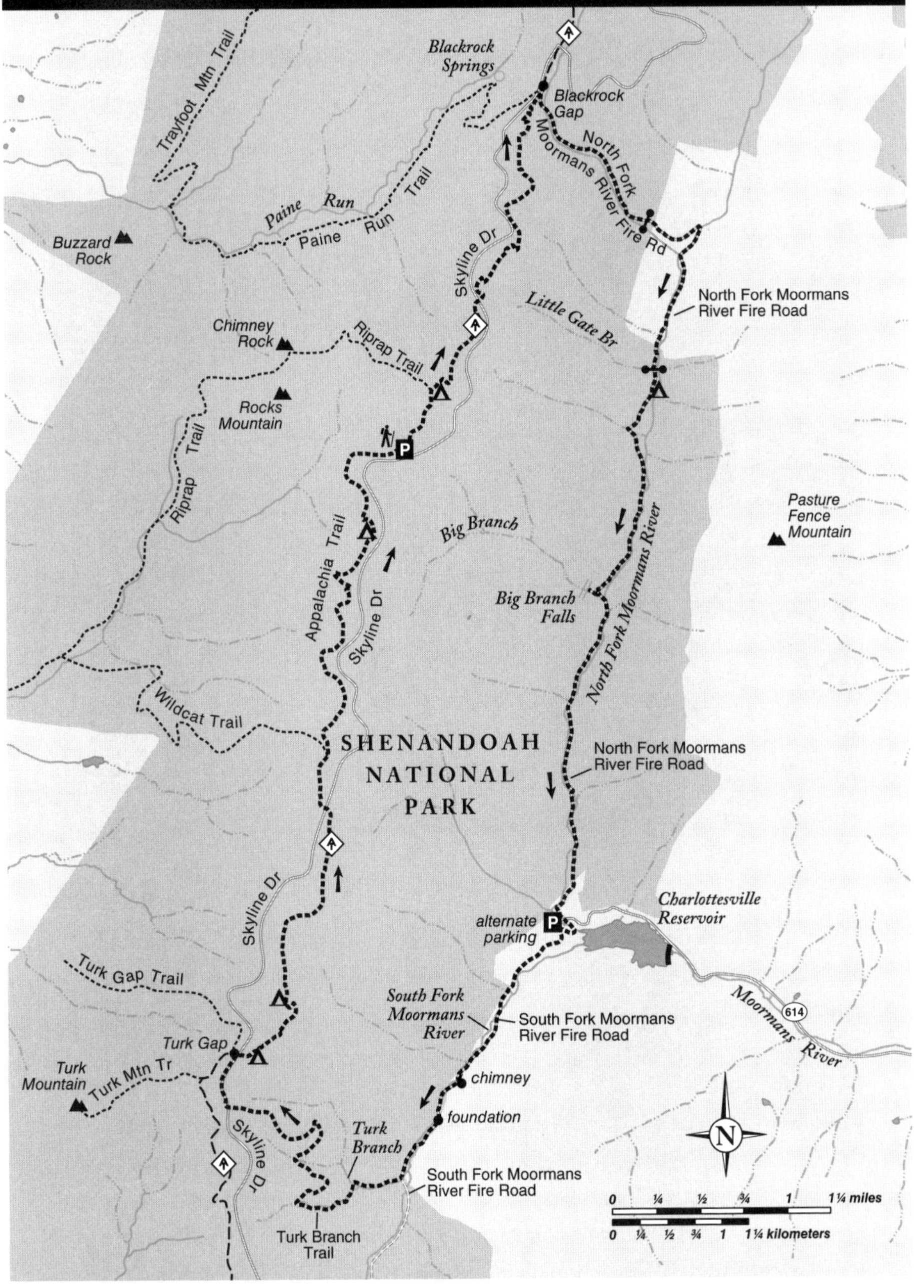

Trailside settler chimneys like this lend historical perspective to our backpacking trips.

A gate and Little Gate Branch mark your reentry into the park at 5.0 miles on a now-standard hiking trail. Find campsites in the flats along both sides of the river in the next mile or so. (You must be at least a quarter-mile within the park boundary to legally camp.) Some sites offer adjacent swimming holes.

Cross Big Branch at 6.6 miles. Here, the bouldery stream cascades toward North Fork Moormans River. A side trail leads upstream .1 mile to the official Big Branch Falls, tumbling in multiple 20-plus-foot segments over scoured gray stone with a final drop just below the trail crossing. Beyond Big Branch, continue paralleling North Fork Moormans River, dotted with huge boulders in the river and bluffs overlooking it. You may see day hikers on the trail, coming up from the parking area at Charlottesville Reservoir.

Cross North Fork Moormans River at 7.4 miles. Stay close along the watercourse, nearing rock slabs that provide quick access to the alluring river. At 8.0 miles, rock-hop the river twice in succession, working around a picturesque multicolored bluff. The valley begins to widen as the trail soon leaves the park, bypassing vehicle barrier boulders. Keep straight on a roadbed to reach VA 614 and a parking area at 8.8 miles. As VA 614 climbs left, you angle right on the gated South Fork Moormans River Fire Road. Shortly reach a concrete ford, crossing North Fork Moormans River a final time near the Charlottesville Reservoir, also known as Sugar Hollow Reservoir. The trail turns up along North Fork, then angles south, entering the South Fork Moormans River valley. Rock-hop South Fork at 9.7 miles, then come alongside a standing chimney of a former homestead at 10.2 miles. Ahead, look for a huge rock outcrop to the left and a deep pool below a cascade. A deeper pool and bigger waterfall are just upstream of this point. The water beckons.

Ahead, look for the rock foundation and an old stone fence marking a homesite. Step over South Fork Moormans River at 10.7 miles. Soon, fully reenter the park past a gate. (The park has been on the other side of the river for some distance.) Meet the Turk Gap Trail at 10.9 miles. A USGS survey marker has been embedded into a boulder at the junction. You can look for campsites either up Turk Branch hollow to your right or ahead on flats of the South Fork Moormans River.

Join the Turk Branch Trail. Pass an old homesite on your right to cross Turk Branch at 11.2 miles. Notice the stonework to level the old roadbed. Ascend a feeder branch of Turk Branch, crossing the feeder branch twice near more stonework. Curve uphill back to Turk Branch, stepping over its upper reaches at 12.2 miles. Ascend through pines mixed with mountain laurel to near Skyline Drive. Parallel the drive north to reach Turk Gap at 13.4 miles. Keep straight across the Turk Gap parking area to intersect the AT. Head northbound on the AT in oak woods. Come near a dry campsite just ahead. Enjoy the mostly level ramble in low-slung oaks and pines. Pass some waterless campsites on the left around mile 14. Drift downward to cross Skyline Drive at 15.3 miles, then pass the Wildcat Trail junction at 15.6 miles. An often-open canopy can make this trail hot on a summer afternoon.

However, the sparse but scenic pine forests allow far-reaching views to the west before the AT crosses over to the east side of the ridge. Curve around the ridgeline to the right and climb, intersecting the Riprap Trail at 18.3 miles. Turn right here and walk just a few feet to the Riprap parking area, completing the backpack.

Mileages

0.0 Riprap Trail, then northbound on AT.
0.4 Riprap Trail leaves left. Stay with AT. Campsites in vicinity.
1.1 Cross Skyline Drive.
2.9 Blackrock Gap; right on North Fork Moormans River Fire Road.
4.0 Pass around gate.
4.3 Right at intersection; cross North Fork.
5.0 Gate, reenter park, campsites ahead.
6.6 Big Branch Falls.
8.8 VA 614 parking lot; pass around gate, cross North Fork, briefly turn upstream.
10.2 Pass chimney.
10.9 Right on Turk Gap Trail; campsites in area, ascend.
12.2 Last trailside water.
13.4 Turk Gap; right on AT, campsite ahead.
14.0 Campsites.
15.3 Cross Skyline Drive.
15.6 Pass Wildcat Trail intersection.
17.4 Poor campsites.
18.3 Return to the trailhead, completing the backpack.

18 • LAUREL FORK BACKCOUNTRY

The Backpack: *Bordered by West Virginia on two sides, this high and rugged parcel of the George Washington National Forest presents a network of trails amid spruce thickets, meadows, beaver ponds, and deep woods in a perched watershed with a cool climate more like neighboring West Virginia's than the Old Dominion's. Start high at remote Locust Spring, dipping along Locust Spring Run before returning to the ridge dividing the two Virginias. After tracing a quiet forest road, dip along Bearwallow Run, with its beaver ponds and spruce, before reaching the scenically superlative valley of Laurel Fork. Turn down the stream, passing campsites. Two crossings of the trout waters lead you to Buck Run and a return climb to the trailhead.*

This loop backpack takes place in a remote corner of Virginia and has unusual terrain for the Old Dominion: high-elevation meadows, beaver ponds, spruce forests, and a generally elevated watershed, of which Laurel Fork is the primary stream. Luckily for us backpackers,

18 LAUREL FORK BACKCOUNTRY

Distance & configuration: 14.0-mile loop

Difficulty: Moderate

Backpacking time: 6.5 to 7.5 hours

Outstanding features: Beaver ponds, spruce woods, Laurel Fork

Elevation: 2,860′ low point, 3,720′ high point

Scenery: 5

Solitude: 3

Family friendly: 3

Canine friendly: 3

Fees/permits: No fees or permits required

Best season: Late spring through early winter

Maps: National Geographic #791 Staunton Shenandoah Mountain

For more info: George Washington National Forest, North River Ranger District, 401 Oakwood Drive, Harrisonburg, VA 22801, 866-904-0240, www.fs.usda.gov/gwj

Finding the trailhead: From the intersection of US 250 and US 220 in Monterey, Va., take US 250 west for 20.6 miles—entering the state of West Virginia after 14 miles—to reach WV 28. Turn right on WV 28 toward Seneca Rocks; continue for 6.6 miles to turn right onto FR 106, at the sign for Locust Springs Recreation Area. Follow FR 106 for .4 mile, then turn right on FR 60. Follow FR 60 for .2 mile, then turn right on FR 142. Drive for .6 mile to reach Locust Springs Recreation Area, reentering Virginia (state line not signed). **GPS trailhead coordinates:** N38° 35.133′, W79° 38.568′

the Laurel Fork backcountry is laced with trails along its streams and ridges. The backcountry camping is good—with most campsites along Laurel Fork—and the trails are in mostly good shape. However, expect sections where the trails may be faint or be overlain with blowdowns. Most trail intersections are signed. By midsummer, expect to deal with brush, briers, and stinging nettle. I recommend a one- or two-night trip. Laurel Fork backcountry is a great place to be when summertime is scorching the lowlands.

This loop does have two fords of Laurel Fork, but I have simply waded sans boots in cool conditions. Don't let this prevent you from coming here when the temperatures are down, though the smaller tributaries of Laurel Fork also have stream crossings.

The circuit leaves the lower end of the Locust Springs Recreation Area picnic area, westerly on the Locust Spring Run Trail, immediately descending past the actual Locust Spring on your right. Mountain laurel, pine, and red spruce rise above, along with northern hardwoods of

18 Laurel Fork Backcountry

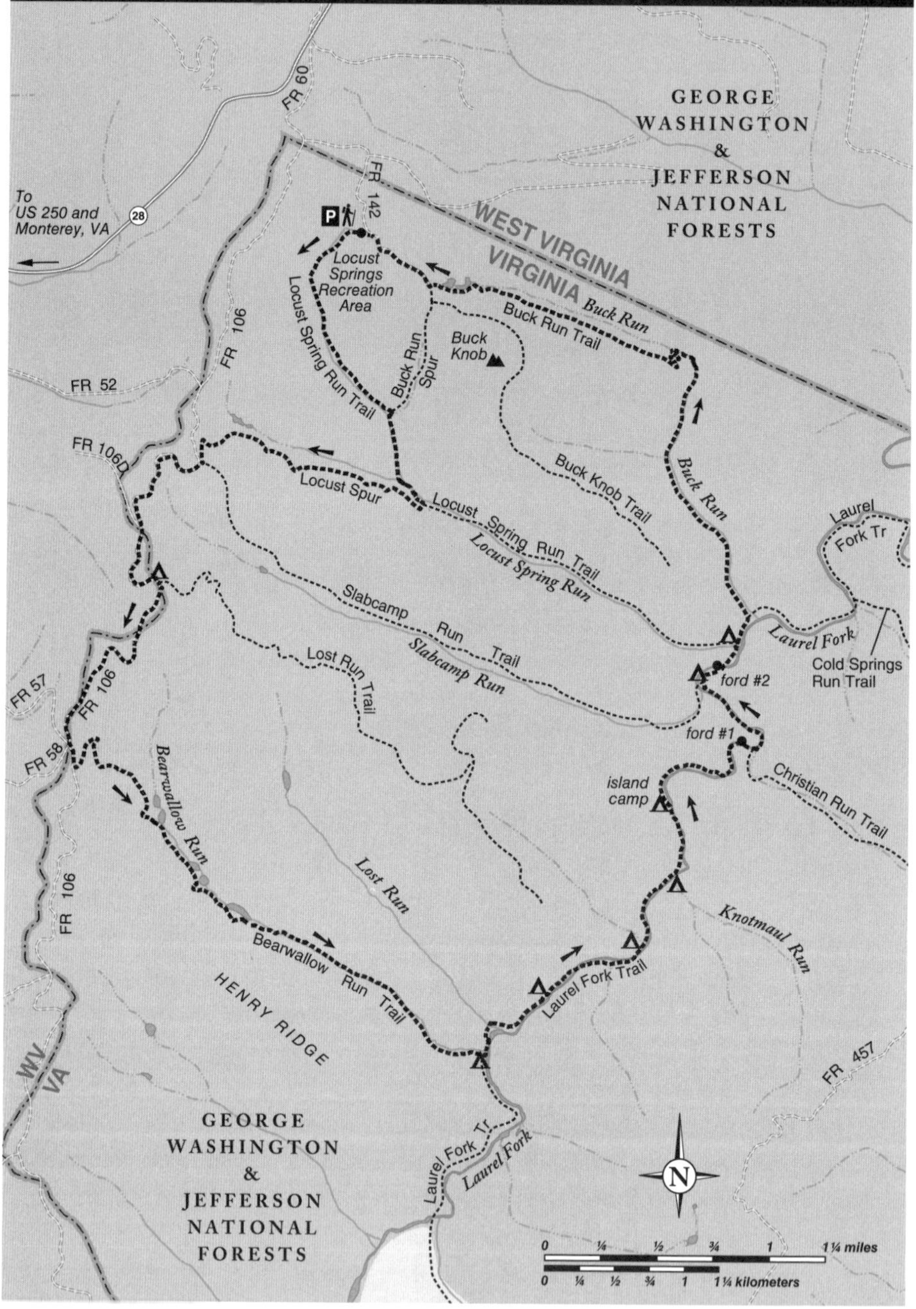

Laurel Fork Backcountry is a remote backpacking destination.

yellow birch, beech, and maple. Pass through dusky planted groves of red spruce and Norway pine. Ahead, cross Locust Spring Run several times.

Before long, the loop curves back up to the stateline ridge, via the signed Locust Spur, which briefly climbs to join an old logging road and make FR 106. Cruise the gravel road, running around 3,400 feet, roughly paralleling the Virginia–West Virginia state line. Reach the unmistakable intersection of FR 106, FR 57, and FR 58. Stay left with FR 106 and look for an old metal gate and the Bearwallow Run Trail. Descend, circling into the watershed, crossing old wooden footbridges and entering upper flats of Bearwallow Run, where beaver ponds and spruce thickets are found. Hike off and on an old railroad logging grade before meeting glistening Laurel Fork, cutting a gorgeous vale of forest, glade, and bluffs, broken with tributaries contributing their flow.

The Laurel Fork Trail traces a sometimes washed-out railroad grade, heading down the west bank among wooded bottoms, rhododendron thickets, brushy meadows, and even river islands. Come to the first inevitable ford at a bluff and switch to the right bank. Ahead, the

Light Options for the Long Nights of Winter

A friend and I were backpacking deep in the Jefferson National Forest. At noon, a low December sun stretched low overhead, then fell to the west, elongating the shadows of leafless, skeletal trees. A creeping chill pushed into our campsite with the darkening dusk.

It wasn't even 6 o'clock. But it was time to light our campsite.

For this backpacker, camping goes on, despite the short days and long nights, when autumn's golden light turns to winter's pale weak rays and don't even stick around that long. In Lynchburg, the geographic center of Virginia, the hours of daylight reach a low of 9 hours, 37 minutes of light per day. That leaves 13-plus hours of darkness. And for the backpacker that can be a long time.

However, backpackers have an array of light options, from old-fashioned candles to ultralight headlamps to solar-charged LED lanterns. Depending on the situation, I use them all to illuminate the night, not only to help me stay awake, but also to gather wood, cook dinner, slip into the sleeping bag, and keep from stumbling around the campsite.

Plastic solar-charged LED lights weigh mere ounces, don't require batteries, and can be pre-charged before your trip and then recharged during your trip simply by hooking them onto your backpack. Candles still have their place. They give a soft light, perfect for general illumination. A little foil will enhance a candle's brightness as well as block a breeze that makes it burn fast or blow out. An upside: candle wax dripped onto kindling makes for a good emergency fire starter. A downside: their subjectivity to wind—also, you simply can't carry them around. This leads to the candle lantern, basically a candle inside a glass and metal housing, solving the wind problem. Larger lamp-oil lanterns can still be found, but the lamp oil seems to leak whenever it is transported. Small, battery-operated lanterns are yet another option. They use two to three small batteries and provide decent illumination.

Headlamps are the best all-around backpacking light. Here, a battery-operated light is connected to a strap fitting around your head. The headlamp is hands free, and the beam shines wherever the user is looking. These generally operate on three AAA batteries, leaving them lightweight. Variations of this include small lights operated by nickel-sized watch batteries that clip onto the bill of a ball cap. Headlamps are best for backpackers because they weigh so little.

The old-fashioned white-gas-operated Coleman lanterns are good for car or canoe camping, but they are too heavy for foot-powered travel. Other large lanterns are battery powered (not as bright) or use fuel canisters. The problem with the canisters is that you never know how much fuel is in them, so you have to take spare canisters when it may not be necessary.

What about a hand-held flashlight? They are still used by a declining number of backpackers and have their place, mostly as a backup for the other light options during the long nights of winter. One more thing: be sure to include fresh batteries *before* starting your backpack.

Christian Run Trail leaves right. The rapids and pools of the creek are alluring among this curving stream segment. The grade is washed out, and you traverse naked rock slabs before returning to wooded banks.

Make your second ford of Laurel Fork, then enter a popular camping area, at the greater confluence of Laurel Fork, Locust Spring Run, and Buck Run. This is the backpack's low point. Work your way up this deep valley on the Buck Run Trail, then make a series of switchbacks to join an old logging road. The upper part of the track passes by more beaver ponds and meadows, as well as spruce thickets, before returning to Locust Springs Recreation Area, completing the backpacking adventure.

Mileages

0.0 Locust Springs Recreation Area Trailhead.
1.1 Buck Run Spur leaves left.
1.6 Right on signed Locust Spring Spur.
2.8 Meet Slabcamp Run Trail and FR 106. Left on FR 106.
3.4 Pass FR 106D.
3.8 Car-accessible campsite.
3.9 Lost Run Trail leaves left.
4.8 Intersection of FR 106, FR 57, and FR 58; stay on FR 106 toward Lake Buffalo.
4.9 Left on Bearwallow Run Trail.
7.5 Drop sharply left off old railroad grade.
7.6 Reach Laurel Fork Trail and streamside campsite.
7.8 Step over Lost Run.
8.1 Campsite.
8.4 Squeeze by rock outcrop with built-in stone block wall along stream.
8.6 Campsite; ahead grade is pinched in, then washed away.
9.0 Campsite across Laurel Fork on Knotmaul Run.
9.3 Campsite on island.
10.0 Pass a small rockhouse before reaching Laurel Fork ford #1.
10.1 Christian Run Trail leaves acutely right.
10.5 Slabcamp Run Trail enters across Laurel Fork; popular campsite just ahead.
10.6 Laurel Fork ford #2.
10.7 Locust Spring Run Trail comes in on the left; popular campsites.
10.8 Left on Buck Run Trail.

12.2 Trail switchbacks up hillside above Buck Run; join old logging road, westbound.
13.6 Buck Run Spur and Buck Knob Trail come in on left; continue west.
14.0 Return to Locust Springs Trailhead beyond a metal road gate.

19 • SHENANDOAH MOUNTAIN

The Backpack: *This exciting 40-mile circuit offers a little bit of everything. Starting on the North River near Bridgewater, the backpack winds through a gorge before joining the Wild Oak Trail for some extensive ridge-running up to Ramseys Draft Wilderness, where it meets Shenandoah Mountain. The hike dips to explore the gorgeous headwaters of the North River before cutting across Buck Mountain, then dropping to the Little River, closing the loop. Though it does use a few forest roads to fashion the circuit, the trek explores wild and scenic terrain sure to please the eye, including overlooks and streams. Campsites can be found throughout the loop.*

This grand adventure takes place on the western side of the Shenandoah Valley, under the mantle of Shenandoah Mountain, big wild country in the George Washington National Forest. With a little planning, the loop can be stretched anywhere from three to six days. Since it does cross—and sometimes use—forest roads, bailout options are numerous. The recommended national forest map is necessary. Some high-country stretches are waterless and require toting your water. Yet other portions are rich with aqua, as along North River and North Fork Little River, often with tall bluffs beside them forcing you to cross them numerous times without footbridges. Ironically, the upper North Fork Little River can run dry in fall. Keep hiking downstream to find above-surface water flow. Some of the ridges are graced with cleared grassy meadows, adding to wildlife-viewing possibilities. The only places where you might see other backpackers will be along the North River near North River Campground and in the Hiner Spring area, in Ramseys Draft Wilderness.

To plan your trip, review the mileages below and work out the distance you want to travel each day as well as where you want to camp each night. Here is a suggested itinerary: First night, camp along North River at 4.7 miles; second night, camp at mile 19.5 Hiner Spring; third night, camp at mile 30.2, North River. The second day is long, but you can shorten it by adding a fourth night.

19 SHENANDOAH MOUNTAIN

Distance & configuration: 40.5-mile loop

Difficulty: Difficult due to distance

Backpacking time: 22 hours

Outstanding features: North River gorge, overlooks, Ramseys Draft Wilderness, North River headwaters

Elevation: 1,580′ low point, 4,140′ high point

Scenery: 5

Solitude: 4

Family friendly: 1

Canine friendly: 2

Fees/permits: No fees or permits required

Best season: Spring through late fall

Maps: National Geographic #791 Staunton Shenandoah Mountain

For more info: George Washington National Forest, North River Ranger District, 401 Oakwood Drive, Harrisonburg, VA 22801, 866-904-0240, www.fs.usda.gov/gwj

Finding the trailhead: From the intersection of VA 257 and VA 42 in Bridgewater, southwest of Harrisonburg, take VA 42 south for .3 mile, then turn right onto VA 727, Spring Creek Road. Follow VA 727 for 3.4 miles, then turn left, staying on VA 727, now called Sangersville Road. Continue for 2.5 miles, then turn left on VA 730, North River Road. Stay with VA 730 for a total of 6 miles, then turn right onto VA 718. Follow it for 1 mile, then veer left onto FR 95, which you follow for .1 mile to reach the Wild Oak trailhead on your right. **GPS trailhead coordinates:** N38° 22.014′, W79° 9.877′

Mileages

0.0 Wild Oak Trailhead, join singletrack Wild Oak Trail.

0.1 Stay left as Wild Oak Trail splits; ahead cross FR 95.

0.4 Reach North River, turn right, upstream, well above waterway on old roadbed.

0.8 Hiker bridge over North River.

1.0 Wild Oak Trail leaves left; keep straight on North River Gorge Trail.

1.1 Campsite, good for late arrivers.

2.0 Cross North River, then cross twice more within .4 mile.

2.7 Cross North River; cross again in .3 mile.

4.5 Cross North River; reach campsite just before next crossing in .2 mile.

4.9 Last river crossing, now on left-hand bank.

19 Shenandoah Mountain

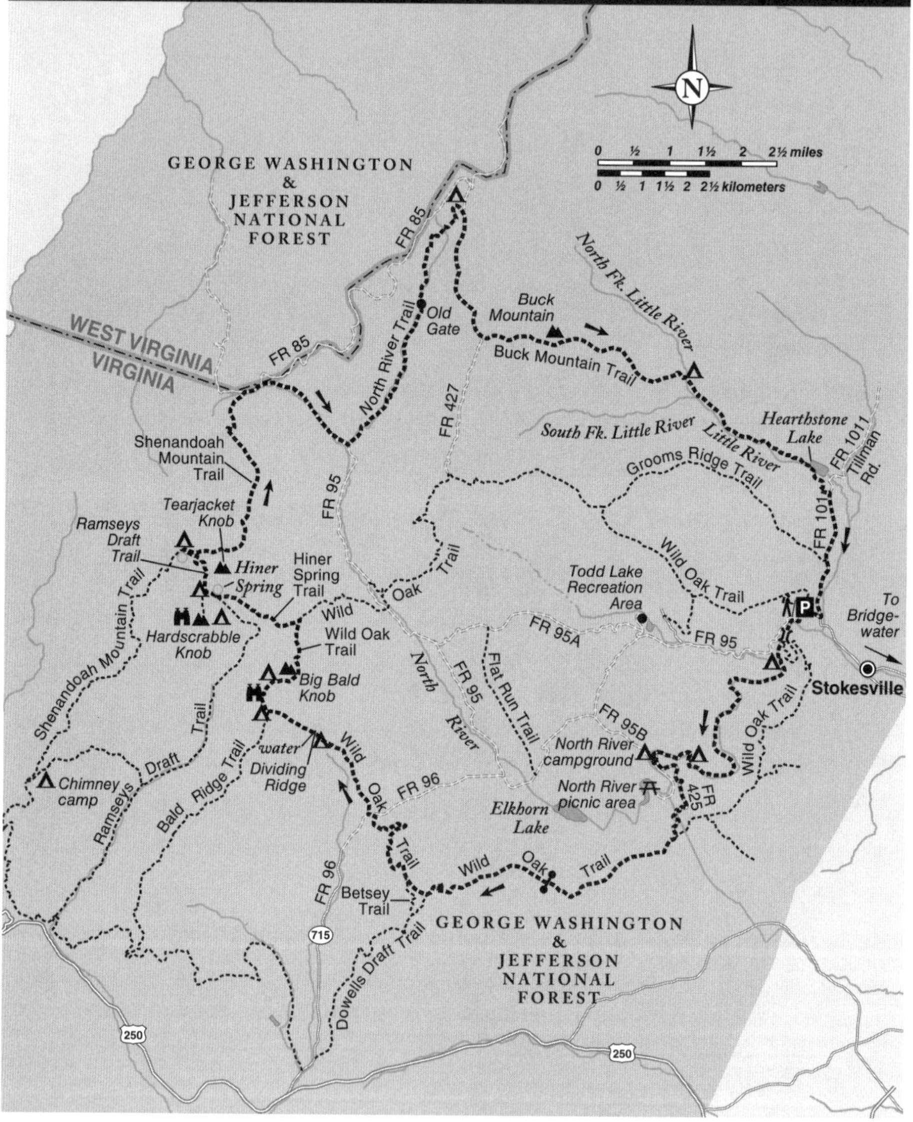

This hiker bridge takes you across the North River.

5.3 Spur trail right to North River Campground; stay left by bluff, get water.

5.4 Emerge onto FR 95B, turn left, then quickly turn left again, ascending seasonally gated FR 425. Curve upward.

7.4 Meet Wild Oak Trail atop Lookout Mountain. Turn right, still following FR 425.

9.6 Pass around permanent gate; Wild Oak Trail becomes footpath.

10.4 Faint White Oak Draft Trail leaves left; wildlife pond ahead.

11.3 Views to the south from outcrop.

11.7 Dowells Draft Trail leaves left. Top a knob, then make 500-foot descent.

12.2 Betsey Trail goes left. Continue descending on Wild Oak Trail.

14.0 Cross FR 96, trail parking. Potential bailout spot. Keep straight in gorgeous pine-oak-hickory woods.

Autumn view from the Wild Oak Trail near Big Bald Knob.

15.5 Small campsite, seasonal stream to the northeast.

15.6 Spur leads down to perennial part of stream as it flows over a 6-foot ledge.

16.3 Reach campsite, wildlife pond, and Bald Ridge Trail after steep climb up Dividing Ridge. Turn right, still ascending on Wild Oak Trail, view east of Elkhorn Lake ahead.

16.9 Dry campsite in a wide gap; break 4,000-foot barrier.

18.0 Trail intersection. Head left on Hiner Spring Trail. Wild Oak Trail leaves right.

19.5 Meet Ramseys Draft Trail coming in from the left at lower tier of Hiner Spring campsite. Rocked-in Hiner Spring is to left. Join Ramseys Draft Trail ascending through upper tier of Hiner Spring campsite.

19.7 Hardscrabble Trail leads left .4 mile to campsite, fallen down tower, and view.

Choose the Right Backpack for Your Hike

Backpacks have come a long way over the past forty years. I'm talking about backpacks used for overnight excursions as opposed to daypacks, used for school, work, and day hiking. In the bad old days, backpacks were a simple aluminum frame holding a nylon pack with a few pockets. Unpadded straps went over your shoulders and around your waist. Known as external packs (due to the external aluminum frame), these became more deluxe, with padded shoulder straps, waist belt, and a dizzying array of pockets for stowing your gear.

External packs once served me well. My longest non-resupplied backpack ever—15 nights in Great Smoky Mountains National Park—was done with an external pack. As time rolled on, the internal backpack came into vogue. As its name implies, the frame is built into the pack.

For the past couple of decades, internal frame packs have completely supplanted external frame packs in popularity. Sure, there are still plenty of external frame backpacks out there, but internal frames rule the roost.

I own only internal packs these days, and recommend them. Internal packs fit closer to your body and are more compact, whereas external frame packs are generally bigger and bulkier; but they have more pockets, which help organization and loading. Internal pack users have to take more of a "duffel bag" approach to their loading, though assorted pockets and pouches are well incorporated into most internal packs. Most importantly, internal packs are significantly lighter, the lightest being a mere 1.5 pounds, more often around 3 pounds, versus 6 pounds for your average external pack.

For the backpacker, which pack you choose is a matter of personal taste. For example, when going off trail or on shorter trips, I prefer a sturdy internal pack. Internal packs are narrower and can squeeze through brush and between boulders without catching. The sturdier internals are more durable.

The ultralight internal packs are designed for longer treks, typically Appalachian Trail thru-hikers going ultralight head-to-toe. The ultralight internals are glorified uberlight duffel bags, with fewer pockets and zippers, but they are also designed to be carried on cleared, maintained trails and are less sturdy or durable. Consider a more durable internal pack when backpacking through Virginia's national forests and wildernesses, where lesser-maintained trails can be rough on a pack.

Your starting point for choosing a backpack is fit. Head to your nearest outdoor store and try on various packs, or borrow a friend's pack. Switch packs with someone while on a trip. The more types of packs you try, the more likely you are to find one suiting your needs. Specialty outdoor retailers often rent packs.

Ask yourself the following questions: How much money do you want to spend? How often do you plan to backpack? How much room do you need in your pack? How long is your typical trip? Name-brand packs offer quality and durability. Consider how much gear you like to carry. Do you like to bring everything but the kitchen sink? Or do you carry only the barest of necessities?

If you want to pare down your gear, buy a smaller pack. Far too often, I see backpackers with huge packs designed for a two-week trip when their average trip is two days. No matter how long you go, be very discerning when choosing the right pack for your backpacking adventures.

20.6 Meet Shenandoah Mountain Trail at campsite with planted spruce and small spring off ridge to west. Acute right on the Shenandoah Mountain Trail, aka Tearjacket Trail, per sign. Circle around Tearjacket Knob, mostly descend. Distant views into West Virginia.

23.3 Curve off the crest of Shenandoah Mountain into a cove.

24.0 Right on FR 95 at West Virginia state line, descend; FR 85 leaves left in .2 mile.

26.0 Cross bridge over North River; left on North River Trail in rich woods.

26.3 Make first of several creek crossings of North River.

28.4 Hike past long-abandoned forest service gate; climb well above now-small stream.

30.2 Trail intersection, campsite, top of North River. Here, a trail goes left to a good campsite, then on to FR 85. This loop turns right, crosses North River, then climbs.

30.4 Right on FR 427; roll along ridge through occasional wildlife clearings.

32.1 Signed Buck Mountain Trail, #434, leaves left, at first following forest road. Soon open onto a wildlife clearing, then join footpath. Descend, then climb over Buck Mountain.

34.1 Buck Mountain Trail begins very sharp descent amid rocks and pines with views.

35.6 Reach campsite and North Fork Little River after 1,500-foot drop. Cross North Fork Little River, then turn right, into stream-braided flat with gorgeous pines and hardwoods.

37.2 Squeeze past cliff on far left side of hollow; keep down the flat.

37.9 Final crossing of Little River.

38.0 Emerge at FR 1177, very near Hearthstone Lake. Head right on FR 1177, climbing above Hearthstone Lake, then descend.

38.6 Right on FR 101; pass private cabin inholdings.

39.5 Pass intersection with Grooms Ridge Trail.

40.4 Right on FR 95.

40.5 Return to the trailhead, completing the backpack.

20 • RAMSEYS DRAFT WILDERNESS

The Backpack: *Make a loop through beautiful and challenging terrain centered by the valley of Ramseys Draft, an alluring mountain stream. Start the trek along trouty Ramseys Draft, then work your way up Jerrys Run to make Shenandoah Mountain. Cruise a ridgeline, then climb to Hardscrabble Knob. From there, stop at Hiner Spring, a popular high-country camp. The last half of the loop stays atop Bald Ridge, replete with vistas, before dropping to the trailhead. Campsites are spread throughout the circuit, though water is a consideration on the ridges. Being a wilderness, trails receive lesser management and can be a little faint or rough in places.*

This two- to three-night circuit backpack explores the lows and highs of Ramseys Draft Wilderness, mostly circling the upper ridges of the Ramseys Draft watershed. However, the initial part of the hike works along Ramseys Draft but does require fords. The valley of Jerrys Run leads you to the high country. The Shenandoah Mountain Trail is a gorgeous path connecting to the Hiner Spring area, where hikers can make

20 RAMSEYS DRAFT WILDERNESS

Distance & configuration: 21.4-mile loop

Difficulty: Moderate to difficult

Backpacking time: 12 hours

Outstanding features: Ramseys Draft, views aplenty

Elevation: 2,280′ low point, 4,282′ high point

Scenery: 5

Solitude: 2

Family friendly: 2

Canine friendly: 3

Fees/permits: No fees or permits required

Best season: Year-round, though trails can be brushy in August

Maps: National Geographic #791 Staunton Shenandoah Mountain

For more info: George Washington National Forest, North River Ranger District, 401 Oakwood Drive, Harrisonburg, VA 22801, 866-904-0240, www.fs.usda.gov/gwj

Finding the trailhead: From exit 220 on I-81 near Staunton, take VA 262 north (the loop road around Staunton) for 6.7 miles to exit at US 250 west. Take US 250 west for 21 miles to Mountain House Picnic Area. Turn right toward the picnic area, then keep straight to dead end at the trailhead after .2 mile. **GPS trailhead coordinates:** N38° 18.495′, W79° 21.653′

20 Ramseys Draft Wilderness

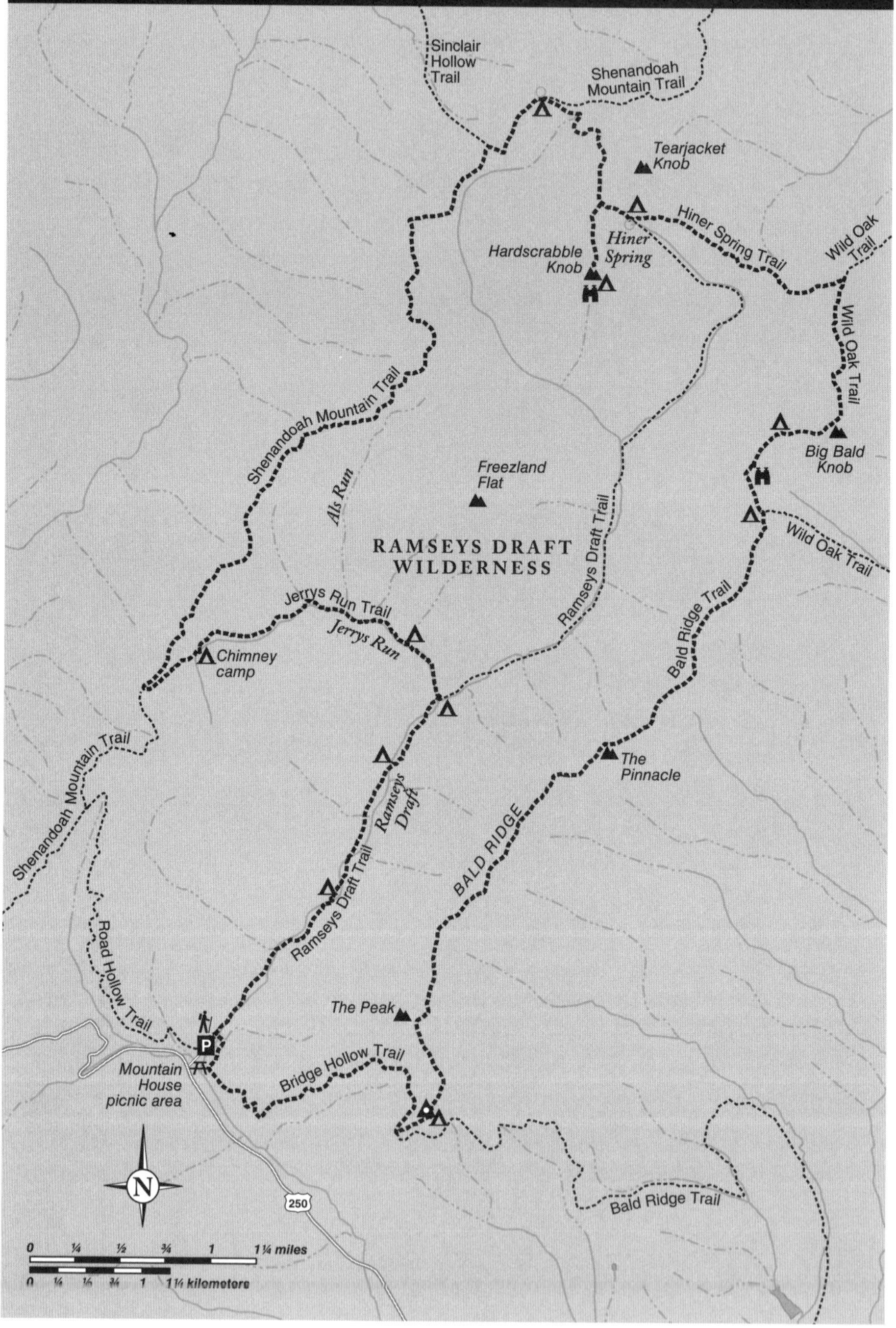

Looking south from Hardscrabble Knob.

a side trip to Hardscrabble Knob. The hike along Bald Ridge presents plentiful views of the Shenandoah Valley to the east.

Campsites can be found nearly the entirety of the circuit, allowing you to vary your daily distances on a whim. Ridgetop campsites are located near springs and wildlife ponds. Others are simply dry campsites requiring you to bring water. Hiner Spring is the most popular highland camp. Expect company up there on weekends, as well as at the "chimney campsite" on Jerrys Run.

The fords on Ramseys Draft can be avoided by taking the Road Hollow Trail up to Shenandoah Mountain. Additionally, hikers must factor in sometimes overgrown or faint paths that are in keeping with wilderness trail maintenance standards. Fallen trees are common along streamside trails. Most—but not all—trail intersections are signed. Intuition, a map, and a GPS will be helpful. By midsummer, long pants are needed; some trails can be lined with briers and stinging nettle.

The hike starts by heading up Ramseys Draft in deep woods of sycamore, musclewood, oak, maple, and white pine. Pass an old building, then enter the wilderness, often cruising up big flats. Six crossings of Ramseys Draft are made before heading up Jerrys Run Trail, with its own crossings. Trekking poles help here.

Jerrys Run Trail is lesser-used, though the chimney campsite, in an

Outfitting Your Backpacker Kitchen

Backcountry cooks, since they are transporting their food and cooking implements on their back, must judiciously consider the weight and space of said items. My backpack always contains a small grill, an aluminum pot that I do not mind putting over the fire, a pot grabber, a small knife, and a plastic spoon. If going on short, lazy summertime trips, I sometimes tote an aluminum frying pan for cooking pancakes or fish. Don't forget the spatula!

If two or more of you are backpacking together, then y'all can split the cooking items: one takes the grill and the other takes the frying pan; one person carries the pot, the other person carries the stove. Aluminum pie tins make great lightweight and reusable plates.

Don't be afraid to tweak your cook kit for different seasons and circumstances. For example, if you are going on a long-distance Appalachian Trail backpack, you might want to pare down your cook kit, whereas on a relaxing, shorter-distance summer trip you can bring the extras and engage in some serious campfire cookery.

Consider the following items for your backpacking adventure.

Camp stove: Backpacking camp stoves range from white gas models with built-in tanks to those with canisters and a whole cook kit built around the stove. All backcountry models should be single burner. Stoves using canisters can be problematic, since unless you are using a brand-new canister, you never know exactly how much fuel is in the canister. Alcohol stoves are very lightweight and use less fuel, but backpackers are limited by the energy output of the alcohol stove. They can boil water for coffee or reconstituting a freeze-dried meal, but forget any actual cooking over them. Alcohol stoves are the number one choice of long-distance backpackers.

attractive area of grass and pines, is popular. The chimney and concrete foundation of a homesite and later a shelter denote the spot. To make Shenandoah Mountain, do not continue upstream beyond the chimney campsite (as many misguided backpackers have, enough to create a faint trail). Backtrack just a bit and look for the official part of the Jerrys Run Trail leading to Shenandoah Mountain.

Once atop Shenandoah Mountain, the walking is relatively easy, gently rising amid the pines and oaks, often working around knobs. You will join the Ramseys Draft Trail at an intersection amid planted red spruce, where stands a campsite and small spring. Ahead, you can take the .4-mile side trip to Hardscrabble Knob, with a view, crumbling cabin, fallen-down tower, and dry campsite.

Cook kit: Cook kits come in a wide variety of sizes and weights, from nearly weightless titanium sets to sets so big and bulky they belong on a wagon train. Just make sure you have enough pots, plates, and cups for everyone on the trip. Also, remember you will be handling hot stuff, so bring a pot grabber, a bandanna, or a small chef mitt.

Grill: Have a grill big enough to cook your meats and other goodies for everyone in the party. Visualize how you will be using a grill. Will you be setting it up on rocks? Does it have legs? I use a very small, titanium grill when going solo but a little bigger one when in a group.

Frying pan: Frying pans can be used for more than pancakes and fish. They can be used to sauté vegetables, to stir-fry rice, to make quesadillas, and of course to make eggy breakfasts. Backpacking-size aluminum frying pans with folding handles are easy for backpackers to tote and stow.

Cup: Plastic cups are preferred. Make sure they are durable enough, can be used for hot or cold drinks, and can hold adequate amounts. Insulated cups are good for winter. No glass in the backcountry.

Utensils: The spoon is the most versatile utensil in the backcountry. It can do almost anything a fork can, yet a fork cannot quite do what a spoon can. That must be why they invented what is known as a spork, which looks like a spoon, except it has tines on the front. Plastic ones are lightest.

I bring an ultralight, one-blade knife when by myself but a more elaborate one if in a group. Make sure your knife includes a can opener if you are toting canned goods.

Cooking in the backcountry can be challenging. However, with the right utensils and frame of mind, it can not only be fun but also enhance your backpacking experience.

Then you reach two-tiered, popular Hiner Spring campsite, under some big oaks. The rocked-in spring is on the lower tier. The hike then joins the Hiner Spring Trail, at the lower end of the Hiner Spring campsite. It continues circling the watershed's ridgeline beyond the intersection with the Hiner Spring Trail.

The views really open up after the hike turns south on the Wild Oak Trail, atop Bald Ridge. Here, gain easterly views into Shenandoah Valley and Shenandoah National Park beyond. The trail has ups and downs, traversing knobs amid wind-stunted woods. The hike stays on Bald Ridge, even after the Wild Oak Trail splits east at a wildlife pond. Pay close attention upon joining the fainter Bald Ridge Trail. After passing around The Pinnacle, the path drops left through a rocky break in the ridge and works along the east slope before returning to the ridgecrest. Keep south, gaining more trailside views along the rim of the Bald Ridge.

Downtrail, a dry campsite near an overlook presents exciting looks southeast into the Calfpasture River valley and mountains beyond. A steady descent on the Bridge Hollow Trail returns you to the trailhead, after one final ford of Ramseys Draft.

Mileages

0.0 Ramseys Draft Trailhead.
0.1 Bridge Hollow Trail leaves right; Road Hollow Trail leaves left just ahead.
0.3 Pass old building in the woods.
0.6 Officially enter wilderness, first creek crossing.
1.1 Cross to left bank, then reach late-arrival campsite; cross again to right bank.
1.4 Cross to left bank, enter big flat; cross to right bank in .6 mile.
2.3 Cross to left bank, then cross Jerrys Run.
2.5 Campsite; left on Jerrys Run Trail.
2.8 Campsite.
4.3 Well-used spur leaves left to grass and pine chimney campsite.
4.8 Right on Shenandoah Mountain Trail.
9.0 Sinclair Hollow Trail leaves left.
9.5 Campsite, small spring; right on Ramseys Draft Trail.
10.4 Spur to Hardscrabble Knob, campsite.
11.5 Hiner Spring, campsite; left on Hiner Spring Trail.
12.8 Right on Wild Oak Trail; climb over Bald Knob, views.
14.6 Wildlife pond, campsite; keep straight, joining Bald Ridge Trail.
16.7 Trail cuts to east side of slope at a rocky break in the ridge.
17.1 Return to ridgecrest in a gap.
18.3 Pass below The Peak.
18.9 Campsite and open outcrop with majestic southeasterly views.
19.1 Right on Bridge Hollow Trail, southward views.
21.0 Turn north into Ramseys Draft valley, stone steps.
21.3 Cross Ramseys Draft.
21.4 Return to the trailhead, completing the backpack.

Heart of Virginia

21 • SAINT MARYS WILDERNESS

The Backpack: *Mix waterfalls, wilderness, and history in one scenic trek and you have a fun, interesting backpacking adventure at Saint Marys Wilderness. Leave the Blue Ridge Parkway, finding waterfalls on Mine Bank Creek. Once along the Saint Marys River, head upstream to find ore-processing remains and good camping. Downstream, visit Saint Marys Falls. Along the way, view more century-old ore-processing remains and the falls and cool, deep pools along Sugartree Branch and Saint Marys River. Campsites are situated throughout the trek.*

The popular Saint Marys area was federally designated a wilderness in 1984. Decades before, the rugged Saint Marys River valley was mined for iron ore and manganese. A series of mine openings as well as processing areas sprang up in 1910, and the extraction continued into the 1950s. To this day, backpackers can find locales where mining, processing, and transporting the ore took place.

This does not detract from the experience. The land has recovered well, and the streams flow crystal clear and clean and are arguably the primary draw for backpackers. Swimming, waterfalling, and fishing are regular pastimes at Saint Marys Wilderness. Campsites are abundant throughout the trek, and you can stretch a trip out here to as many as three nights.

Most hikers start at the trailhead at the bottom of Saint Marys Run, but I recommend starting on the Blue Ridge Parkway to see more waterfalls and more of the wilderness. Leave the Mine Bank Creek Trailhead and soon pass the Bald Mountain Trail intersection. The singletrack Mine Bank Creek Trail dips into its lush namesake valley, thick with rhododendron, where waterfalls, cascades, and cataracts are a constant companion, lorded over by massive boulders and rock ramparts. At .9 mile, the trail crosses Mine Bank Creek twice in succession, the last one just above an 18-foot tiered fall. Come to a small, late-arrival campsite at 1.1 miles. Cut through the heart of the gorge, passing Mine Bank Cascade, a long, 60-foot slide, at 1.4 miles.

The Saint Marys canyon opens, and you intersect the Saint Marys Trail at 1.9 miles. First, head right, up the Saint Marys River. At 2.3 miles, discover a mine site and processing area in a flat nestled between the Saint Marys River and a tributary. Look for timeworn concrete walls of a processing area, metal relics, and now-vegetated slag piles. Campsites are ample in this locale. From here, you can head upstream to explore

21 SAINT MARYS WILDERNESS

Distance & configuration: 10.6-mile there and back, additional mileage possibilities

Difficulty: Moderate, does have two fords en route to Saint Marys Falls

Backpacking time: 5.5 hours

Outstanding features: Saint Marys Falls, other falls, historic ore-processing remains

Elevation: 1,920′ low point, 3,290′ high point

Scenery: 5

Solitude: 2

Family friendly: 3

Canine friendly: 3

Fees/permits: No fees or permits required

Best season: Warm season to visit falls and swim

Maps: National Geographic #789 Lexington/Blue Ridge Mountains

For more info: George Washington National Forest, Glenwood-Pedlar Ranger District, 27 Ranger Lane, Natural Bridge Station, VA 24579, 540-291-2188, www.fs.fed.us/

Finding the trailhead: From exit 205 on I-81/I-64, take VA 606 east for 1.5 miles to Steeles Tavern and US 11. Turn left on US 11 north for .1 mile, then turn right on VA 56 east. Follow VA 56 east for 5.4 miles to the Blue Ridge Parkway. Join the Blue Ridge Parkway northbound and follow it for 4.1 miles to the Mine Bank Creek Trailhead on your left, just before reaching the more easily identifiable Fork Mountain Overlook, which will be on your right. **GPS trailhead coordinates:** N37° 54.721′, W79° 5.214′

botanically rich Green Pond, or simply head downstream, making this a base camp.

The next phase of the adventure heads downstream toward Saint Marys Falls. The Saint Marys Trail stays away from the river much of the time but crosses tributaries of the Saint Marys, often with campsites, such as the pine-needle-carpet site with small creek nearby at 2.9 miles. Talus-covered slopes of the Saint Marys gorge can be seen through the trees. At 4.1 miles, the trail curves around a mine area, dotted with campsites. Next, the trail abruptly dives along and through a streamlet to meet gorgeous Sugartree Branch and small campsites at 4.4 miles. Downstream, find Sugartree Branch Falls, a 10-foot, two-tier plunger filling a deep and chilly pool. More pools beckon the summer swimmer and campsites call the backpacker before you make an intersection at 4.8 miles. Here, the Saint Marys Trail leaves left to the popular lower wilderness parking area. Our hike takes the spur leading right to Saint Marys Falls. Quickly reach a ford. Wade the stream and trace what once

21 Saint Marys Wilderness

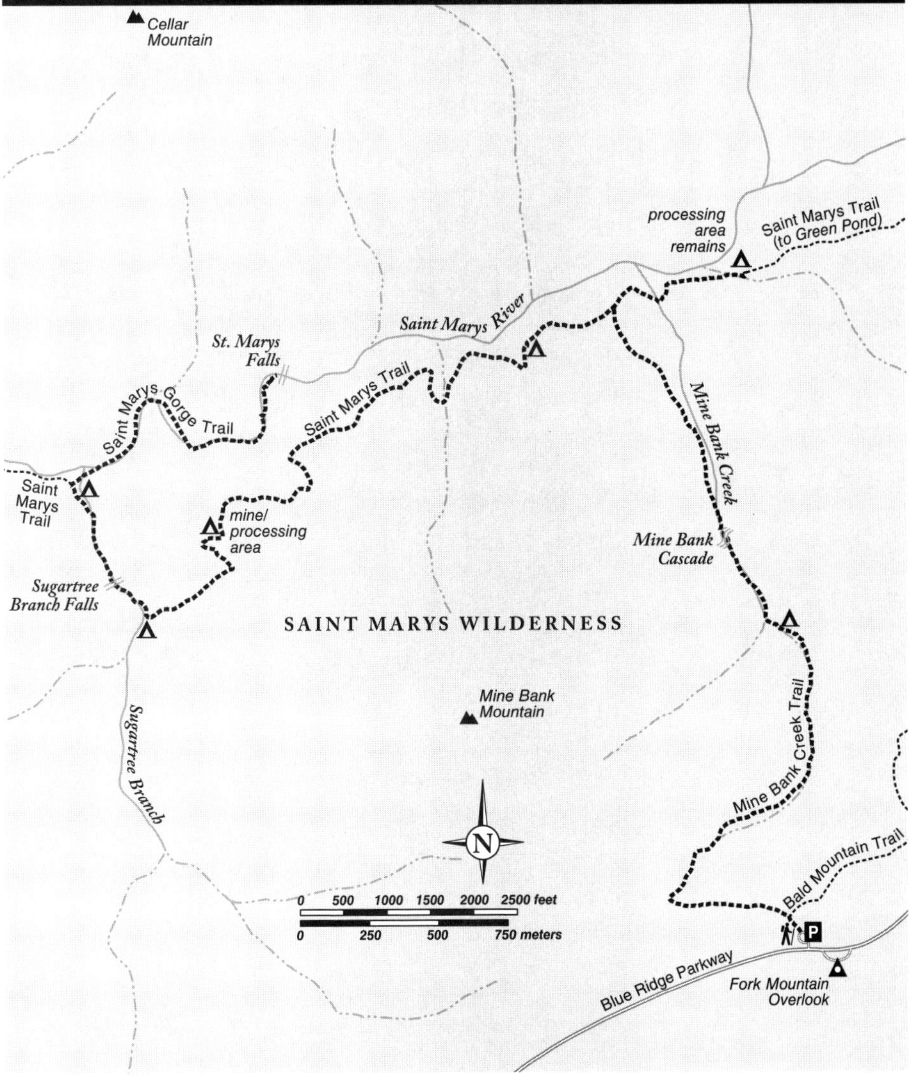

was an old railroad grade from the mining days. Much of the grade has been washed out from multiple floods. Wildfires have burned here, too.

Continue up the closing gorge with rising cliffs. Deep, alluring pools and sunning rocks beckon, while talus slopes rise above. Nonrecommended campsites can be found here. Expect no privacy as day hikers stroll through your camp en route to the falls.

Approaching Saint Marys waterfall.

At 5.6 miles, the trail dead-ends at Saint Marys Falls. The 25-foot spiller makes an initial curtain drop, then splashes and flows over an angled skirtlike rock to end in a pool. Do not camp here as the area sees heavy use, and you will get no privacy whatsoever. From the falls it is a 5-mile backtrack to the trailhead.

Mileages

0.0 Mine Bank Creek Trailhead off Blue Ridge Parkway.
0.9 Cross Mine Bank Creek twice in succession above a waterfall.
1.1 Small, late-arrival campsite; cross creek, then cross tributary.
1.9 Intersect Saint Marys Trail.
2.1 Hop Mine Bank Creek.
2.3 Cross tributary, reach mine ruins and camping flat; backtrack.
2.6 Pass Mine Bank Creek Trail again; continue downstream on Saint Marys Trail.
2.9 Pine-needle-covered campsite, small creek.

4.1 Mine/processing area to right of trail, campsites.
4.4 Cross Sugartree Creek, campsites.
4.5 Sugartree Branch Falls.
4.8 Intersection; right on spur toward Saint Marys Falls, ford river.
5.4 Ford the river again.
5.6 Saint Marys Falls; backtrack.
10.6 Return to Mine Bank Creek Trailhead and Blue Ridge Parkway.

22 • TORRY RIDGE LOOP

The Backpack: *Experience waterfalls, views, ridgetops, and creeks on this classic backpacking circuit. Leave the Blue Ridge Parkway, visiting frothy White Rock Falls, then dip into North Fork Back Creek. Visit Sherando Lake Recreation Area before climbing to rocky Torry Ridge. Drop to the serene Mills Creek watershed before climbing again to the high country, where more views can be garnered en route to the trailhead.*

This two- to three-night backpack has plentiful highlights and plentiful ups and downs. Beginning at the Blue Ridge Parkway, your first downhill takes you to an overlook and White Rock Falls. After rising to cross the parkway, you drop to North Fork Back Creek. There, Sherando Lake Recreation Area offers developed campsites, water, and hot showers if you choose to undertake more refined camping. The ascent to Torry Ridge includes a rewarding vista at Overlook Rock. Then down to Orebank Creek you go. From there, surmount a gentle gap to reach Mills Creek, a long, narrow, but relatively flat wooded valley exuding serenity. A steep climb earns Bald Mountain. The final descent leads you back to the trailhead, aggregately a little over 4,800 feet of climbing and descending.

Campsites with water can be found along North Fork Back Creek, Orebank Creek, and Mills Creek. Developed camping can be had at Sherando Lake Recreation Area. No camping or open fires are allowed on the first 2.7 miles of the trek—the White Rock Falls Trail along the Blue Ridge Parkway.

Find the singletrack White Rock Falls Trail across the parkway and just a little south from The Slacks Overlook. Begin descending a tributary of White Rock Creek in classic hickory-oak woods. Bridge a creek,

22 TORRY RIDGE LOOP

Distance & configuration: 19.4-mile loop

Difficulty: Difficult due to rocky trails and elevation changes

Backpacking time: 11 hours

Outstanding features: White Rock Falls, views, Sherando Lake Recreation Area

Elevation: 1,760′ low point, 3,560′ high point

Scenery: 4

Solitude: 3

Family friendly: 2

Canine friendly: 2

Fees/permits: No fees or permits required

Best season: Year-round as long as parkway is open

Maps: National Geographic #789 Lexington/Blue Ridge Mountains

For more info: George Washington National Forest, Glenwood-Pedlar Ranger District, 27 Ranger Lane, Natural Bridge Station, VA 24579, 540-291-2188, www.fs.fed.us/

Finding the trailhead: From exit 205 on I-81/I-64, take VA 606 east for 1.5 miles to Steeles Tavern and US 11. Turn left on US 11 north for .1 mile, then turn right on VA 56 east. Follow VA 56 east for 5.4 miles to the Blue Ridge Parkway. Join the Blue Ridge Parkway northbound and follow it for 7.3 miles to The Slacks Overlook on your left. **GPS trailhead coordinates:** N37° 54.484′, W79° 3.059′

then reach an overlook at .5 mile. Gaze down into the Tye River Valley. White Rock Falls is below, but stay with the maintained trail along a cliffline, then switchback to reach the spur to White Rock Falls at .9 mile. Shortly view the 30-foot, slender spiller frothing into a rock-walled amphitheater complete with a dunking pool.

The main trail passes more cascades before crossing White Rock Creek at 1.4 miles. Ascend through a cove to reach White Rock Gap and cross the parkway. Join the signed White Rock Gap Trail, descending past The Slacks Overlook Trail at 3.0 miles. Cross North Fork Back Creek and find a campsite at 3.3 miles. Next, continue descending to cross a large tributary of North Fork. Open to an upper impoundment, then reach Sherando Lake Campground at 5.2 miles. From there, trace the campground road through the recreation area. Reach a picnic area at 5.9 miles, very near Sherando Lake. Take the Blue Loop up past the recreation area office and scramble up dry and rocky Torry Ridge (another option is to walk along Sherando Lake, then climb the Dam Trail) onward to Lookout Rock, with the lake in the fore and Three Ridges Wilderness in the yon.

22 Torry Ridge Loop

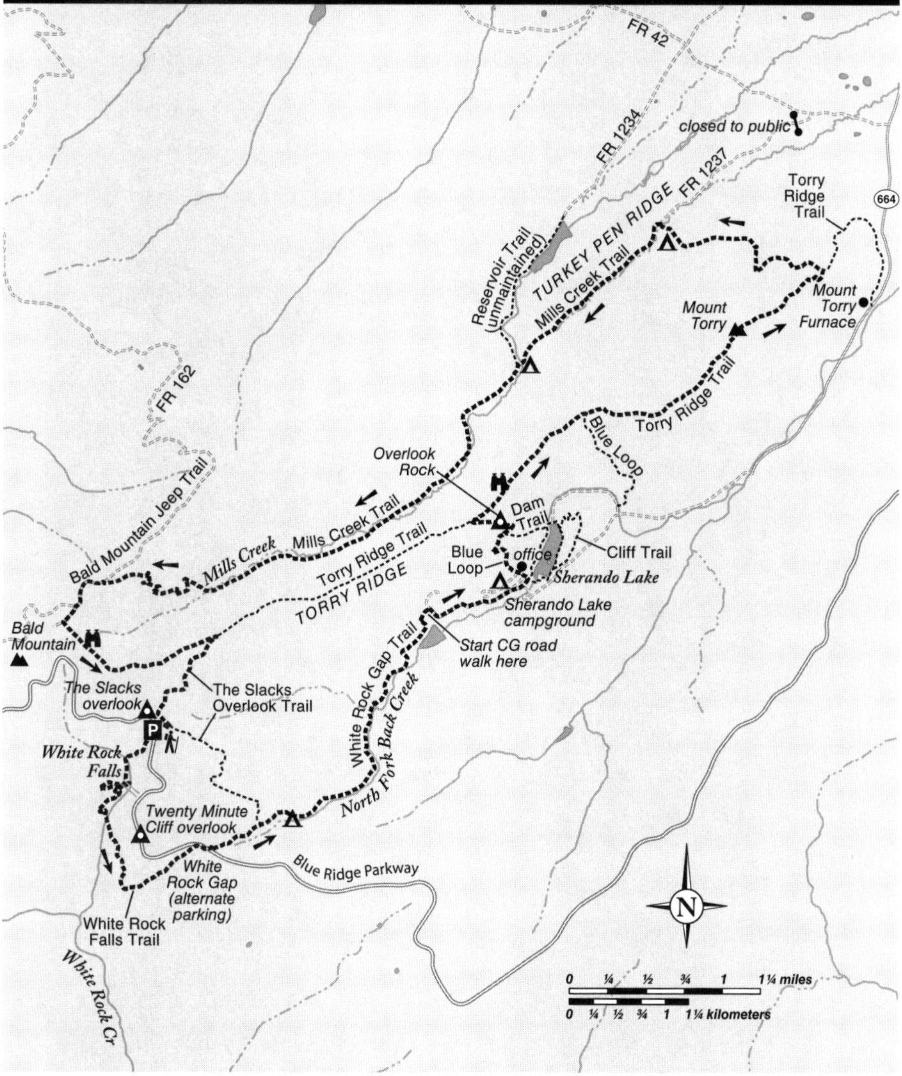

Trekking along clear North Fork Back Creek.

Make Torry Ridge at 6.9 miles. Turn right, easterly on the slow, stony, but mostly level trail. Views open north and south near talus slopes and outcrops. Pass the Blue Loop at 8.0 miles, then top out on Mount Torry at 9.3 miles. An extended downgrade leads to Mills Creek Trail at 10.1 miles. This path turns west to cross a small creek at 10.8 miles, then keeps west to meet Orebank Creek and a campsite at 11.5 miles.

From there, cross Orebank Creek at the dead end of FR 1237, open only to forest personnel. Turn left up the stream, topping out amid marshy meadows, then quickly reach Mills Creek and a streamside campsite at 12.9 miles. From there, cross Mills Creek, then keep up a scenic valley cloaked in deep forest. Isolated campsites can be found here, well away from the trail. Hop Mills Creek a few times. The last crossing is at 15.6 miles. Water up, then make the switchback-laden, 1,000-foot piney ascent to reach a non-recommended campsite and the Bald Mountain Jeep Trail at 16.9 miles. Head left on the rough dirt road, then split left on a signed spur road at 17.1 miles. Rejoin footpath and the Torry Ridge Trail at 17.2 miles, descending through pines and laurel, with views. After circling upper Mills Creek on a sometimes-rocky trail, split right on The Slacks Overlook Trail at 18.6 miles. At 19.2 miles, a user-created trail leads right to The Slacks Overlook. The official trail goes .2 mile farther, then you cut acutely right on a spur to officially complete the backpacking circuit at 19.4 miles.

Mileages

0.0 The Slacks Overlook.
0.5 Overlook.
0.9 Spur to White Rock Falls.
1.4 Hop White Rock Creek.
2.7 Cross parkway; join White Rock Gap Trail.
3.0 Slacks Overlook Trail.
3.3 Campsite.
5.0 Upper dam control lake.
5.2 Sherando Lake Campground.
6.0 Left on Blue Loop.
6.5 Stay left at intersection with Dam Trail.
6.7 Lookout Rock.
6.9 Right on Torry Ridge Trail.
8.0 Blue Loop leaves right.
10.1 Left on Mills Creek Trail.
11.5 Orebank Creek and campsite.
12.9 Mills Creek and campsite.
15.6 Cross Mills Creek a final time, then ascend.
16.9 Campsite and Bald Mountain Jeep Trail.
17.1 Left on signed road spur.
17.2 Left on Torry Ridge Trail.
18.6 Right on Slacks Overlook Trail.
19.4 Official spur trail to The Slacks Overlook, backpack's end.

Backpackers Have Food Choices

People often ask me, "What do you eat while in the backcountry?" The answer: "It depends." What type of trip am I going on? How long is it? I want foods that have as little water weight as possible, are packaged for travel, are nutritious (or at least filling), and are easy to make. Place a grain of salt in your pack when you read this and don't blame me for food poisoning.

When I started backpacking, I tried freeze-dried meals. Generally coming in pouches to which you add boiling water and wait, freeze-dried meals are tastier than they used to be but are pricey. After examining my pocketbook, I brought my indoor pantry outdoors.

First, why the paranoia on spoiled food? If it smells bad, don't eat it. Few backpacking trips last longer than a week, and most, unfortunately, last only for a weekend. So why eat like an Appalachian Trail thru-hiker?

Furthermore, backcountry meals are often more important to novice backpackers than to veterans. In fact, when introducing new backpackers, be sure to include at least one fun and tasty meal they like, such as brats cooked over the coals, or pancakes with their favorite syrup. Consider the special meal a prize for first-time backpackers entering the backcountry. Also, when taking kids backpacking, be sure to include their favorite dinners and snacks as a reward for their efforts.

Breakfast. Simple Quaker Oats are light and filling. Traditional, long-cooking oats taste better and are more nutritious than individual packets. Raisins lend flavor and add some nutritious fruit to your wilderness diet. Other lightweight breakfasts include country ham, bagels, and cream cheese. My baseline backpacking breakfast is home-mixed cereal—mainly Cheerios and Grape Nuts with raisins, cranberries, and an assortment of nuts—then add reconstituted dried milk to the whole shebang. If you have a short first day, bring bananas to enhance your next morning's breakfast.

The base of my lunches: flat flour tortillas. Think of tortillas as pre-smashed bread. Other packable breads include bagels, English muffins, and pita bread. Add peanut butter and fruit preserves to make a roll-up sandwich. You have to work to get fruit into an outback diet. Or put in smoked oysters, then add mozzarella slices to munch a nice greasy, filling lunch.

To meat or not to meat? (If you are vegetarian, skip to the next paragraph.) Even on the trail, my first night's fare features heavy perishables to cook over hot coals, such as hamburgers, boneless chicken, or steak and whole baked potatoes, sweet potatoes, or baked onions. Microwave the taters or onions at home, then wrap in foil after smearing them with butter and spices. Reheat in coals. If you are suspicious about meat going bad, do this: freeze it at home and wrap it in foil, and it will be thawed by the time you arrive at camp.

Spam and Vienna sausages are no-brainers, so let's skip to hot dogs, kielbasa, and other precooked links. You would think that kielbasa and dogs are for the first or second night, but they will keep up to a week. Salami and summer sausages are good choices that don't require refrigeration.

Cheese: My tests show that cream cheese keeps decently not refrigerated. Regular cheese keeps better. It might get a little greasy or malformed in warmer weather, but it neither scares me nor makes me sick. Also consider string cheese or wax-covered cheese.

Snacks: dried fruit, nuts, hummus, or sardines. Don't forget the bars—candy, granola, nutrition, or energy bars. Other standards, like jerky and dried fruit, are standards for a reason. They work. They're light. Also consider sweet treats as a reward and lightweight dessert, such as chocolate, licorice, and hard candy.

Backpackers carry easy dinners: macaroni and cheese, instant mashed potatoes, couscous, stuffing, rice, Ramen noodles (or Remain noodles, since they remain in your pack until all else is gone). Add freeze-dried vegetables to make the dinners healthier.

Finally, consider packaging. The less packaging the better in the backcountry. If you can't completely burn the packaging in the fire then carry it out.

The most important thing is your backcountry experience. There's no reason you can't enjoy what you normally eat, and even look to it as a reward at the end of a hard day. After all, "an army travels on its stomach" . . . well, so does a backpacker.

23 • THREE RIDGES WILDERNESS

The Backpack: *Enjoy this scenic, untamed—and popular—loop, combining the Appalachian Trail (AT) and the Mau Tar Trail. First, climb from the Blue Ridge Parkway along Meadow Mountain, then reach the Maupin Field area, with camping possibilities including a trail shelter. Begin the loop portion of the hike, ascending Bee Mountain. Pass numerous overlooks before making Harpers Creek and another trail shelter. After leaving the AT, reach the geologically rich gorge of Campbell Creek, with two waterfalls and a swimming hole in a rugged canyon. Close the loop by returning to the Maupin Field area. A final backtrack leads you back to the trailhead.*

Three Ridges Wilderness deserves its popularity. With the AT being the primary pathway already making the wilderness popular, add in a connector trail creating a quality loop, and then you are going to have a desirable circuit hike. Sprinkle in several expansive panoramas of the Blue Ridge from trailside overlooks, then throw in a couple of trail shelters. Finally, fold in a rugged gorge replete with waterfalls, and you create one of Virginia's most scenic yet busiest backpacking loops. Be apprised that backpackers will experience over aggregate 5,000 feet each of ascending and descending on often-rocky paths.

I'm not saying don't go. On the contrary, I am saying choose your visitation times carefully to maximize your experience. I would stay away from here during good weather weekends, including winter, and especially holidays. However, backpackers making this circuit during the week will find adequate solitude possible.

Not only is Three Ridges Wilderness scenery outstanding, but the camping setup is good for both one- or two-night trips. Several camping options are available for late arrivers in the first 1.5 miles (bring your own water). Start your hike by leaving Reeds Gap, southbound on the AT, walking a mown grass path, paralleling the Blue Ridge Parkway to your right. The walking is easy; then you climb into hickory-oak woods, stair-stepping uphill, then roll into now-wooded Maupin Field, with campsites aplenty and water. A gated forest road enters on your right. The Maupin Field shelter and a spring are right, down the Mau Tar Trail, your return route. This is your last water for 6 miles, until the Harpers Creek shelter.

From there, keep south on the AT, officially entering Three Ridges

23 THREE RIDGES WILDERNESS

Distance & configuration: 13.1-mile balloon loop

Difficulty: Difficult due to elevation changes and rocky trail

Backpacking time: 7.5 hours

Outstanding features: Wilderness, views, waterfalls, abundance of campsites

Elevation: 1,760′ low point, 3,960′ high point

Scenery: 5

Solitude: 1

Family friendly: 3

Canine friendly: 2

Fees/permits: No fees or permits required

Best season: Weekdays any time of year

Maps: National Geographic #789 Lexington/Blue Ridge Mountains

For more info: George Washington National Forest, Glenwood-Pedlar Ranger District, 27 Ranger Lane, Natural Bridge Station, VA 24579, 540-291-2188, www.fs.fed.us/

Finding the trailhead: From exit 96 on I-64 near Waynesboro, take Mount Torry Road, VA 624, north for 1.5 miles, then keep left, south at Lyndhurst, where Mount Torry Road changes to VA 664. Stay with VA 664 for 11.3 miles to emerge onto the Blue Ridge Parkway at Reeds Gap. The trailhead parking area is on the east side of the Blue Ridge Parkway. **GPS trailhead coordinates:** N37° 54.085′, W78° 59.123′

Wilderness, flanked by rhododendron. Ascend Bee Mountain, passing westerly views ahead from rock outcrops. The stone-riddled AT tops out, then descends south, very steeply, despite switchbacks. Views into the Piedmont open as you zigzag downward. Eventually, the path turns northwest into Harpers Creek, a clear mountain stream, home to a three-sided, wooden trail shelter and additional campsites.

Ahead, join the also-rough Mau Tar Trail, traversing a stony mountainside en route to the even more stone-strewn Campbell Creek canyon. You'll hear the stream before you see it. A spur heads downstream to 30-foot Lower Campbell Creek Falls. This cataract dives from a stone lip into a narrow cut, then makes an angled slide to end in a deep pool, then crashes out of sight. The Mau Tar Trail heads past a small camp, then up the canyon, reaching Upper Campbell Creek Falls, a 25-foot harder-to-reach sloped cascade. Your final aquatic treat is a deep, dipping hole for mountain stream swimmers, far bigger than you would expect from the smallish size of Campbell Creek. The boulders and cliffs flanking

23 Three Ridges Wilderness

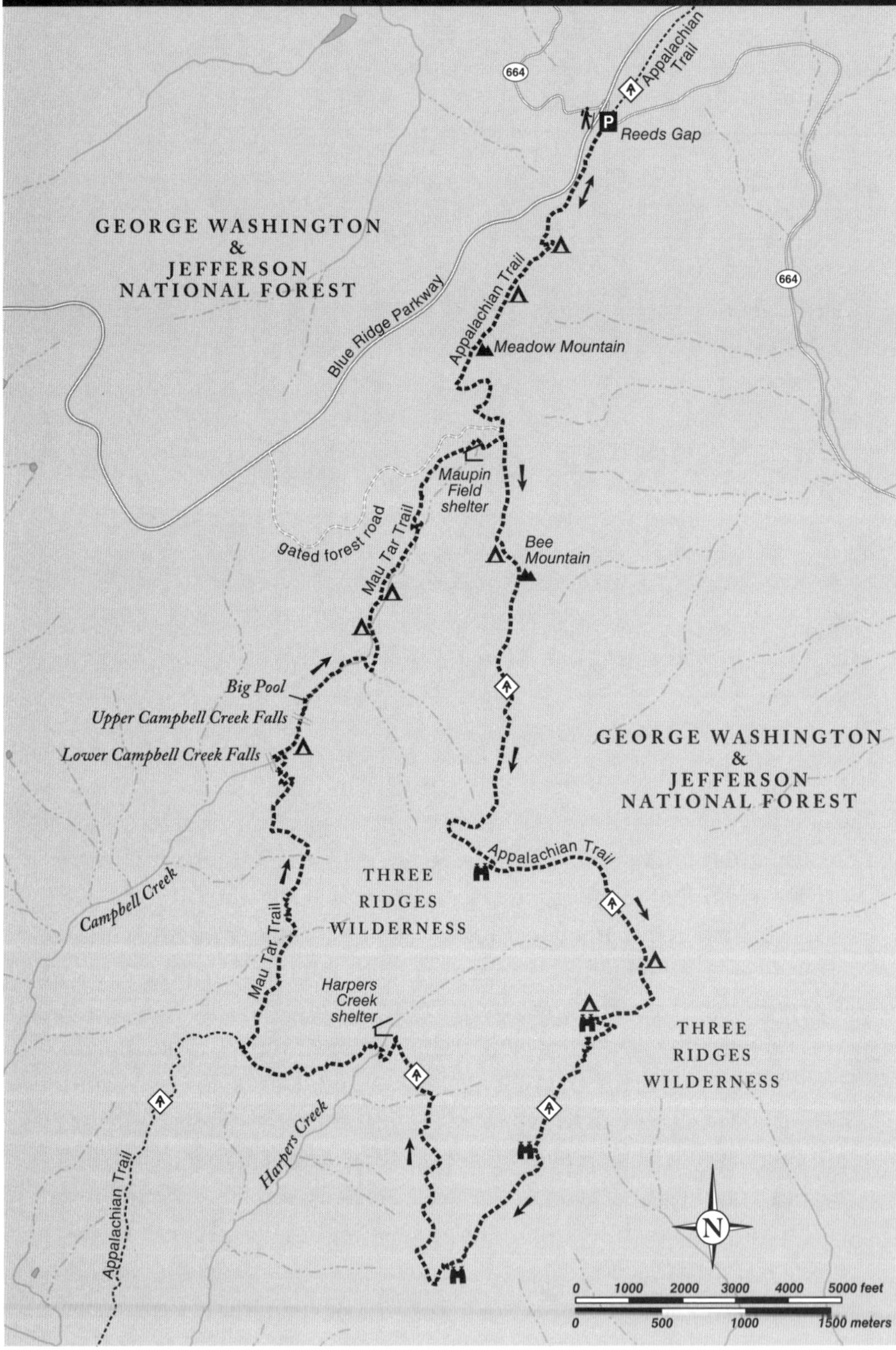

the creek seem bigger than life, too. The Mau Tar Trail breaks out of the canyon, then ascends past a couple of campsites in its calmer upper stream valley before reaching Maupin Field shelter, another three-sided wooden hut. From here, it is a simple backtrack, northbound on the AT, to reach Reeds Gap and adventure's end.

Mileages

0.0 VA 664, Reeds Gap.
0.6 Dry campsite.
0.8 Dry campsite.
1.4 Maupin Field area, shelter, campsites, woods.
2.0 Dry campsite.
3.5 Westerly vista.
4.3 Dry mountaintop campsite.
4.5 Trail sign at turn.
4.7 View from outcrop with small campsite.
5.6 Westerly view from open rock slab.
6.2 Southeasterly view amid switchbacks.
7.5 Spur trail leads right to Harpers Creek shelter, campsites nearby, too.
8.3 Right on Mau Tar Trail.
9.8 Campbell Creek and camping area; spur left to Lower Campbell Creek Falls.
9.9 Lower Campbell Creek Falls.
10.0 Upper Campbell Creek Falls.
10.7 Campsite.
10.8 Campsite.
11.6 Maupin Field shelter, campsites, spring.
11.7 Reach AT, head northbound.
13.1 Return to the Reeds Gap Trailhead, completing the backpack.

About Outdoor Sleeping Arrangements

One winter night I was on Wilburn Ridge in the Mount Rogers High Country. My friend John Cox and I were on night one of a three-night trip. The next two nights we were heading to trail shelters, so we didn't bring a tent for this first night of backpacking.

While I was lying in the open, under star-filled, clear skies, snug in my bag, the wind began to blow, increasing so fiercely I could feel the cold air push into my sleeping bag. I began to chill, then get colder and colder, until by dawn it seemed as if I was sleeping in the open without a bag. What a long night.

Having the proper sleeping bag can mean the difference between a good night's rest and a miserable night followed by an exhausted next day. The primary concerns for backpackers when choosing a sleeping bag are warmth, space, and weight. Match your sleeping bag to the season and the situation.

For example, in summer, use a fairly warm sleeping bag on a backpacking trip in the high and cool Laurel Fork Backcountry. If you are trekking along the Atlantic at False Cape State Park in August, choose the lightest bag possible.

For most backpacking adventures, I recommend a sleeping bag—with a full zipper going down the bag—comfort rated to around 40°F. These can handle local cold fronts in spring and cool Appalachian mountain nights, without weighing too much. If the temperature dips, just put on more clothes and you'll be fine. In warmer conditions you can use it unzipped as a blanket. However, during high-country winter trips or other extreme cold spells, a more substantial sleeping bag is recommended. A toboggan, gloves, and extra socks can also help keep you warm in your bag.

In warm, summertime conditions, use a simple zippered fleece blanket—one item you can get cheaply. Don't pay too much by purchasing a name-brand fleece bag that performs no better than an inexpensive one.

When going on one-night trips, backpackers can worry less about the weight and space of the sleeping bag. However, take note that newer sleeping bags—especially those with down fill—can compress to the size of a large water bottle.

For additional comfort, consider carrying a small camp pillow and bundling your clothes up under your head. Don't underestimate the importance of a pillow. This is one item that novice backpackers overlook. A lightweight air pillow you blow up is another possibility.

Sleeping pads are every bit as critical to a good night's rest as are a pillow and a sleeping bag. For quality sleeping while backpacking, I combine a simple closed-cell foam pad, 6 feet in length, with a lightweight, three-quarter-length, 48-inch, self-inflating air mattress on top of it. In colder conditions I put the closed-cell foam pad over the air mattress.

Lighter-model air mattresses come

in under a pound each. Full-length air mattresses don't weigh much and are more comfortable. I often use them in warmer conditions. These are rising in popularity as they are less cold.

A closed-cell foam pad can be used not only under you while sleeping but also around the campsite. It will prevent you from popping a hole in your air mattress should you use it sitting around camp or by the fire. The foam pad provides protection from a hard rock or wet ground and can be rolled up for extra padding. By the way, a thin ground sheet cut a little larger than the size of your sleeping pad helps keep you and your stuff dry from ground moisture.

Hammock campers have the advantage of not having to find an acceptable flat spot to overnight, but they do need two properly placed trees to string up their haven. Sleeping in a hammock can be comfortable, but cold; the sleeper is exposed to the air all around his or her body. Therefore, consider using an "underquilt," a down blanket of sorts that warms your underside. Hammocks perform best in mild conditions.

Whether you are sleeping under the stars, in a tent, or in a hammock—or even in a trail shelter—proper sleeping arrangements can enhance or diminish your backpacking experience.

Trail shelters such as this one in Three Ridges Wilderness are strung along the entire Appalachian Trail.

24 • MOUNT PLEASANT NATIONAL SCENIC AREA

The Backpack: *This is a first-rate but popular adventure. A near-double loop starts with the Appalachian Trail (AT) to roll over an open panoramic ridgetop. Leave the AT, passing a trail shelter, then experience more meadows before almost returning to the trailhead. Make a second loop highlighted with the twin lookouts atop 4,021-foot Mount Pleasant before returning to the trailhead along ridgetops.*

This locale truly lives up to its name. Mount Pleasant National Scenic Area contains a wealth of views from both meadows and mountaintops. Campsites are abundant and well dispersed. Furthermore, since the hike makes a near-figure-eight double loop, backpackers can treat this as a two-night trip or separate one-night adventures. Either way you cannot go wrong. Nice-weather weekends can be busy, so get there early to snag your preferred camp.

Campsites can be found throughout the loops, including one near the meadows of Cole Mountain, at and around Cowcamp Gap shelter, at a highland gap near Floyd's Mountain, and at Mount Pleasant. Be apprised that camping and campfires are prohibited on the meadows and mown areas of Cole Mountain. Water is available but limited; fill up where you can.

Start the adventure by climbing from Hog Camp Gap—on the list of top-ten all-time Appalachian names—in fern-floored woods of oak and hickory. Wend your way up to the meadows of Cole Mountain at .7 mile. The Forest Service keeps these former grazing lands open by mowing. Soak in 360-degree views from the linear meadows of the surrounding Blue Ridge countryside, including Mount Pleasant. Blackberries grow rife in summertime. Roll through a menagerie of meadows and woods, accompanied by vistas of Virginia's mountains fading into the yon.

Beyond here, the AT straddles a rocky spine before working downhill, passing a pair of westerly overlooks of the Blue Ridge Parkway and the Shenandoah Valley at 1.8 and 2.1 miles, respectively. Leave the AT at Cowcamp Gap to join the Old Hotel Trail. Reach Little Cove Creek and the wooden Cowcamp trail shelter, as well as nearby tent sites, at 2.9 miles. This camping area can be busy. Continuing, curve along the side slope of Cole Mountain on a sometimes rocky track. Look for a pioneer stone fence along the headwaters of Rocky Branch at 4.3 miles. Rise to a

24 MOUNT PLEASANT NATIONAL SCENIC AREA

Distance & configuration: 12.1-mile loop

Difficulty: Moderate

Backpacking time: 5.5 hours

Outstanding features: Views galore, shorter loop possibilities

Elevation: 3,050′ low point, 4,021′ high point

Scenery: 5

Solitude: 3

Family friendly: 4

Canine friendly: 2

Fees/permits: No fees or permits required

Best season: Whenever the skies are clear

Maps: National Geographic #789 Lexington/Blue Ridge Mountains

For more info: George Washington National Forest, Glenwood-Pedlar Ranger District, 27 Ranger Lane, Natural Bridge Station, VA 24579, 540-291-2188, www.fs.fed.us/

Finding the trailhead: From exit 188 on I-81 near Buena Vista, take US 60 east through Buena Vista and to the Blue Ridge Parkway. Stay with US 60 beyond the Blue Ridge Parkway for 4.3 miles, then turn left on VA 634. Stay with VA 634 for 1.6 miles, then split right with CR 755, Wiggins Spring Road. Continue for 1.3 miles and keep straight as the road becomes FR 48. Drive for 1.5 more miles to cross the AT at Hog Camp Gap, where there is parking on the left. **GPS trailhead coordinates:** N37° 45.585′, W79° 11.724′

gorgeous grass-and-tree-pocked gap and camp lying between Cole and Floyds Mountains at 4.5 miles. Water can be had down Rocky Branch.

Beyond the gap, the Old Hotel Trail winds through formerly inhabited meadows and woods, delivering stellar views of Mount Pleasant. The inhabitants of the valley housed traveling guests, hence the trail name.

Come to a T intersection and head right a short piece to reach Henry Lanum Trail parking area at 5.7 miles. It is .4 mile left to the Hog Camp Gap parking area from the T intersection, should you decide to do only one loop. And if you left something in your vehicle, access is easy.

Otherwise, join the Henry Lanum Trail, heading counterclockwise on a level track that starts next to gated FR 51. Enjoy an easy grade until reaching the headwaters of North Fork Buffalo River at 7.0 miles. The path turns to singletrack and climbs to a wide gap and campsite below Mount Pleasant at 7.9 miles. A spring serves this large and attractive camp.

24 Mount Pleasant National Scenic Area

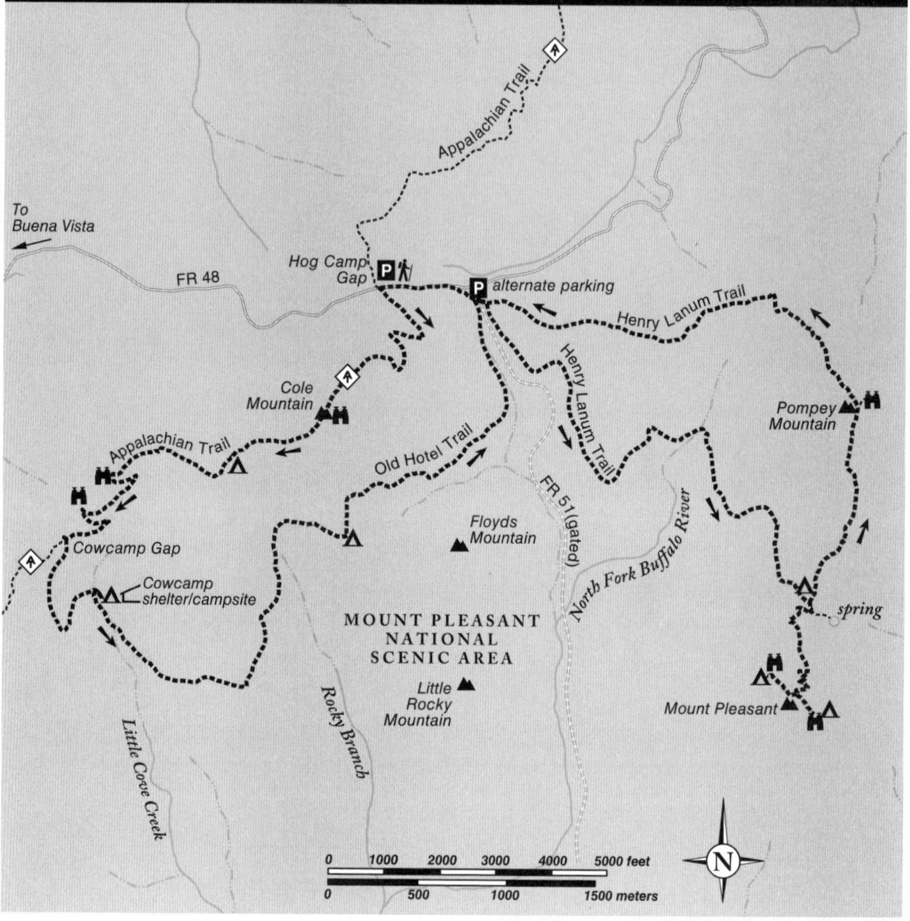

A spur switchbacks through low-hanging witch hazel trees up Mount Pleasant, then splits to east and west overlooks, where the views from rock outcrops at 8.5 and 8.8 miles are worth every step, including seeing the Cole Mountain meadows where you were earlier. Heavily used campsites accompany each overlook. Bring your water to these camps.

Return to the camp and gap below Mount Pleasant at 9.4 miles. Roll to Mount Pompey. A faint spur leads right to an outcrop and northeasterly view. More ridge-running takes you to the Henry Lanum Trail parking area. From here, take the Old Hotel Trail to pop out on FR 48, then shortly reach the parking area at Hog Camp Gap.

The views from this truly scenic area are phenomenal.

Mileages

0.0 FR 48, Hog Camp Gap.
0.3 Cross gated forest road.
0.7 Emerge onto the meadows of Cole Mountain.
1.2 Campsite in woods to left of meadows; no water.
1.4 Leave Cole Mountain meadows.
1.8 Westerly views from outcrop.
2.1 Westerly views from outcrop.
2.4 Cowcamp Gap; left on Old Hotel Trail.
2.9 Cowcamp trail shelter, campsites, Little Cove Creek.
4.5 Gap and campsite in gap between Cole and Floyds Mountains.
5.7 Henry Lanum Trail parking area; right on Henry Lanum Trail.
6.9 Curve left along headwaters of North Fork while unmaintained trail goes straight.
7.0 Step over North Fork.

7.9 Gap and campsite below Mount Pleasant; right on spur to Mount Pleasant.
8.5 Mount Pleasant west overlook.
8.8 Mount Pleasant east overlook.
9.4 Continue Henry Lanum Trail, northbound from gap/campsite.
10.1 Right spur to outcrop and view near Mount Pompey; undulate ridgeline.
11.7 Leave Henry Lanum Trail parking area, join Old Hotel Trail.
11.8 Emerge onto FR 48.
12.1 Return to the Hog Camp Gap Trailhead, completing the backpack.

25 • LAKE MOOMAW

The Backpack: *This short but surprisingly undulating hike leads you through steep hills and hollows above the shores of mountain-rimmed Lake Moomaw, past views of the impoundment, and ultimately to a backcountry campsite along its shores. The backpack is scenic from the first step to the last. The combination of Virginia's Appalachians and a scenic lake are hard to beat.*

Lake Moomaw in western Virginia is a gem of a recreation destination for a host of outdoor lovers, including campers, anglers, boaters, hikers—and backpackers. Ensconced in high mountains of the George Washington National Forest fast against the West Virginia border, backpackers can take a 3-mile trek to the Greenwood Point Campground overlooking and accessing Lake Moomaw.

This is a fee campsite. And it is first-come, first-serve, so upon arriving at Bolar Mountain Recreation Area (where the hike starts), let the entrance gate personnel or campgrounds host know you are heading for Greenwood Point Campground. Then you can pay your fee and get parking instructions (overnight parking areas change with the seasons).

Greenwood Point Campground, where Greenwood Point Trail ends, has six sites available. The primitive camp is set on a grassy, tree-bordered hill in a cove of Lake Moomaw. Backpackers will find the campground views of the lake and mountains rewarding. Be apprised that auto campers cannot access Greenwood Point Campground, but boaters can. They keep Greenwood Point hopping during summer, especially on weekends. Therefore, I recommend backpacking here during spring, fall, and winter.

25 LAKE MOOMAW

Distance & configuration: 6.2-mile there-and-back

Difficulty: Moderate

Backpacking time: 3.5 hours

Outstanding features: Lake views, lakeside camping

Elevation: 1,590′ low point, 1,870′ high point

Scenery: 4

Solitude: 2

Family friendly: 4

Canine friendly: 5

Fees/permits: Fee required

Best season: Spring, fall, and winter for quiet and solitude

Maps: National Geographic #788 Covington/Allegheny Highlands

For more info: George Washington National Forest, 422 Forestry Road, Hot Springs, VA 24445, 540-839-2521, www.fs.fed.us/

Finding the trailhead: From the intersection of VA 39 and US 220 in Warm Springs, take VA 39 west for 10.5 miles to VA 600. Turn left on VA 600 and follow it about 7 miles to the intersection with Twin Ridge Drive. SR 600 bears left and becomes SR 603.

GPS trailhead coordinates: N37° 58.549′, W79° 59.130′

During winter, some roads within the greater Bolar Mountain Recreation Area may be closed, adding a little distance to your hike.

The hike to Greenwood Point is a good break-in trip for novice backpackers. The trek features ample hills to challenge but isn't far distance-wise. Furthermore, Lake Moomaw adds an aquatic dimension sure to please. Speaking of water, there is no potable water available; therefore, you must treat your water from the lake or bring your own.

To reach the backcountry campground at Greenwood Point from the Campground 3 turnaround, follow the campground road past campsite #59 and then reach the Greenwood Point Trail. The singletrack path leaves right and uphill on a steep slope characteristic of the hills and hollows around Lake Moomaw. Top out at .2 mile, then drop down a partly grassy slope, revealing views of Lake Moomaw. At .4 mile, turn up a seasonal stream, then curve back to the lakeshore.

The trail turns up a hollow, where oaks and tulip trees reign. The sharp slopes of the hollow will surprise. At 1.1 miles, the trail rises to a knob and first-rate panorama. Here, Lake Moomaw expands within a sea of mountains rising tall in the near and rolling northward to the horizon.

25 Lake Moomaw

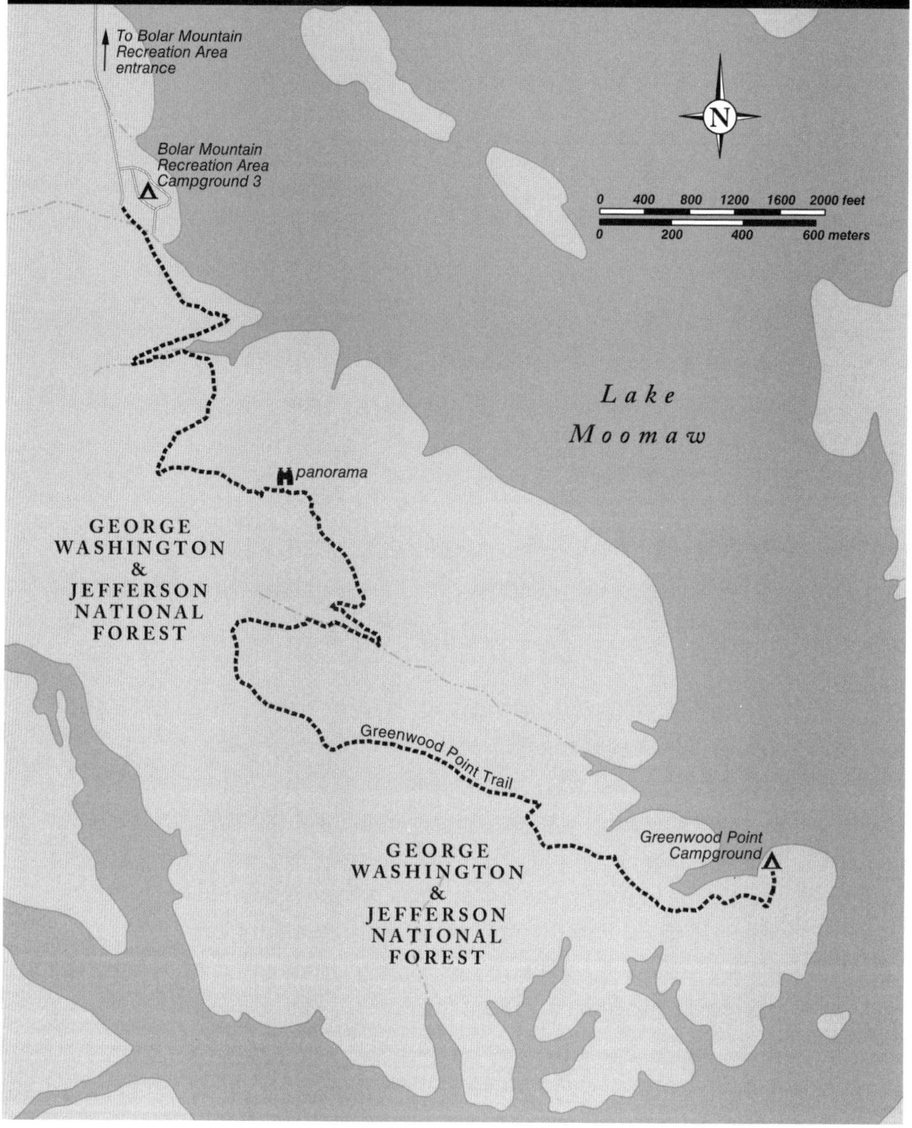

Your waterside camping area on Lake Moomaw.

Note the two islands in Lake Moomaw. The path proceeds to dive off the shale-covered knob into another hollow so steep the sun seldom shines there. A sharp climb ensues, and you are once again rambling amid the oaks. The Greenwood Point Trail turns easterly, cruising uplands while gaining occasional looks into lake coves. A long, slow descent leads to Greenwood Point Campground. The large grassy area bordered by trees beckons. Picnic tables are scattered about, delineating the six campsites. A small beach shows itself at lower lake levels. Pick your spot and enjoy lakeside camping at Lake Moomaw, backpacker style.

Mileages

0.0 Join Greenwood Point Trail past campsite #59 at Campground 3.
0.8 Bridge a normally dry streambed.
1.1 Impressive vista of Lake Moomaw.
1.5 Reach the bottom of a steep hollow.
1.8 Level off after a climb.
3.1 Greenwood Point Campground.
6.2 Return to trailhead.

Tent, Tarp, or Under the Stars While Backpacking?

Whenever possible, I sleep out in the open, under the stars, partly because I am lazy and do not want to carry, set up, or take down a tent. On short trips with a reliable weather forecast, I bring no shelter at all, saving weight and space, and get to hike, camp—and sleep—in the great outdoors. However, on longer trips or with rain in the forecast, I bring a tarp.

Nevertheless, tents are the time-honored shelter of choice for backpackers. Before pitching a tent, ask yourself why you are staying in a nylon bubble. There are five good reasons for taking a tent with you: bugs, precipitation, cold, wind, and privacy. A tent will keep the bugs out and the rain away, will make it a little warmer, and will block the wind.

It also allows for privacy when at crowded campsites. However, a tent is an *exclosure* that divides you from the outdoors. Why not sleep in nature if you can, under the stars? If taking a newbie backpacker, I do recommend a tent. Tents can provide mental protection as well as physical shelter for first-time campers. It takes time to get used to sleeping out under the stars, cowboy-style.

Backpackers have to consider smaller tents, sacrificing tent space for weight. Be prepared for a tight squeeze when sharing a tent that weighs under 5 pounds, but don't bring a heavier one, since you are carrying the tent on your back. Ultralight tents cost a pretty penny, but there are also some adequately performing mid-priced tents out there. Do stay away from low-end tents found at megastores. They have questionable waterproofness and limited life span.

Consider a tarp. Tarps can be used as your primary shelter if not in bug country. I exclusively use a tarp in the mountains of Virginia. Today's silicon-impregnated nylon tarps can be 10′ by 12′ and weigh a little over a pound. Since tarps are so light, go for a larger size. This will allow extra room for you, your gear, and perhaps a little kindling to keep dry. Tarps can be configured in a variety of ways. If the wind is high and rain is coming, set your tarp low. Otherwise, you can set one end low with the other end a little higher, allowing you to get under the shelter more easily.

Tarps allow you to have shelter yet still enjoy nature. Contrastingly, when inside a tent, you invariably lie down, and when you lie down, you invariably go to sleep. Tarps can also be used for sun protection when at camp. Bring plenty of cord to string up your tarp—at least 15 feet for each corner to be on the safe side, with a separate 40-foot cord to string a main line between trees.

Backpackers have a weight-saving option while in places where mosquitoes can be a problem: a tarp and bug screen combination. A single-person bug screen weighs mere ounces. Add an ultra-lightweight tarp. This entire setup is very small and packable and can weigh less than 2 pounds. If there is no rain, set up the bug screen by itself. If rain is a possibility, set up the bug screen under the tarp.

Next time you are considering your backpacking shelter, think outside the tent.

26 • HOOP HOLE

The Backpack: *Explore the Hoop Hole trail system, conveniently starting at historic and scenic Roaring Run Recreation Area. Day-hike the falls of Roaring Run, then set out on the Iron Ore Trail, backpacking into the Rich Patch Mountains, where you enter the high country before descending to the cascade-rich Hipes Branch. The last part of the hike takes you up geologically fascinating Stony Run, where outcrops and more cascades enhance the trek. Campsites are scattered throughout the circuit, allowing you flexibility as to length and difficulty of the adventure.*

Take the time to walk the Roaring Run Furnace area via a 1.6-mile nature trail loop before the Hoop Hole backpack. You will already be at the trailhead. See the 1830s-era Roaring Run Furnace where iron was once made, then view cascades aplenty, with impressive Roaring Run Falls crashing through the Roaring Run gorge. An alluring picnic area enhances the trailhead.

You will see more cascades and waterfalls on the Hoop Hole backpack, in the Jefferson National Forest. Overall, the trails are clearly indicated with plastic diamond blazes and signs at intersections, yet the trailbed can be faint on the Upper Hoop Hole Trail. First, climb out of Roaring Run on the Iron Ore Trail, passing some early campsites in case you need a short day (bring water to these sites). Then comes the ascent of the Rich Patch Mountains, where you climb 2,200 feet on a steady but not brutal grade.

Look for exposed iron ore as well as other stone outliers while rising. Worthwhile views are limited to winter only. After topping out, you make the passage through the legendary Upper Hoop Hole stinging nettle zone where the itchy plants line the path during late summer (no kidding, the stinging nettle in this particular area is the thickest I've ever encountered in the Appalachians). During the warm season, long pants are recommended on this stretch to avoid the trailside brush and stinging nettles. Camping in the high county is limited to one gap on the ridgecrest. Bring water to this spot straddling the Botetourt–Allegheny county line.

The nettle gauntlet leads into the Hipes Branch watershed, a gorgeous Virginia vale where outcrops, vegetation, and moving water unite to create one impressive scene after another, including cascades, waterfalls,

26 HOOP HOLE

Distance & configuration: 13.9-mile balloon loop

Difficulty: Moderate to difficult, does have major elevation gain and loss

Backpacking time: 8 hours

Outstanding features: Falls and geology on Hipes Branch and Stony Run

Elevation: 1,190′ low point, 3,330′ high point

Scenery: 4

Solitude: 3

Family friendly: 2

Canine friendly: 3

Fees/permits: No fees or permits required

Best season: Spring for waterfalls, winter for geology

Maps: National Geographic #788 Covington Allegheny Highlands

For more info: George Washington National Forest, Eastern Divide Ranger District, 110 Southpark Drive, Blacksburg, VA 24060, 540-552-4641, www.fs.fed.us

Finding the trailhead: From exit 150B on I-81 just north of Roanoke, take US 220 north 8 miles to Fincastle and continue on US 220 for 12 more miles to VA 615, Craig Creek Road, near Eagle Rock. Turn left on VA 615 and follow it 5.5 miles to turn right on Roaring Run Road, VA 621. Follow Roaring Run Road for .9 mile, then turn left into the Roaring Run Recreation Area, following it for .3 mile to dead end at the trailhead. **GPS trailhead coordinates:** N37° 42.396′, W79° 53.592′

and chilly pools ideal for a summertime dip. A well-used waterside campsite is nestled among rhododendron thickets down here.

The backpack bottoms out near VA 615 (an alternate trailhead where you could make a 3.3-mile backpacking mini-circuit by exclusively using the Lower Hoop Hole Trail). A slightly sloped camp lies down here but is very close to the VA 615 trailhead, reducing the wilderness aspect. The trek then turns up fittingly named Stony Run, a declivitous gorge of rock and water sporting its own pools, cataracts, and imposing rock crags. A small campsite at the top of the gorge allows overnighting along the creek—after you cross the watercourse eleven times. At normal flows these will be simple rock-hops.

The circuit then rejoins the Upper Hoop Hole Trail in the wooded and calmer upper reaches of Stony Run, where a final campsite can be found. The camp is a bit sloped but bigger than most sites on the circuit. From there, you traverse a pine-oak-mountain-laurel-covered mountainside, then retrace your steps back to Roaring Run. You might be too tired to explore Roaring Run Falls and Furnace on the tail end

26 Hoop Hole

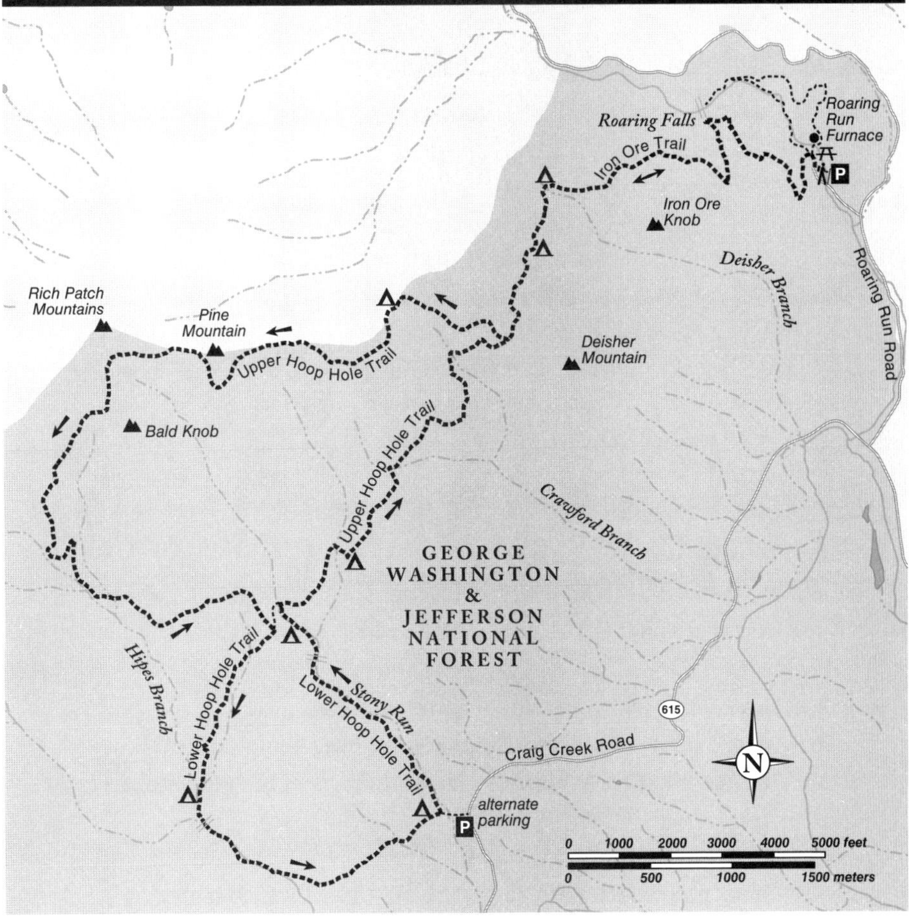

of the trip. I would make sure to walk the nature trail loop before you backpack. I guarantee it will be worth it—and so will the backpack.

Mileages

0.0 Roaring Run Trailhead, picnic area, nature trails.

0.3 Reach a better-than-nothing, very sloped late-arrival campsite in pines.

0.7 Come near yet well above Roaring Run after crossing powerlines.

1.9 Level campsite on potentially dry upper reaches of Deisher Branch.

You will find this waterfall on the Lower Hoop Hole Trail.

2.2 Campsite in man-made flat, no water.
2.5 Right on much fainter Upper Hoop Hole Trail; climb.
3.0 Reach gap and seldom-used campsite on Pine Mountain, no water.
4.3 Reach hike high point of 3,330 feet.
4.7 Bisect gap with Bald Knob to left; enter infamous nettle section on sloped trailbed.
5.4 Come near streambed.
5.8 Step over perennial section of Hipes Branch, walk away from stream.
6.6 Intersect Lower Hoop Hole Trail, turn right, descend.
7.1 Return to Hipes Creek; pass rusted machine parts.
7.3 Streamside campsite on Hipes Branch; cross stream twice.
7.4 10-foot waterfall, deep chilly swimming hole, outcrops ahead.
7.8 Turn away from Hipes Branch.
8.5 Campsite just before reaching trail junction; right turn goes to VA 615; turn left.
8.8 Enter the uber-rocky Stony Run gorge; begin stream crossings, impressive pools.

9.4 12-foot waterfall with deep hole downhill to your right, below the trail.
9.5 Small streamside campsite between trail and Stony Run.
9.6 Trail junction; turn right on Upper Hoop Hole Trail.
10.0 Campsite just up the hill just after stepping over upper Stony Run in woods.
10.5 Cross upper tributary of Crawford Branch, walk among pines.
11.4 Complete Upper Hoop Hole Trail; backtrack on Iron Ore Trail.
13.9 Return to Roaring Run Trailhead, completing the backpack.

27 • JAMES RIVER FACE WILDERNESS

The Backpack: *This wilderness adventure is packed with superlatives and possibilities. Start at the lowest spot on the Appalachian Trail (AT) in Virginia, crossing the longest hiker bridge on the entire AT. After spanning the James River, cruise the riverside, then climb to Hickory Stand via Matts Creek. Drop back to the river on the Balcony Falls Trail, then circle through lowlands to climb past the Devils Marbleyard, an amazing boulder field with a view. Rejoin the AT for more upland backpacking before returning to the lowlands. Campsites are abundant, and additional connecting trails make altering your adventure easy.*

James River Face Wilderness offers a network of rewarding trails linked to the AT coursing through its heart. Here, backpackers can make a rewarding three- to five-day loop hike exploring lands high and low. Moreover, the camping possibilities are excellent, with established sites throughout the circuit, allowing you to vary the camping. The loop hike is challenging: it climbs to the mountain crest, descends to the lowlands, then enjoys a relatively level stretch before climbing to the mountain crest a second time on a steep, rocky path. Wander the wilderness peaks before returning to the lowlands. Be apprised that water is very limited in the higher terrain; only the ridgetop camp near Marble Springs has readily accessible water.

The outlined backpack is a moving highlight reel of this special swath of Virginia. However, trips can be shortened or altered to suit your desires, namely, hiking just the first 2 miles to the Matts Creek trail shelter, an ideal quick family trip or laid-back overnighter. Parts of the backpack use bridle trails; but worry not, for the paths are firm, doubletrack trails. The hike is relatively low elevation, making it best for fall through spring, and potentially too warm for summer.

27 JAMES RIVER FACE WILDERNESS

Distance & configuration: 26.8-mile balloon loop

Difficulty: Difficult due to distance and elevation changes

Backpacking time: 15 hours

Outstanding features: Wilderness, views, James River hiker bridge, Devils Marbleyard

Elevation: 638′ low point, 2,630′ high point

Scenery: 5

Solitude: 3

Family friendly: 2

Canine friendly: 3

Fees/permits: No fees or permits required

Best season: Early fall through late spring

Maps: National Geographic #789 Lexington/Blue Ridge Mountains

For more info: George Washington National Forest, Glenwood-Pedlar Ranger District, 27 Ranger Lane, Natural Bridge Station, VA 24579, 540-291-2188, www.fs.fed.us/

Finding the trailhead: From exit 175, Natural Bridge, on I-81 near Lexington, take US 11 north for 1.7 miles to VA 130. Turn right on VA 130 east and follow it 6.2 miles to US 501, passing through Glasgow. Turn right on US 501 east and follow it for 5.5 miles to the parking lot on your right, near the hiker bridge and railroad bridge crossing the James River. **GPS trailhead coordinates:** N37° 35.801′, W79° 23.463′

The highlights come immediately as you cross the hiker bridge over the James River, the lowest point of the AT in Virginia, using the longest hiker bridge on the entire AT (no camping allowed until Matts Creek). The hike then cruises beneath bluffs along the James River before turning up Matts Creek, a noisy, wildflowery mountain rill. Matts Creek Trail shelter and campsite provide an overnighting opportunity. The AT climbs a ridge above the rapids of the James, with the Blue Ridge rising across the waterway. Ascending further still, the backpack detours on the lesser-used Balcony Falls Trail, presenting views into Big Hellgate Creek gorge and the James River valley beyond.

A series of switchbacks drops you to the lowlands sloping toward the James River, across from Glasgow. Here, join the Glenwood Horse Trail, a former forest road, as it crosses small streams flowing off the Blue Ridge, sometimes passing near private property as well as the Hellgate Trailhead. The circuit then turns up the Belfast Trail, up the rocky and scenic Belfast Creek canyon. The stony, steep ascent culminates at the Devils Marbleyard, an incredible, sun-bleached rock slope full of big boulders with rewarding views across the Elk Creek valley. The climb

27 James River Face Wilderness

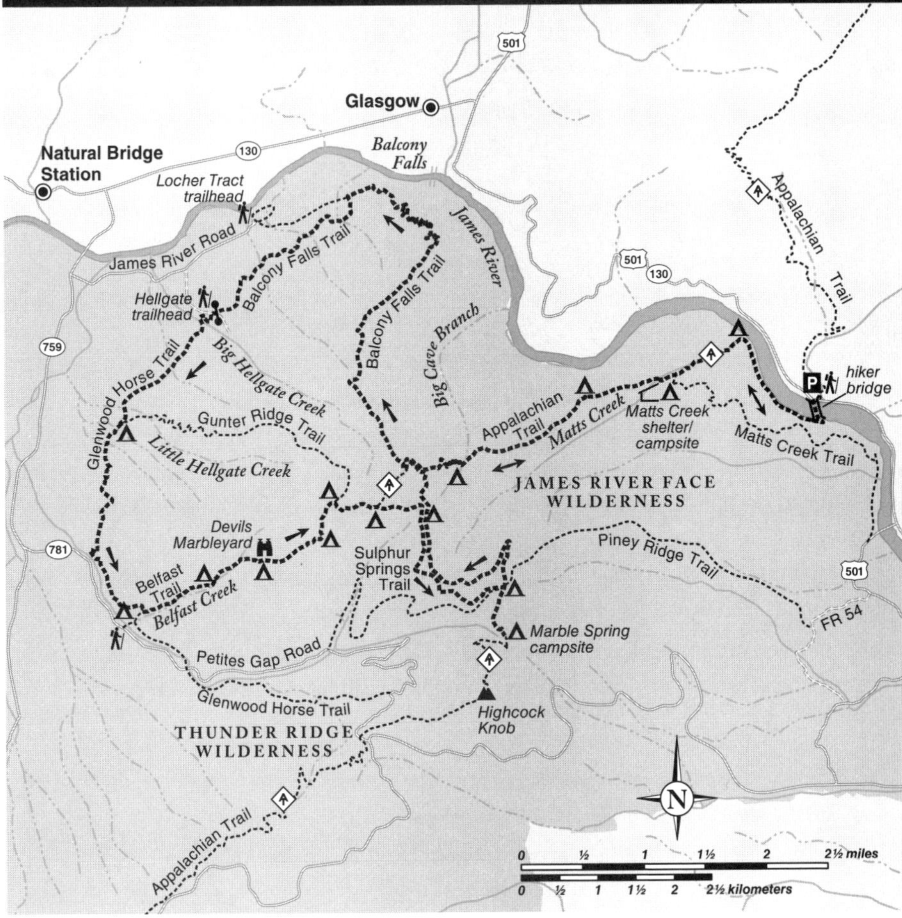

continues in more moderate fashion to meet the Gunter Ridge Trail. From here, the loop stays in the high country, where ridgetop campsites reign.

Rejoin the renowned AT. The world's most famous footpath rolls between gaps and peaks en route to the Marble Springs campsite, former site of an AT shelter (removed when James River Face was declared a wilderness). Your return route joins the wide Sulphur Springs Trail, rising proudly as it circles the upper Matts Creek watershed amid pines with scattered views. Finally, the loop closes upon returning to the AT a final time, followed by a little less than 5-mile backtrack to the trailhead. You could extend the trip by camping at Matts Creek on the way out.

Start your James River Face Wilderness adventure by crossing the longest hiker bridge on the entire Appalachian Trail.

Mileages

0.0 US 501 trailhead; cross James River on hiker bridge; no camping.

0.2 Right on AT beneath cliffs; undulate upstream along James River.

1.1 Enter James River Face Wilderness.

1.3 Turn up Matts Creek; camping allowed.

2.0 Matts Creek Trail leaves left for US 501.

2.1 Matts Creek trail shelter, creek crossing, campsites across creek; climb.

2.8 Reach ridgecrest, campsite to right, views of James River below.

4.0 Big Cove Creek, very small campsite; climb by switchbacks.

4.8 Trail intersection 1,900 feet above James River; right on Balcony Falls Trail; curve northwest among pines; views of Big Hellgate gorge.

6.2 Gap and old trail sign. Ahead, trail turns northeast.
7.3 Extended descent by numerous switchbacks; views through the pines.
8.4 Temporarily leave James River Wilderness; roll through lesser-sloped ground; pass a tumbled-down chimney.
9.1 Split left onto Glenwood Horse Trail (Balcony Falls Trail keeps straight to Locher Tract Trailhead); ascend to a little clearing, then join old FR 3110, crossing small creeks divided by low ridges.
10.9 Glenwood Horse Trail reaches a gate. Bypass the first road, bearing hard left beyond the gate. Follow main road straight a short distance, then turn left into the signed Hellgate Trailhead, popular with equestrians. Leave Hellgate Trailhead parking area southwest, still on signed Glenwood Horse Trail. Quickly turn left on doubletrack continuation of Glenwood Horse Trail, then cross normally dry bed of Big Hellgate Creek at a concrete ford. Keep southwest through lowlands.
12.3 Meet Gunter Ridge Trail leaving left just after crossing Little Hellgate Creek by culvert. Campsite a short distance up Gunter Ridge Trail to right at leveled, former cabin site. Glenwood Horse Trail curves southerly, rolling through hills near private property.
14.4 Intersect Belfast Trail. Campsite downtrail to right. Loop goes left, up rocky Belfast Trail.
14.7 Reenter James River Face Wilderness.
15.0 Pass small campsite uphill to the left just prior to two quick crossings of Belfast Creek. No water until Marble Springs 4 miles distant.
15.6 Open onto Devils Marbleyard after short, very steep section. Look left for access to open talus slope with excellent views. Small, sloped campsite across Belfast Creek.
16.2 Reach a gap. Lesser-used campsite to right in gap; potential solitude.
16.5 Meet Gunter Ridge Trail in a gap and level campsite. Right on Gunter Ridge Trail.
16.9 Meet AT. Campsite near intersection. Right on AT, southbound.
17.3 AT curves south in gap, coming very near Sulphur Springs Trail. Views into Elk Creek valley and Thunder Ridge beyond.

18.0 Views amid pines. Spur trail leads left, just a few feet up to Sulphur Springs Trail.

18.8 Reach a gap and official trail intersection with Sulphur Springs Trail. Small campsite in low pines and hardwoods. Turn right, still southbound on AT.

19.2 Reach gap amid grasses and taller hardwoods. Former site of Marble Springs Trail shelter. Spring downhill to west. Backtrack.

19.6 Join the doubletrack Sulphur Springs Trail ascending north.

20.0 Curve back south around a point; begin circling around upper Matts Creek drainage.

20.8 Come back again near AT in pines; run parallel with AT.

21.4 Small camp between AT and Sulphur Springs Trail in gap, unseen from AT. Sulphur Springs Trail and AT diverge; climb.

22.0 Return to AT, completing the loop portion of the backpack. Turn right on AT, now backtracking.

26.8 Reach the US 501 trailhead on the James River, completing the backpack.

28 • APPLE ORCHARD FALLS LOOP

The Backpack: *This short but lively circuit is long on aquatic beauty and offers views, too. Climb along a dashing mountain stream to make Apple Orchard Falls, a 200-foot cataract. Pass a second upper fall, then join the Appalachian Trail (AT) before descending along cataract-heavy Cornelius Creek. Campsites are scattered along the loop, ideal for a one-night highlight-heavy trip or two nights of relaxing by the abundant water.*

This is a highlight-heavy backpack, so it draws in day hikers, too, especially around Apple Orchard Falls. Backpackers, however, will find the circuit rewarding as well—just expect company on the trail. The water lover's loop first heads up the unnamed stream of Apple Orchard Falls. Enjoy everywhere-you-look beauty while climbing toward the Blue Ridge. Apple Orchard Falls is a long cataract, and it is hard to see the entire thing. Nevertheless, a bridge and observation platform allow you to admire the main part of cataract.

Beyond Apple Orchard Falls, the trail climbs past a lesser waterfall with a campsite. The loop, which circles Backbone Ridge, then joins the AT and does some highland wandering. No campsites are available

28 APPLE ORCHARD FALLS LOOP

Distance & configuration: 7.1-mile loop

Difficulty: Moderate, does have major elevation gain and loss

Backpacking time: 4.5 hours

Outstanding features: Apple Orchard Falls, views, Cornelius Creek Cascades

Elevation: 1,470′ low point, 3,320′ high point

Scenery: 5

Solitude: 2

Family friendly: 2

Canine friendly: 3

Fees/permits: No fees or permits required

Best season: Spring through fall to enjoy the streams

Maps: National Geographic #789 Lexington/Blue Ridge Mountains

For more info: George Washington National Forest, Glenwood-Pedlar Ranger District, 27 Ranger Lane, Natural Bridge Station, VA 24579, 540-291-2188, www.fs.fed.us/

Finding the trailhead: From exit 168, Arcadia, on I-81 near Buchanan, take VA 614 east for 3.2 miles, then turn left on North Creek Road, FR 59. Follow North Creek Road for 2.8 miles, passing North Creek Campground, then continue straight as the road becomes gravel. Drive 1.7 more miles to dead end at the trailhead. **GPS trailhead coordinates:** N37° 31.788′, W79° 33.192′

along the AT, but after you descend to Cornelius Creek, then camping is once again a possibility.

Multiple waterfalls can be enjoyed on Cornelius Creek, and it is arguably an even more scenic watershed; it does have good campsites, too. Being only 7 miles in length, this circuit limits most backpackers to one-night trips, but do be apprised that anglers and mountain creek enthusiasts could spend one night along each watercourse with no fear of boredom. Take note that there is a nearly 2,000-foot differential between low and high points along the trek, so expect some challenge despite the short distance.

Your clockwise loop immediately bridges Cornelius Creek on the Apple Orchard Falls Trail. Cruise the upper reaches of North Creek in hardwoods on a well-trod path. Pass a series of heavily used streamside camps for late arrivals at .1 mile. At .3 mile, the Apple Orchard Falls Trail splits right, away from North Creek, while an abandoned trail keeps straight to a defunct bridge on North Creek.

The valley closes as you turn up the unnamed stream of Apple Orchard Falls. Scope for pools and cascades along the way. Reach the FR

28 Apple Orchard Falls Loop

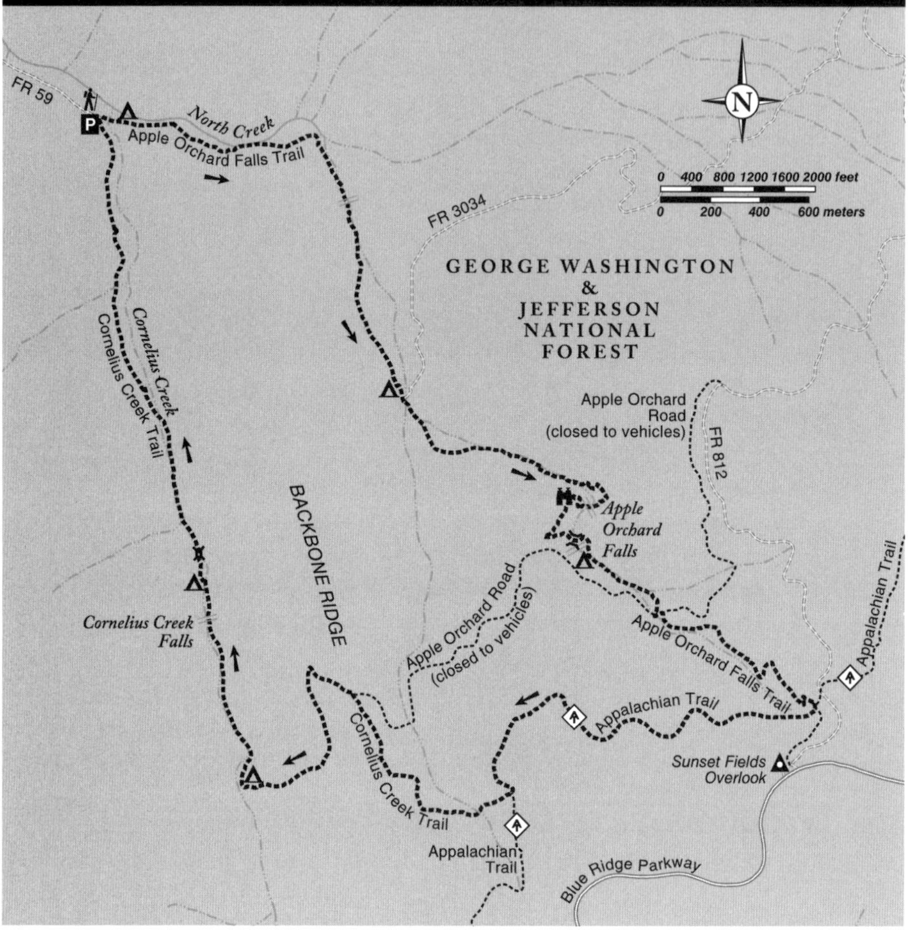

3034 access (across the creek) and a campsite (on this side of the creek) and continue ascending the stream. The trail steepens. The waterway and woods become quite bouldery. Wind among outcrops, crashing water, and woods. A pair of bridges marks the main viewing area of Apple Orchard Falls, which spills over an irregular surface of boulders, flat slabs of stone, and rock jumbles. Some hikers will have come down from the Blue Ridge Parkway.

After admiring one of the highest falls in the Old Dominion, climb away to a fine vista looking west over the James River valley. Ahead, return to the creek, where you find a 12-foot curtain-type fall and heavily used

This scenic cataract spills upstream of Apple Orchard Falls.

campsite. After crossing closed Apple Orchard Falls Road—a potential shortcut—continue in a highland cove to meet the AT. Undulate the slope of the Blue Ridge (no campsites), then take the Cornelius Creek Trail. It leads down pine-oak-mountain-laurel-clad Backbone Ridge, then drops to a gorgeous waterway chock full of sliding cascades and chilly plunge pools. A campsite can be found as soon as you reach Cornelius Creek.

The rest of the hike follows Cornelius Creek. Small falls and pools will attract your attention. At 5.7 miles, pass 10-foot Cornelius Creek Falls. Here, the stream pours over a weathered stone face into a plunge pool replete with hardy trout. At 5.8 miles, rock-hop to the left-hand bank and find a small campsite. Just ahead, cross Cornelius Creek again by bridge above a sliding cascade and plunge pool. Cross to the left-hand bank at 6.3 miles. The stream valley widens, and you could hunt for a site in the flat between you and the creek. Lesser-visited pools and rapids lie out of sight. The end comes soon, and you are back at the trailhead at 7.1 miles.

Helpful Hints for Photographing Waterfalls

When backpacking, I often seek out waterfalls (I have written five waterfall guides). I photograph just about every waterfall visited, digitally preserving the collection.

Getting excellent shots of waterfalls like those found on this loop takes time, effort, and luck. For the best shots, you need a tripod, a digital camera with manual settings, and early morning or late afternoon light. Capturing the personality of a waterfall may mean several visits during different times of the year.

Here are a few hints that may help you become a better waterfall photographer:

Tripod. You need a sturdy tripod because you cannot hold a camera sufficiently steady when using slow shutter speeds. Be sure the tripod is compact and lightweight so you will be willing to carry it while backpacking. Set your camera and use a timer, reducing shake caused by pressing the shutter button. Ultralight, backpacker-friendly tripods are available.

ISO speed. The ISO setting on most modern digital cameras is designed to approximate the ISO speed of a chosen film and corresponding camera setting used in a traditional film camera. The lowest ISO number you'll find on a digital camera, usually 100 but sometimes lower, is generally the preferred setting for shooting waterfalls. This number will yield the greatest detail, sharpness, effects, and color accuracy.

Shutter speed. Slow shutter speeds give a sense of movement. So you know, movement of flowing water is completely stopped at 1/2000 second. The fastest water will soften starting at 1/60 second. At 1/15 second, water movement will be clearly seen, but not completely blurred. Most waterfall photographs are shot at 1/10 second or slower to produce a soft quality.

Time of day. Midday sun can create harsh lighting and shadows. Visit a waterfall at daybreak or an hour before sunset, and use the wonderful quality of the light. Cloudy days afford more photo opportunities.

Exposure. The white water of a falls will often cause underexposure of your shot, making the water gray and the foliage slightly dark. With digital cameras, you can see what you just shot and adjust aperture, shutter speed, or ISO setting.

Perspective. Waterfall photographs need a reference to indicate their size. To give a feeling of depth and space, use foreground elements, such as trees, rocks, and people. Try to frame the waterfall with a fellow backpacker in the foreground.

Position. Shoot from the top, bottom, or side of the falls. Treat the waterfall like a piece of architecture. Be creative while shooting the waterfall from different perspectives.

People. The high reflectance of water tends to underexpose people in a waterfall photograph. When positioning people, consider proper lighting for both them and the waterfall. Make sure they are still when undertaking a long exposure.

Rainbows. If you are lucky enough to find a rainbow at the end of a waterfall, take as many pictures as you can. Shoot at different settings, then delete pictures back at home.

Watch the horizon. Horizon lines should be level and, in general, not placed in the center of the composition. In the image area, look for wasted space, light and dark areas, and distracting elements.

Using the above tips will increase your chances for a spectacular waterfall photograph while backpacking Virginia.

Mileages

0.0 Apple Orchard Falls Trail at FR 59 dead end.
0.1 Campsites.
0.3 Right, away from North Creek.
0.7 Cascade, pool.
1.2 Streamside campsite, bridge, FR 3034 across creek; bridge second stream.
1.6 Bridge stream near the base of Apple Orchard Falls; keep climbing.
1.9 Bridge stream at upper end of Apple Orchard Falls, viewing platform.
2.0 View across James River valley.
2.2 Campsite, 10-foot waterfall, bridge.
2.5 Reach Apple Orchard Falls Road (closed to public vehicles); shortcut opportunity.
3.1 Right on AT, southbound.
4.2 Right on Cornelius Creek Trail.
4.8 Intersect other end of Apple Orchard Falls Road; drop off Backbone Ridge.
5.3 Reach Cornelius Creek and a slightly sloped campsite.
5.7 Cornelius Creek Falls.
5.8 Rock-hop to left-hand bank, small campsite.
5.9 Cross bridge over Cornelius Creek above slide cascade.
6.3 Rock-hop to the left hand bank; valley widens.
7.1 Return to the trailhead, completing the backpack.

29 • ROANOKE TRIPLE CROWN CIRCUIT

The Backpack: *This highlight-laden trek visits three Virginia Appalachian Trail (AT) icons on one loop—McAfee Knob, Tinker Cliffs, and the Dragons Tooth—while circling the Catawba Creek valley. Start your adventure on the AT; make the popular hike to McAfee Knob, the most photographed overlook in Virginia. Leave the crowds behind en route to extensive vistas along Tinker Cliffs. Descend to cross the Catawba Creek valley, then rise to knife-edge North Mountain. The slender ridge leads you back to the AT and the Dragons Tooth, where yet another stunning vista awaits from this stone prominence. A final stretch of the AT closes the loop. Campsites are prevalent throughout the circuit, but camping is restricted by regulation in certain locations. Furthermore,*

29 ROANOKE TRIPLE CROWN CIRCUIT

Distance & configuration: 35.1-mile loop

Difficulty: Difficult due to distance

Backpacking time: 19 hours

Outstanding features: Views from McAfee Knob, Tinker Cliffs, and Dragons Tooth

Elevation: 1,340′ low point, 3,197′ high point

Scenery: 5

Solitude: 2

Family friendly: 2

Canine friendly: 1

Fees/permits: No fees or permits required

Best season: Early fall through early summer

Maps: National Geographic #788 Covington Allegheny Highlands

For more info: George Washington & Jefferson National Forests, Eastern Divide Ranger District, 110 Southpark Drive, Blacksburg, VA 24060, 540-552-4641, www.fs.usda.gov/gwj

Finding the trailhead: From exit 141 on I-81 just south of Roanoke, take VA 419 north for .3 mile, then turn right on VA 311 north and follow it for 5 miles. As you approach the gap on Catawba Mountain, look for the yellow hiker road crossing sign, then turn left into the large parking area for McAfee Knob. **GPS trailhead coordinates:** N37° 22.812′, W80° 5.360′

backpackers need to watch their water needs and for crowds around the three elements of the Roanoke Triple Crown.

This is one of Virginia's grand backpacking circuits—a must-do overnighter to which we should all aspire. A few things to know: The three primary highlights—the Triple Crown—can be very busy with day hikers, especially McAfee Knob and Dragons Tooth. The loop primarily uses the AT and the North Mountain Trail. The AT will generally be busier, but North Mountain Trail presents solitude. Camping is restricted on the start and finish of the loop. For the initial 13 miles—from the VA 311 trailhead to Catawba Road—camping is limited to designated shelters and campsites. Beyond Catawba Road, on Catawba Valley Trail and North Mountain Trail, camping is unrestricted. However, there is no water atop North Mountain. Backpackers can water up on a small stream near Catawba Road or cache water nearby before ascending North Mountain.

Beyond North Mountain, the Dragons Tooth area has additional

29 Roanoke Triple Crown Circuit

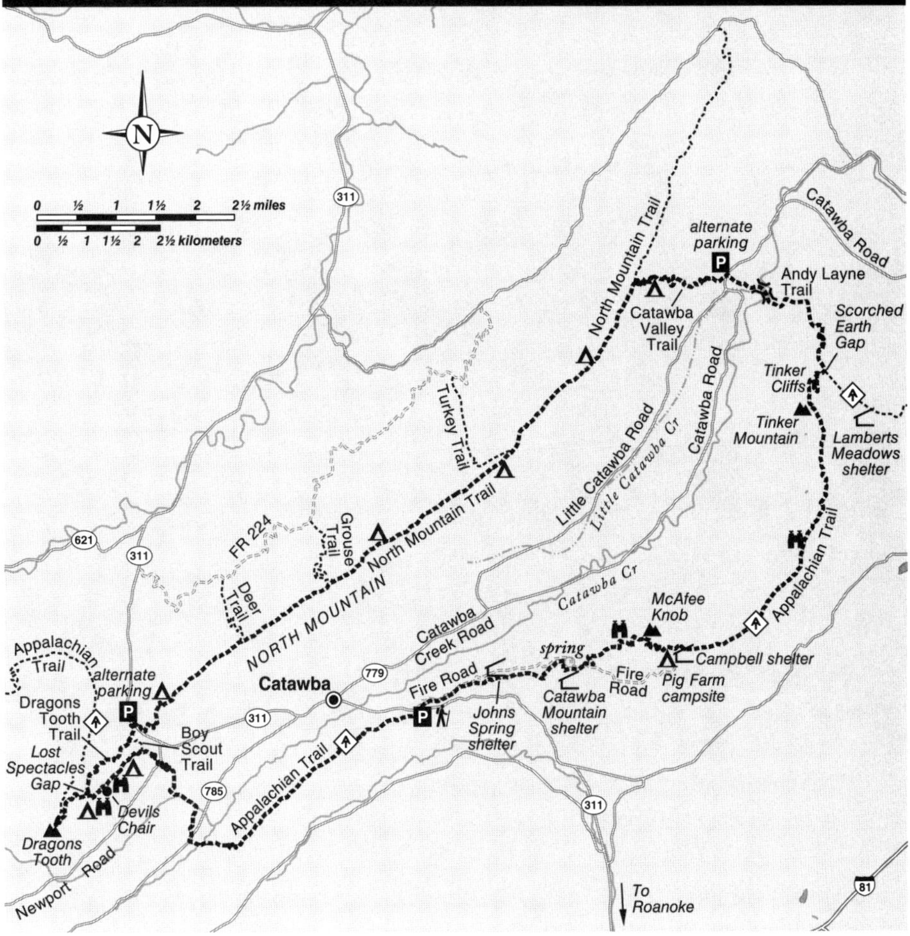

camping options. Sloped but heavily used campsites can be found along a small stream just beyond the Dragons Tooth parking area. Two other camping options can be found at saddles on the AT beyond the Dragons Tooth; then that's it, since camping is prohibited on the AT beyond Newport Road, the last 6 miles of the loop.

Other things to know: Water up when you can and avoid watering up on Catawba Creek—an agricultural stream—if possible. This loop uses one of three major trailheads: VA 311 atop Catawba Mountain. However, the loop could be executed from either the Andy Layne Trailhead or the Dragons Tooth Trailhead. If you choose these options, plan your camp-

Wintertime view from McAfee Knob.

sites ahead as much as possible, considering the restrictions. Finally, summer is the least attractive option for this circuit, since the crowds are thick, elevations aren't that high, and waterside camps are scarce.

The "Mileages" section below is comprehensive and details step-by-step turns for this adventure. Here is a suggested itinerary: first night, mile 2.1 Catawba Mountain shelter/campsites; second night, mile 13.1, campsites past Andy Layne Trailhead; third night, campsites at miles 25.0 and 26.2, Lost Spectacles Gap.

Mileages

0.0 Join AT northbound from VA 311 parking area.

0.3 Trail intersection and informational kiosk. Stay right with AT, passing overlook.

1.0 Reach Johns Spring trail shelter.
2.1 Curve just below a box spring, then reach spur to the Catawba Mountain shelter, with bearproof food storage box. Designated campsites just ahead. Climb.
2.6 Cross fire road, then bisect a powerline clearing .5 mile ahead.
3.6 Reach what seems a trail intersection; turn left. Curve through an agglomeration of giant boulders into brushy, wind-stunted woodland.
3.9 Short spur left to outcrop atop McAfee Knob. The area is truly picturesque—a large upthrust outcrop overlooking the Catawba Creek valley and a host of ridges and valleys to the north and west.
4.4 Pass powerline clearing, then Pig Farm campsite, spur to water.
4.7 Campbell trail shelter, spur to water.
6.3 AT slices between boulders.
6.9 Easterly view of Carvins Cove Reservoir.
7.7 Grassy gap; climb.
9.0 Boulders, open to Tinker Cliffs; hike along cliffs.
9.6 Descend to flats.
10.2 Left on Andy Layne Trail at Scorched Earth Gap. Lamberts Meadow trail shelter is .6 mile east on AT.
12.0 Reach Catawba Creek tributary, open onto meadows, then bridge Catawba Creek.
12.5 Bridge Little Catawba Creek; climb through cedars.
13.1 Andy Layne Trailhead. Cross Catawba Road to join the Catawba Valley Trail. Potential campsites ahead.
13.3 Cross small stream; switchback at low-flow cascade. Climb via switchbacks.
14.6 Reach camping flat, no water, on shoulder of North Mountain.
15.0 Left on North Mountain Trail.
16.2 Dry campsite; other seldom-used campsites along North Mountain Trail.
18.0 Turkey Trail descends right to FR 224; campsite .2 mile ahead.
20.1 Campsite.
20.9 Grouse Trail descends right to FR 224.
22.3 Deer Trail descends right to FR 224.

23.1 Begin descending off North Mountain; campsite .6 mile ahead; switchbacks.

24.7 Cross VA 311, ascend road to Dragons Tooth Trailhead, join Dragons Tooth Trail.

25.0 Step over creek; campsites. Boy Scout Trail leaves left. Stay right with the Dragons Tooth Trail.

26.2 Lost Spectacles Gap; campsite. Join the AT right, southbound toward Dragons Tooth, join extremely rocky trail ahead. Pass views of the Catawba Creek valley and Fort Lewis Mountain to the southeast. Manage two spots with iron rungs placed into the rock for hands and feet.

26.9 Leave the AT left, joining spur to Dragons Tooth.

27.1 Reach the Dragons Tooth. Views can be had from its base, but 360-degree views await atop the tooth. Carefully descend the Dragons Tooth, then backtrack on AT.

28.0 Pass through Lost Spectacles Gap again. Continue northbound on AT.

28.3 Reach spur to Devils Chair after passing view. North Mountain stands tall from Devils Chair. Pass another view.

28.6 Last legal camping area in gap on AT.

29.1 Pass the other end of Boy Scout Trail.

29.4 Cross Newport Road; camping restrictions rest of hike. Ascend by switchbacks.

30.3 Cross tributary of Catawba Creek; open onto pastures ahead.

31.1 Cross VA 785, reenter pastures, views.

31.2 Bridge Catawba Creek, turn downstream, cross small creek, then climb meadow.

32.0 Reach crest of Catawba Mountain above Beckner Gap, turn northeast. AT alternates between easy, level stretches and rocky, narrow segments.

35.1 Reach parking area on VA 311.

30 • MOUNTAIN LAKE WILDERNESS

The Backpack: *Mountain Lake Wilderness makes for a fine escape from summer's heat or for a pleasant fall backpack. The entire circuit stays above 3,400 feet. Campsites are well dispersed, too, along the route. Join the Appalachian Trail (AT) northbound to quickly reach Wind Rock, with extensive views and a late-arrival campsite. Next, travel high country with little elevation change in highland forest mixed with rare spruce trees. Drop a ways, then leave the AT for War Spur Lookout and a rewarding view with a nearby campsite. From War Spur Lookout, either backtrack or make a loop using the forest road accessing the trailhead.*

Potts Mountain and Salt Pond Mountain—where this backpack takes place—are high enough to harbor pockets of red spruce, very uncommon in the Old Dominion. Combine this cool highland with views and ample campsites and you have a rewarding loop, especially when summertime

30 MOUNTAIN LAKE WILDERNESS

Distance & configuration: 9.0-mile loop or 11.0-mile out-and-back

Difficulty: Moderate

Backpacking time: 5.5 hours

Outstanding features: High country, multiple views, spruce

Elevation: 3,410′ low point, 4,110′ high point

Scenery: 5

Solitude: 3

Family friendly: 2

Canine friendly: 3

Fees/permits: No fees or permits required

Best season: Mid-spring through fall

Maps: National Geographic #787 Blacksburg New River Valley

For more info: George Washington & Jefferson National Forests, Eastern Divide Ranger District, 110 Southpark Drive, Blacksburg, VA 24060, 540-552-4641, www.fs.usda.gov/gwj

Finding the trailhead: From exit 118 on I-81 near Christiansburg, take US 460 west for 19 miles to VA 700, Mountain Lake Road. Turn right onto VA 700 east toward Mountain Lake. Follow VA 700 east for 7.3 miles to Mountain Lake. Here, Mountain Lake Road becomes VA 613. Stay with it another 4.6 miles for a total of 11.9 miles from US 460 to the AT crossing. The parking area is on the left just before the crossing. **GPS trailhead coordinates:** N37° 24.717′, W80° 31.361′

30 Mountain Lake Wilderness

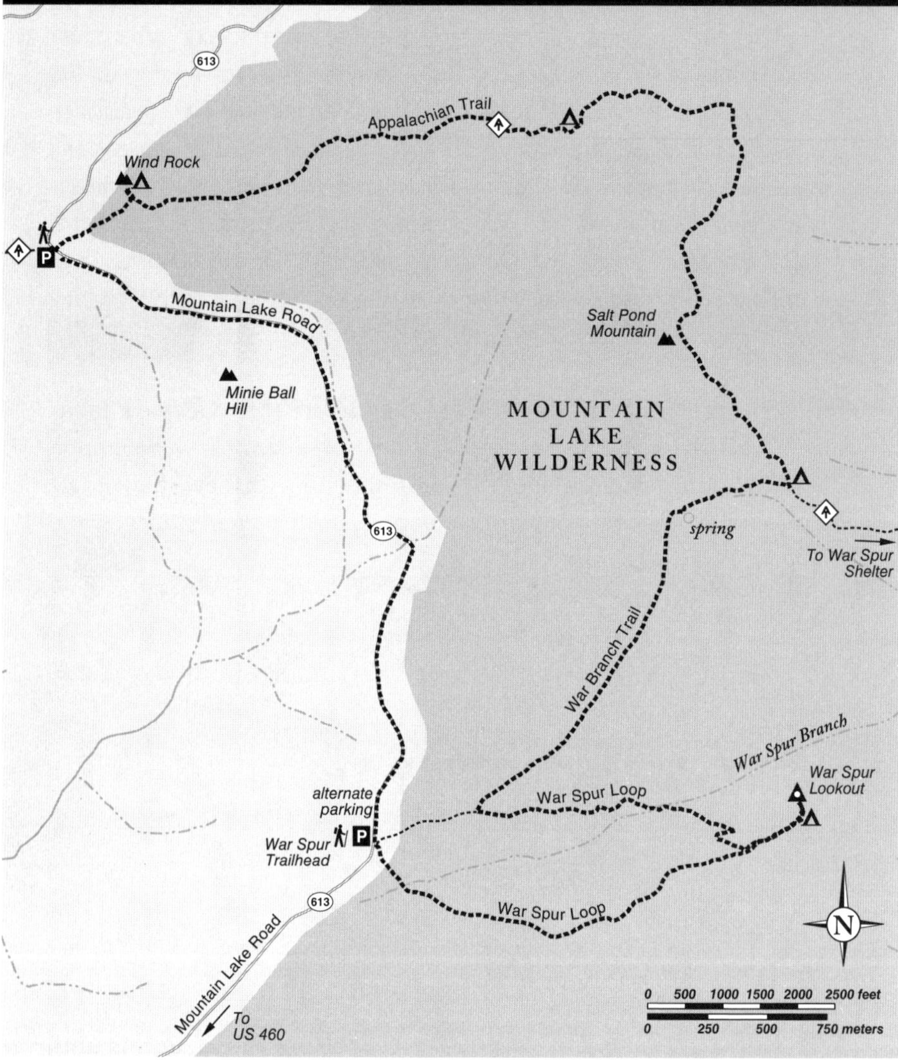

is in full swelter. An array of campsites along the route allows you to tailor the backpack to your distances and desires.

Leave VA 613, easterly, northbound on the AT, entering 10,753-acre Mountain Lake Wilderness. Part of the wild area is in West Virginia. Rise through hardwoods to reach the spur left to Wind Rock at .2 mile, passing through a few campsites good for late arrivals. Bring water, however. Gaze north, west, and east from Wind Rock. Peters Mountain stretches

Gazing out from Wind Rock.

wide across the Stony Creek valley. To your left, Big Mountain extends toward the New River. Potts Mountain keeps going to the northeast.

The now decidedly less-used AT keeps east just below the crest of Potts Mountain. In the forest, scan for occasional spruce trees and some hemlocks mixed amid wind-stunted hardwoods in this Old Dominion highland. Ferns will carpet the forest in summer. At 1.6 miles, reach a slightly sloped campsite and spring just beyond.

At 2.0 miles, the AT turns sharply right, joining Salt Pond Mountain. The trail remains easy, allowing you to look for the rare spruce, as well as hemlocks. Red spruce are rare in Virginia, found in pockets of Shenandoah National Park and a few other high points like this until they grow in relatively large numbers in the Mount Rogers High Country. Rise a bit, passing an outcrop at 2.7 miles, just before diving off Salt Pond Mountain. Drop 500 feet in .5 mile to find a trail intersection and a sloped, waterless campsite.

Turn right onto the War Branch Trail, rising back on Salt Pond Mountain, passing a spring at 3.5 miles (if you continue northbound on the AT, it is 1.1 miles and another 1,200 feet down to the War Spur Trail shelter and water). Level off, then come near a fully silted-in pond on trail right. Revel in the highland scenery. At 4.5 miles, intersect the

Be Weatherwise When Backpacking

Ominous April clouds rolled in overhead, darkening by the moment. I was backpacking the Iron Mountain Trail in southwest Virginia. The Jefferson National Forest pathway offered mountain scenery towering over lesser hollows. By now, the western sky had turned nearly black, so I pulled out my weather radio from my pack. The monotone computer voice delivered ominous warnings of heavy storms accompanied by heavier rain and copious lightning.

I needed to find a camp—and fast! While hiking downtrail, I scanned each potential campsite closely, looking for signs of ponding on the ground to avoid and high spots on which to pitch my tarp.

I spotted a likely site and dropped my pack. The lesser-used locale offered a mound slightly higher than the surrounding terrain. Tarp drainage. I pitched the tarp and called it camp. Noting the potential for high winds, I looked above for dead standing trees, known as "widow-makers" for their propensity to tumble onto unsuspecting campers. I took extra care in battening down my plastic enclave, despite peals of lightning shooting sideways across the sky.

A line of strong showers rushed toward me in a low rumble. I dove under the low-slung tarp and prepared for the aquatic siege. Soon, rain pelted the plastic, which flapped wildly with each punishing gust as I tried to sleep. Lightning repeatedly illuminated my shelter, followed by ground-shaking thunder loud enough to wake the dead—or at least an Iron Mountain backpacker. Next day, I found out the area had received over 3 inches of rain! Water puddled in places, yet my judicious choice of campsite kept me mostly dry.

Backpackers live and die with the weather and the seasons. Reveling in the changes, we wait with anticipation as each season unfolds, along with its unique conditions, each potentially threatening in its own way: the storms of spring, the heat and lightning of summer, the first cold blasts of fall, the snows and frigid temperatures of winter.

War Spur Loop. Head left here, dropping into War Spur Branch, where outcrops and rhododendron thickets conceal the stream, which you cross at 5.0 miles. Note the spruce in this chilly little vale. Grab water here if you plan to camp on War Spur, then climb to a trail junction at 5.3 miles. Head left for War Spur Lookout, descending. Just as the hike curves left for the vista, a lesser-used path heads right, across stony terrain to reach a sloped, dry campsite. It is just a short distance to War Spur Lookout from the nonlevel camp.

Knowing the weather when backpacking is paramount. When you have an idea of what to expect, you can bring gear and clothing appropriate for the predicted weather—or call it off altogether. However, try to play the weather cards you are dealt. Avoid becoming a slave to weather forecasts, reacting to their declarations as a servant to its master. I call it "weather paralysis," not knowing a course of action when the weather is iffy.

After all, what do you do when there's a 50 percent chance of rain?

Avoid weather paralysis, but be prepared and informed. Know the possibilities and have not only the clothing and gear contingencies covered, but also alternate plans if the weather gets dangerous.

I recommend bringing a portable weather radio. They come in small backpacking sizes and weights, often with AM/FM radio bands included. Weather radio broadcasts originate from the National Oceanic and Atmospheric Administration (NOAA), with over 1,000 transmitters stretching throughout the United States. NOAA broadcasts twenty-four hours a day, seven days a week over seven frequencies that require a special transmitter. Not only does NOAA predict forthcoming weather, but it also gives "short term" forecasts, which, especially during thunderstorm season, can predict strong, potentially life-threatening storms.

A weather radio also broadcasts sunrise and sunset times, as well as weather averages for the given day and temperatures and conditions for regional cities.

No matter what, check the weather before leaving home. Furthermore, learn weather averages well before embarking to a distant destination, so you can get an idea of typical temperatures and precipitation in the area during the time you plan to backpack. That way you will be weatherwise when embarking on your adventure.

Behold the view at the outcrop; Salt Pond Mountain forms a rampart across the War Spur Branch valley. Potts Mountain extends easterly with Johns Creek flowing through the lowlands. Whether or not you camp near War Spur Lookout, you can return the way you came to the trailhead for an 11-mile backpack or continue the War Spur Loop to Mountain Lake Road, then trace the quiet, primitive road back to the trailhead, creating a 9.0-mile circuit. Furthermore, more level campsites can be found on the War Spur Loop after leaving War Spur Lookout.

Mileages

- 0.0 Mountain Lake Wilderness Trailhead.
- 0.2 Wind Rock, campsites.
- 1.6 Campsite, spring.
- 2.7 Leave Salt Pond Mountain.
- 3.2 Right on War Branch Trail; sloped campsite.
- 3.5 Spring to left of path.
- 4.5 Left on War Spur Loop.
- 5.3 Left on side path to War Spur Lookout.
- 5.5 War Spur Lookout, campsite.
- 6.9 Right on VA 613.
- 9.0 Mountain Lake Wilderness Trailhead.

31 • LOCUST KNOB

The Backpack: *Looking for solitude and good scenery? This circuit backpack situated in the New River valley travels up attractive North Fork Stony Creek to reach a venerated streamside camp. The route then wanders up Dixon Branch, shrouded in rhododendron, to reach Huckleberry Ridge. Here, the segment winds among highland hardwoods before returning to the lowlands. Established campsites are restricted to the first half of the loop, but they are good. Backpackers accomplished in route-finding could alter the route and take the formerly maintained Flat Peter Loop.*

I've never seen another soul while backpacking this circuit. This loop hike has undergone name and configuration changes through the years; it was previously the Flat Peter Loop and the Dixon Branch Loop and is now the Locust Knob Loop. The first half of this hike remains as it ever was—up North Fork Stony Creek and Dixon Branch to the edge of the Peters Mountain Wilderness atop Huckleberry Ridge. Formerly the loop then descended Dismal Branch as the watercourse dove for the lowlands, then cut through the scenic Hatfield Meadows, mountain-bordered fields.

However, the Forest Service rerouted the trail, changed the name, and added plastic diamond blazes, making it much easier to follow. The route remains a winner, traversing deeply wooded forested creek valleys and dense rhododendron thickets. The newer portion of the path is mostly in mountainside hardwoods. However, you can still follow the old

31 LOCUST KNOB

Distance & configuration: 8.9-mile loop

Difficulty: Moderate, does have creek crossings

Backpacking time: 5 hours

Outstanding features: Rhododendron thickets, solitude

Elevation: 2,580′ low point, 3,540′ high point

Scenery: 3

Solitude: 5

Family friendly: 3

Canine friendly: 3

Fees/permits: No fees or permits required

Best season: Early spring through late fall

Maps: National Geographic #787 Blacksburg New River Valley

For more info: George Washington & Jefferson National Forests, Eastern Divide Ranger District, 110 Southpark Drive, Blacksburg, VA 24060, 540-552-4641, www.fs.usda.gov/gwj

Finding the trailhead: From exit 118 on I-81 near Christiansburg, take US 460 west for 29 miles to VA 635, Big Stony Creek Road, a little before US 460 bridges the New River near Ripplemead. Turn right onto VA 635 and follow east for 13 miles to turn left on County Road 722, toward Glen Alton. Follow VA 622 for .1 mile. At this point, the road to Glen Alton veers right. Here, stay straight on FR 942 and follow it just a short distance to curve right to a small parking area and gate, just beyond gated FR 10402. Note: During fall big game hunts, the gate on FR 942 will be open. **GPS trailhead coordinates:** N37° 25.586′, W80° 33.336′

route down Dismal Branch. It is not closed, just no longer maintained. If you do choose the old route, have a map-loaded GPS for safety's sake.

The hike's beginning is easy as you walk up FR 942 for .5 mile. Look right for a singletrack footpath marked with plastic diamonds (and old paint blazes). Ascend the nose of Locust Knob. Top out at .8 mile, then descend to soon reach North Fork Stony Creek. Head left, upstream, ensconced in thick rhododendron above which rises black birch. Surmount a bluff, then come along North Fork. Rock-hop its tea-colored waters at 1.2 miles. Watch out for metal splinters on the metal cable at the crossing. Continue up the rocky vale, cleared of stones where a logging grade ran.

At 2.0 miles, cross North Fork a second time and reach a long-established and recommended campsite. This would make an easy

31 Locust Knob

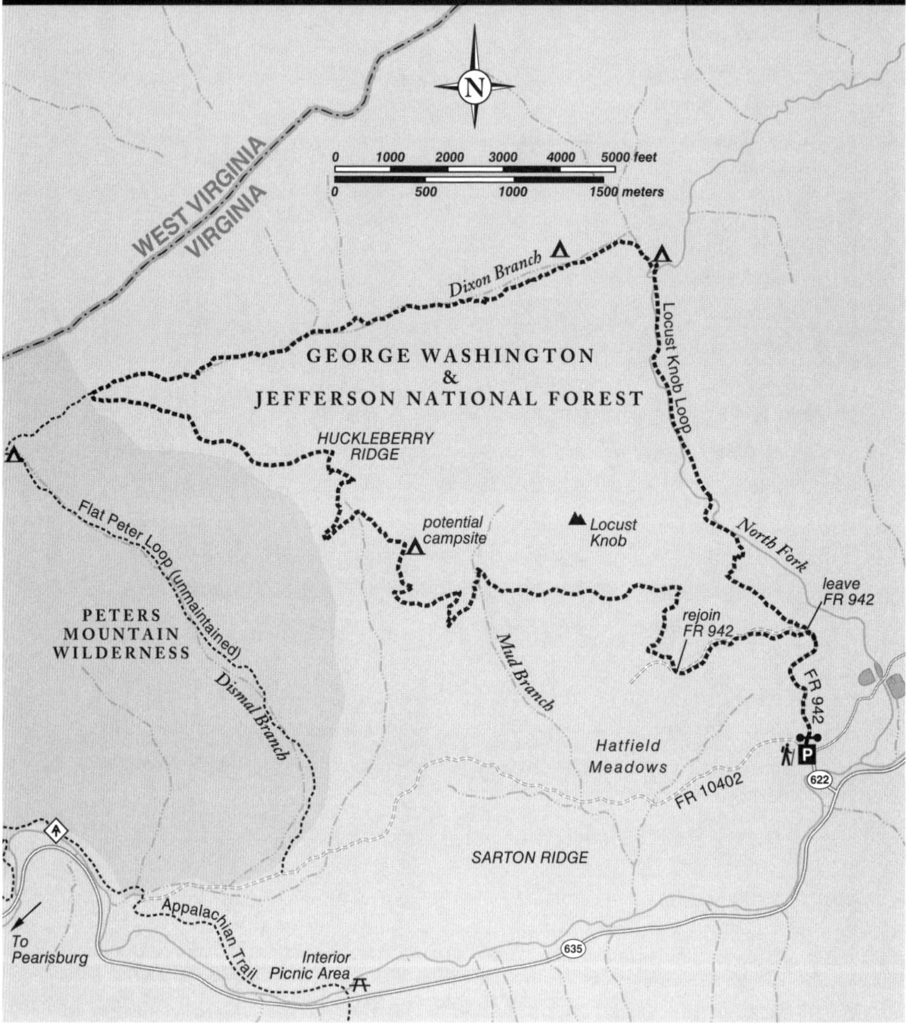

out-and-back one night trip. The Locust Knob Loop turns left. Step over Dixon Branch just above its confluence with North Fork and a pool where you can see the wheels of the logging railcar in the water.

The flora morphs to massive rhododendron thickets as you turn up Dixon Branch. Come to a second campsite at 2.5 miles. A spur trail leads right to the creek here. At 2.7 miles, begin the crisscrossing of Dixon Branch. Gently climb and cross, making the final rock-hop at 3.9 miles.

Ascend a ferny, wooded cove to reach a gap at 4.2 miles. Here is where

Note the cable to help you cross North Fork.

the newer portion of the Locust Knob Loop leaves left. (Accomplished navigators could follow the old Flat Peter Loop. Here are brief instructions: Keep west from the gap, entering Peters Mountain Wilderness. Descend into Dismal Creek. Reach a campsite at 4.6 miles. At this point, the trail turns south and crosses Dismal Branch six times. End up on the east bank 1,000 feet below to find a trail intersection at 6.6 miles. Head left, easterly, entering a patchwork of fields and linear wildlife clearings—the scenic Hatfield Meadows. The trail transforms into a gravel FR 10402 as you continue east. Reach the trailhead parking area at 8.6 miles.)

The much-easier-to-follow official route stays with the newer Locust Knob Loop. The official trail and plastic blazes turn southeasterly here, bisecting deep rhododendron on a wider path, then opens to hardwoods. At 5.1 miles, the path cuts through a gap on Huckleberry Ridge and begins a switchback-laden descent. Partial views open across the Stony Creek valley. At 5.9 miles, reach a saddle with camping potential but no water.

Resume the downgrade, crossing the rhododendron-roofed waters of Mud Branch at 6.8 miles. At 7.2 miles, join a wider linear track. At 7.9 miles, pass around a pole gate, then turn left onto gravel FR 942. Easy walking leads past the point where you left the forest road before. Retrace your steps on FR 942, completing the backpack at 8.9 miles.

Mileages

0.0 Locust Knob Trailhead.
0.5 Split right on singletrack path.
0.9 North Fork Stony Creek.
2.0 Preferred campsite.
2.5 Campsite.
4.2 Gap; old loop goes straight, newer loop heads left.
5.1 Bisect gap on Huckleberry Ridge.
5.9 Dry gap with camping potential.
6.8 Cross Mud Branch.
7.9 Pole gate; left on FR 942.
8.9 Locust Knob Trailhead.

32 • ROCK CASTLE GORGE CIRCUIT

The Backpack: *This backpack is one of the finest overnighters on the entire Blue Ridge Parkway: incredible views, rock formations, cascades, settler history, and wildflowers, too. However, reaping these rewards requires a challenging trek. Start high, rambling over meadows before descending into Rock Castle Creek gorge, where a designated campsite awaits. From there, ascend a steep path, passing settlements of early Virginians, then rejoin the spine of the Blue Ridge. Top off your backpack with views from Rocky Knob, where you will agree this path deserves its designation as a national recreation trail.*

Note: A backpacking permit is required and can be obtained by calling the Blue Ridge Parkway District Ranger Office at 540-745-9660 or Rocky Knob Campground at 540-745-9664, or by stopping at the campground at BRP milepost 167 during the warm season.

Start the backpack at the Twelve O'Clock Knob Overlook. Leave the asphalt parking area, hiking south down the grassy clearing to join the Rock Castle Gorge Trail. Turn right, southbound. The Rock Castle Gorge drops sharply off to your left as you hike the well-maintained, singletrack path under a mantle of oak, locust, hickory, and maple. At .5 mile, cross a stile to enter cattle-grazing pasture where the open terrain allows northerly panoramas of mountains fading into the yon. Stroll across the open expanse of Grassy Knoll, showcasing additional views.

At .9 mile, the Black Ridge Trail leaves right, while our route—Rock Castle Gorge Trail—reenters woods after passing through a stile, then nears a communication tower to surmount another stile. These stiles

32 ROCK CASTLE GORGE CIRCUIT

Distance & configuration: 10.7-mile loop

Difficulty: Difficult due to elevation changes

Backpacking time: 6 hours

Outstanding features: Rock formations, panoramas, deep gorge, settler history

Elevation: 1,720′ low point, 3,560′ high point

Scenery: 5

Solitude: 2

Family friendly: 2

Canine friendly: 2

Fees/permits: Free permit required

Best season: Spring through fall

Maps: Blue Ridge Parkway—Rocky Knob Trails

For more info: Blue Ridge Parkway, 199 Hemphill Knob Road, Asheville, NC 28803-8686, 540-745-9660, www.nps.gov/blri

Finding the trailhead: From Floyd, take VA 8 south 6 miles to the Blue Ridge Parkway and milepost 165.3. From there, take the parkway southbound to milepost 169.1 and the Twelve O'Clock Knob Overlook, on the left, just past the Rocky Knob picnic area and visitor center. **GPS trailhead coordinates:** N36° 48.597′, W80° 21.005′

keep cattle where they are supposed to be. The bovines keep the pastures from growing over with trees. The trail bisects a meadow at 1.2 miles, then begins a near-continual downgrade stretching 4 miles.

At 1.4 miles, come to a rhododendron-choked tributary of Rock Castle Creek. Glance into the chasm the creek has created. You'll follow the stream, then turn away only to return and cross the waterway just above a 100-foot angled waterfall at 2.1 miles.

Beyond the waterfall, keep slanting toward Rock Castle Creek. At 2.5 miles, slowly pick your way through a boulder jumble dubbed the Bare Rocks. At 2.8 miles, surprisingly find an old chimney in the woods. The chimney unintentionally memorializes the thirty-plus families dwelling in the Rock Castle Creek valley before the land was purchased for the parkway. The subsistence farms seem inconceivable, considering how richly the flora and fauna have recovered.

At 2.9 miles, reach Rock Castle Creek. Span the scenic stream at it dances downward amid a stony bed. Meet Rock Castle Fire Road, open only to parkway personnel. Turn left and trace the wide track into the Rock Castle Gorge. At 3.1 miles, meet 70-foot Rock Castle Cascades. This

32 Rock Castle Gorge Circuit

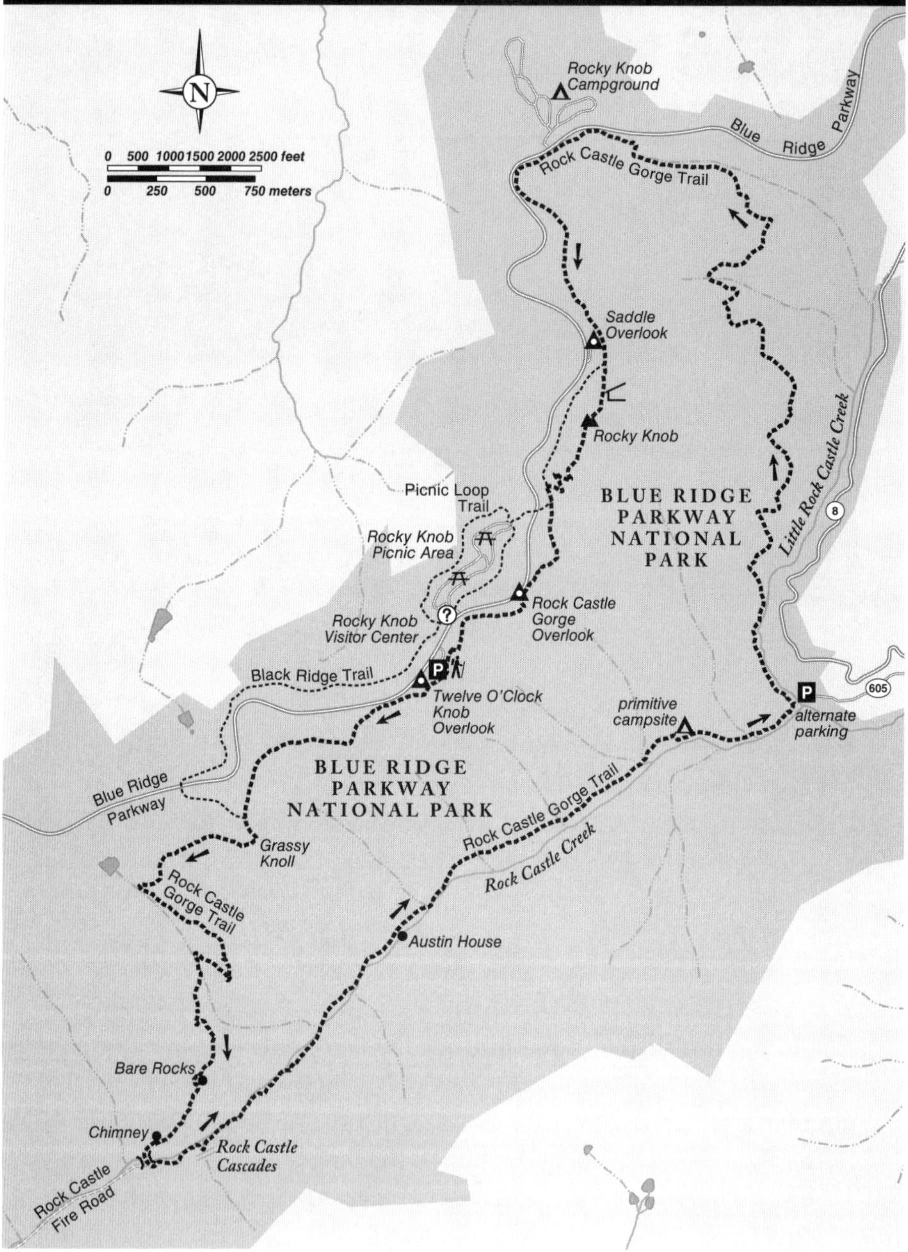

The first part of the backpack crosses this alluring meadow.

tributary of Rock Castle Creek dashes over a rock slope and can be less than thrilling at low water levels.

The track spans Rock Castle Creek at 3.7 miles and again at 3.8 miles. You'll see more signs of human habitation as the gorge widens. Look for rock piles, wooded flats, and old roadbeds. At 4.0 miles, come to the privately held Austin House, built in 1916.

Bridge Rock Castle Creek at 4.3 miles amid a wealth of hardwoods and more former homesites. At 5.2 miles, come to the designated primitive camping area, former site of a Civilian Conservation Corps camp. Look for the stone slab building foundations. The large campsite astride Rock Castle Creek features multiple fire rings and bearproof food storage boxes. This is the only legal campsite on the loop.

At 5.6 miles, watch for the Rock Castle Gorge Trail splitting left, resuming its status as a singletrack path, while the fire road keeps straight a short distance, reaching alternate parking off VA 605.

Hike up the Little Rock Castle Creek valley. The trail steepens at 5.9

miles amid rocky terrain. Get your mojo on, then climb 1,000 feet in the next 1.2 miles. An irregular, steep slope hardens the task. The trail mercifully joins a settler road, bridging a stream at 7.3 miles. Ahead, explore a settler's homestead. You'll see ancient cedars, stone piles, and a crumbled fireplace.

Curve sharply left, west, at 7.6 miles. Enter a cool, stream-centered valley populated by northern hardwoods such as yellow birch. At 8.2 miles, step over what is left of this stream. Pass over a stile, then enter oak-pocked pastures atop the Blue Ridge. A spur leads right a short distance to Rocky Knob Campground, with water, at 8.5 miles.

Views aplenty lie ahead as you wander through view-rich meadows near the Blue Ridge Parkway, guided by posts. Cattle will be present, so watch your feet. Traverse a knob, then enter woods at 9.0 miles, after passing through a small corral and stile.

At 9.1 miles, come to Saddle Overlook on the parkway. Auto tourists have much less perception of the depth and ruggedness of the canyon than does a backpacker who has trekked the Rock Castle Gorge.

Come near the parking area, then reenter woods. At 9.2 miles, reach a trail split. Head left, uphill toward Rocky Knob. The other way bypasses Rocky Knob. Head for Rocky Knob, where you can discover a former Appalachian Trail shelter standing above the Rock Castle Creek abyss. The Appalachian Trail once routed through here. Gaze easterly beyond the gorge to the Piedmont, then keep south on the stony spine of Rocky Knob. At 9.8 miles, reunite with the Rocky Knob bypass.

A spur leads right to Rocky Knob picnic area at 9.9 miles. Stay with the Rock Castle Gorge Trail, running the edge of the incredibly steep canyon. At 10.2 miles, pass the Rock Castle Gorge Overlook and the parkway.

Reenter woods, then pass a spur to the Rocky Knob visitor center at 10.5 miles. At 10.7 miles, emerge at the Twelve O'Clock Knob Overlook and the hike's beginning, completing the backpacking circuit.

Mileages

0.0 Twelve O'Clock Knob Overlook.
0.9 Black Ridge Trail leaves right.
2.1 Cross creek above waterfall.
2.5 Bare Rocks.
2.9 Bridge Rock Castle Creek, turn left.
4.0 Pass Austin House.
5.2 Reach designated primitive campsite with water.

5.6 Split left, ascend Little Rock Castle Creek.

7.3 Settler homesite.

8.5 Pass spur to Rocky Knob Campground.

9.2 Split left for Rocky Knob, old Appalachian Trail shelter.

9.9 Spur to Rocky Knob picnic area.

10.2 Rock Castle Gorge Overlook.

10.5 Spur to Rocky Knob visitor center.

10.7 Twelve O'Clock Knob Overlook.

Southwest Virginia

33 • GARDEN MOUNTAIN WILDERNESS

The Backpack: *This end-to-end adventure on the Appalachian Trail (AT) rolls over ridges and valleys before making a 2,000-foot climb to view-laden meadows and a historic ranger-cabin-turned-shelter. Continue traipsing above Burkes Garden—Virginia's highest valley—on a slender rock ridge. Dip into the Hunting Camp Creek valley before returning to more ridge walking, where additional overlooks reveal more of this slice of the Old Dominion. Along the way, walk by and through three federally designated wildernesses. Numerous campsites and three trail shelters enhance the route.*

This three- to five-day end-to-end AT adventure is full of highlights, is rich with varied camping opportunities, and has plenty of hills to challenge, along with some easy sections and rocky sections. The three wildernesses through which the backpack passes or comes near add an untamed quality to the trek. Furthermore, the vistas and overlooks along the way allow you to appreciate the grandeur of the mountains, including the meadows of Chestnut Ridge and the overlooks of Burkes Garden, Virginia's highest mountain valley.

The camping state of affairs allows for not only varied daily distances while backpacking but also a variety of camping situations. You can overnight at one of three trail shelters along the way, or pitch your tent serenaded by a mountain stream, or sleep beside a mountaintop spring-fed pond or in a highland gap.

Since you are using the AT the entire way, route-finding is an easy proposition. The trip can be made in three to five days depending on how you want to execute the hike. Do you want to undertake big miles, relax at camp, or something in between? Expect to see AT thru-hikers and section hikers on the trip, and don't expect solitude if overnighting at the trail shelters. Solitude seekers should avoid the shelters when camping. However, if you are using the shelters, you will have a 2-mile day, a 9.4-mile day, a 10.8-mile day, and a final 11.3-mile day, when your pack will be its lightest. If you are avoiding the shelters, the trip can be easily stretched to four nights. When embarking for the first night, remember it takes a little extra time to set up the shuttle vehicle.

Scan the following mileages to piece together your daily trip itinerary. Late-arrival campsites are found at 0.0 and 2.0 miles. The following mileage chart details the backpack, including campsites and water sources.

33 GARDEN MOUNTAIN WILDERNESS

Distance & configuration: 33.5-mile end-to-end

Difficulty: Difficult due to distance and elevation changes

Backpacking time: 18 hours

Outstanding features: Views, wildernesses, waterside and mountaintop campsites

Elevation: 2,265′ low point, 4,409′ high point

Scenery: 5

Solitude: 2

Family friendly: 1

Canine friendly: 2

Fees/permits: No fees or permits required

Best season: Year-round; excessive thru-hikers from late April through late May

Maps: National Geographic #787 Blacksburg New River Valley

For more info: George Washington & Jefferson National Forests, Eastern Divide Ranger District, 110 Southpark Drive, Blacksburg, VA 24060, 540-552-4641, www.fs.usda.gov/gwj

Finding the trailhead: From exit 52 on I-77 near Bland, take VA 42 east/US 52 north for .6 mile to a T intersection in Bland. From here, turn left, staying with US 52 north for 2.8 miles to the parking area on your left at the ridgetop, where Wyrick Trail, a gravel road, comes in on your left. Leave a car here. Next, backtrack to exit 52 on I-77, then keep on US 52 south/VA 42 west for 4 miles, then stay right with VA 42 as US 52 splits left. Stay with VA 42 for 14.2 more miles, then look right for the Appalachian Trail parking area, just before the O'Lystery Ruritan picnic shelter. **GPS trailhead coordinates:** US 52 Trailhead: N37° 8.226′, W81° 7.987′; VA 42 Trailhead: N36° 59.078′, W81° 24.370′

Mileages

0.0 Leave the parking area on blue-blazed trail; immediately hit the AT, head right, climb above Possum Jaw Creek. Campsite in hollow below for late arrivers.

0.8 Reach crest of Brushy Mountain, head northeast.

1.4 Drop off north side of Brushy Mountain in rhododendron groves.

2.0 Reach Knot Maul trail shelter, campsites nearby, spring to left downhill.

2.5 Campsite and bridge on Knot Mole Branch (different spelling than shelter).

33 Garden Mountain Wilderness

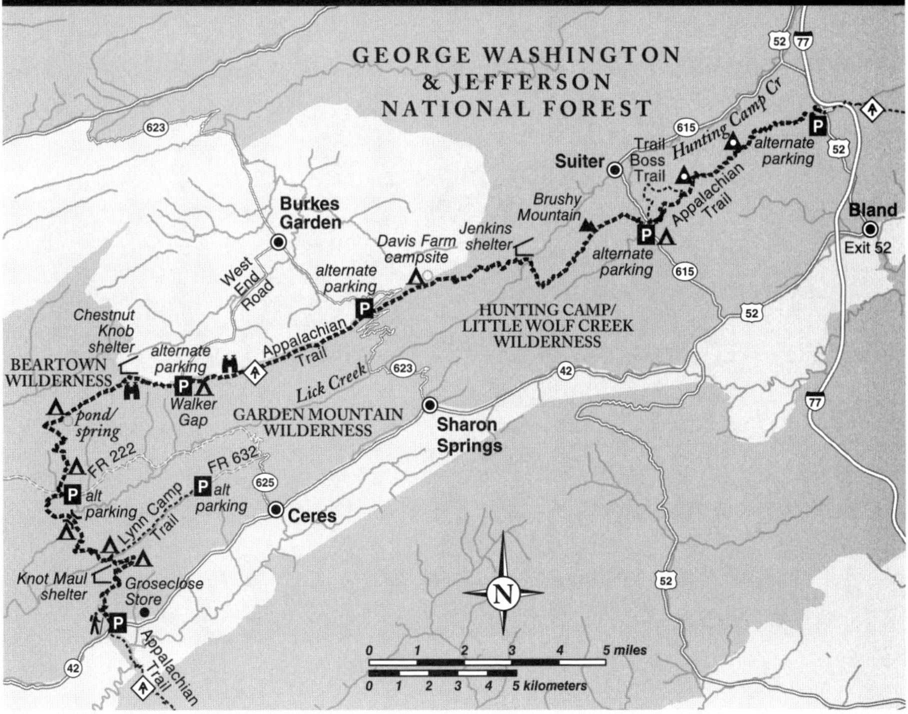

3.3 Bridge Lynn Camp Creek, campsite in flat; Lynn Camp Trail comes in, ascend Lynn Camp Mountain in oaks.

4.3 Bisect a gap on Lynn Camp Mountain, descend a sharp slope.

5.5 Reach bridge and campsite at big Lick Creek, turn up a hollow.

6.7 Hop Laurel Creek after surmounting a hill; get water.

6.8 Cross FR 222. Begin ascent to Chestnut Knob.

7.6 Dry campsite before main climb; pass intermittent streams.

8.2 Big switchback to the right.

9.2 Open onto meadows of Chestnut Ridge; stay with AT through clearings. Big views.

9.3 Pass pond. Spur trail leads left to spring and sloped campsite on far side of pond, Beartown Wilderness to north. Keep ascending through mix of fields and meadows.

The author warms in the November sun at Jenkins shelter.

11.4 Reach Chestnut Knob and four-sided shelter. Former site of fire tower. Shelter, now with six bunks and windows, was once home of fire warden. Has privy but no nearby water. Cleared views of Burkes Garden below; descend past wooded campsites.

12.8 Come to Walker Gap, alternate parking, campsite and covered spring to right; climb from the gap into Garden Mountain Wilderness. Ridgeline narrows and becomes rocky.

13.9 View into Burkes Garden. Continue northeast on Garden Mountain, where upthrust rocks create a sawtooth effect. The drop-off into Burkes Garden is very sharp. Pass abundant boundary markers as you straddle the line between Garden Mountain Wilderness and Burkes Garden to your left. Trail is often rocky.

17.8 Reach a gap and gravel VA 623. Keep northbound on AT, climbing past rock formations, entering Hunting Camp–Little Wolf Creek Wilderness. Keep northeast along Garden Mountain.

Being a Trail Angel Really Can Work Like Magic

Fresh fruit—check. Cookies—check. Candy bars—check. They were just what were needed for an afternoon of magic on the Appalachian Trail (AT). I've been the recipient of this extraordinary generosity several times but had never been on the giving end until recently. I made a last-minute decision for a quick one-night backpack trip on the AT near my home, not only to enjoy the great outdoors but to help out by providing fresh food and snacks to any AT thru-hikers I might encounter. It was spring, and the AT thru-hikers were on the march in the Southern Appalachians.

For many hikers, the term "trail magic" is familiar and may bring back happy memories. Unexpected tasty treats are the most common trail magic and are a welcome sight for those dedicated thru-hikers trudging mile after mile with minimal rations.

To thru-hikers, purveyors of trail magic are known as trail angels. All that is required to be a trail angel is to position yourself somewhere on the AT or other long-distance trail, usually near a trail junction, road crossing, campground, or parking area, with a smorgasbord of edible goodies for the hikers. The good eats can be extravagant, such as grilled hot dogs, hamburgers with all the fixings, ice cream or some perishable dessert, or a simple setup of fresh fruit (too heavy for the hikers to carry as part of their daily meals) and soft drinks.

Cookies and candy bars are always on the menu. Hikers seem to crave sweets and can't get enough. And when they do have them, the treats don't last long enough.

For my afternoon of trail magic, I choose an AT road crossing on a remote road and included a table with the treats upon it as well as extra chairs in case the hikers wanted to take a load off their feet. Even with the iffy weather forecast and the "waiting" for my guests to arrive, I was excited and energized to be sharing fresh fruit and sweet snacks with my fellow backpackers.

It wasn't long before the first hiker came by. He appeared quietly down the trail and made his way across the road before realizing his good fortune. Super Dave (his trail name) was a young man in his early thirties with a trim build and shoulder-length hair, a scruffy beard, and a smile on his face. As Super Dave unloaded his pack, we were able to chat about his hometown (he was from Portland, Maine, and hiking toward "home"), his profession (works on oil rigs all over the world), and his purpose for hiking the full 2,100 miles of the AT (looking for adventure).

Super Dave wasn't your typical thru-hiker—a post-college grad yet to start a career or a mature retired executive. Dave was in that "middle zone," occupied by few. I asked Super Dave all the questions he probably expected. (Have you seen a bear? What has been the most gorgeous scenery on the trail? What do you think about our neck of the woods? Are you staying in touch with your family?) I realized I was living his adventure with him—just two compadres sharing their passion for the outdoors.

I highly recommend becoming a trail angel. Trail magic is not limited to food. Rides into town for supplies are important as well. Where I live, it is an opportunity to show Southern hospitality. I promise any small act of kindness will be so graciously received that it will have a far greater impact on the giver. Try it for yourself.

18.7 Spur leads left .5 mile to Davis Farm campsite and wet-weather spring. Pass a big rock face ahead with easterly views of Walker Mountain.

19.5 Drop off the slope of Garden Mountain into Hunting Camp Creek valley.

21.0 Cross seasonal stream in rhododendron thicket.

22.2 Spur left to Jenkins trail shelter, water, privy nearby.

22.4 Bridge Hunting Camp Creek, ascend Brushy Mountain.

23.6 Reach the crest of Brushy Mountain, cruise the ridgeline on a wide former logging road; easy walking.

25.5 Drop off Brushy Mountain.

26.7 Bridge Laurel Creek, cross gravel VA 615, reenter woods, pass a series of campsites, then come near a parking area. AT turns up hollow, then switchbacks up Brushy Mountain.

27.8 Regain crest of Brushy Mountain, roll along the ridge.

28.6 Trail Boss Trail enters from the left.

29.1 Overlook and view into Hunting Camp Creek valley backed by Round Mountain. Circle around coves and rib ridges.

30.6 Pass another stellar overlook into the Hunting Camp Creek valley.

31.1 Walk under transmission line.

33.0 AT joins gravel road; head left.

33.5 Reach US 52 and parking area, completing the backpack.

34 • LITTLE DRY RUN WILDERNESS

The Backpack: *This vertically challenging yet visually rewarding backpack leaves Comers Rock Campground, then drops off Iron Mountain to enter a deep hollow within Little Dry Run Wilderness. It then regains elevation, ascending Henley Hollow onward to Horse Heaven. Enjoy a view, then roller-coaster yet again, down to the lowlands, then back up to Iron Mountain. A ridge run ultimately leads down to West Fork Dry Run and then back up to Comers Rock. Campsites aren't plentiful, but the scenery is rich.*

This makes a good two-night trip, covering a lot of varied terrain, from cool, stream-cut hollows to the high hardwood ridges above them. The trails are varied, too, from the singletrack, almost faint Little Dry Run Trail to the doubletrack roadlike Virginia Highlands Horse Trail (VHHT). Don't be scared off by using a horse trail. Most segments of the VHHT

34 LITTLE DRY RUN WILDERNESS

Distance & configuration: 19.4-mile loop

Difficulty: Difficult due to elevation changes

Backpacking time: 11.5 hours

Outstanding features: Little Dry Run Wilderness

Elevation: 2,470′ low point, 3,830′ high point

Scenery: 4

Solitude: 4

Family friendly: 2

Canine friendly: 3

Fees/permits: No fees or permits required

Best season: Year-round

Maps: National Geographic #786 Mount Rogers National Recreation Area

For more info: Mount Rogers National Recreation Area, Route 1, Box 303, Marion, VA 24354, 276-783-5196, www.fs.usda.gov/gwj

Finding the trailhead: From exit 70 on I-81 near Wytheville, drive south on US 21 for 17.8 miles to FR 57, passing through Speedwell. Turn right on FR 57 and follow it for 3.6 miles to Comers Rock Recreation Area. Look for a sign indicating the Iron Mountain Trail near the campground restroom. **GPS trailhead coordinates:** N36° 45.781′, W81° 13.445′

are built to handle horse traffic, so your most unpleasant scenario will likely be skirting around a little manure.

A few established campsites dot the circuit, and more can be made using Leave No Trace principles in the hollows and along the ridges. Be prepared to scout for a campsite. Water is abundant, though the ridge walks are dry. Comers Rock Campground makes an excellent late-arrival camp, for departure the next morning. Check out the view from nearby Comers Rock by foot or automobile before your hike.

Starting high, leave Comers Rock Campground from near the restroom and campsite #5 to soon make an intersection. Here, the Iron Mountain Trail leaves left while we stay straight, descending the Little Dry Run Trail along a steep ridge, coming to an intersection in a flat gap at 1.1 miles. Continue on the singletrack Little Dry Run Trail through a rocky segment, then come alongside rhododendron-cloaked Little Dry Run. The path and stream intertwine, resulting in gravel bars and occasional muddy segments under the tall pines. Campable flats can be found trail-side. Be prepared to look for a site; they aren't going to jump out at you.

At 3.5 miles, near the wilderness boundary, the track abruptly turns

34 Little Dry Run Wilderness

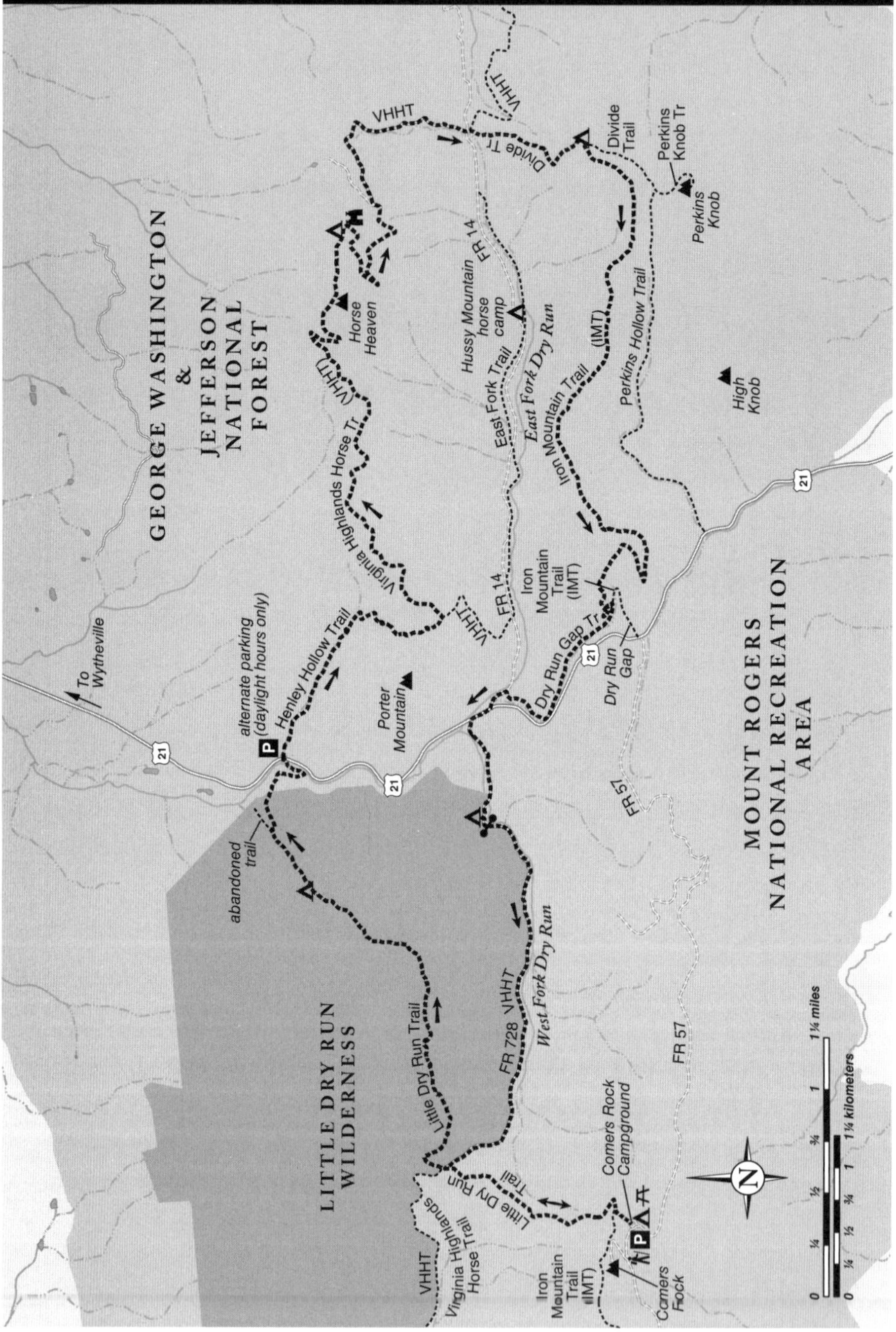

Little Dry Run Wilderness is underused, despite having views like this.

right, away from Little Dry Run. The hike then skirts a slope to switchback down to a rock-hop of Dry Run, then reaches US 21 at 4.1 miles. Angle left, crossing US 21, then pick up the singletrack Henley Hollow Trail. Pass a day-use-only parking area. Climb the richly vegetated, scenic, but very narrow hollow, watering up before reaching the VHHT at 5.6 miles. Head left on this wide doubletrack, a gentle easterly upgrade along the ridge named Horse Heaven. The walking is easy. The flora reflects prescribed fire management by forestry personnel.

Top out at 7.9 miles. Ahead, find a dry, slightly sloped campsite at 8.3 miles on a sharp right turn, then an easterly view opens. Make a long, easy descent to cross FR 14 at 10.4 miles. Water and camps can be had in the hollow just before reaching FR 14.

Night Hiking Is a Viable Option

A gust of wind blustered through Ramseys Draft valley as I sat before the flickering flames of the evening fire. Fallen leaves scattered across my Virginia mountain campsite. Concerned about a change in already sullen late autumn skies, I turned on my weather radio. It predicted showers moving in around daybreak. I was hiking out the next day and amended my plan in order to beat the rain back to the car.

The new plan: night hiking. Yep, walking in the dark, strolling under the stars, trudging in the blackness. I broke camp at 5:00 A.M., strapped on my pack, and logged over 3 miles before dawn lightened the skies, making the trailhead just as heavy rain reached my neck of the woods.

As fall progresses and winter approaches, we have fewer hours of daylight. Hikers should consider adapting to increased darkness. Using the hours after sunset or before sunrise for trekking through the Appalachians can make more trips happen. And isn't that what it's all about—making trips happen? On the above example, I used night hiking simply to escape inclement weather. Consider adding night hiking to your backpacking arsenal.

Most night hiking is done after sunset, rather than before sunrise. Most night hiking is done on Friday evenings, when just-off-work backpackers race to the wilderness, hike to a given point, and set up camp under cover of darkness. Even if you have the car packed, the pack loaded, and the grub bought, it's just hard to get out of work and to your destination before the sun drops. There's the invariable last-minute stop, the wrong turn, and your sidekick being late again.

So what are the advantages of night hiking? First, you can simply travel when you want, 24 hours a day, even if getting a late start, avoiding a rainstorm, or covering more miles than there is daylight. Night hiking presents a completely different experience—an often eerie one. Your auditory senses rise. Every sound of the woodlands seems amplified and takes on more meaning. Was that crack a falling stick or a bear coming? Was that rushing sound moving water or an unseen someone talking? Is that loud splash a beaver or someone coming to get you?

Since your range of sight is limited, you more closely notice that which is near—the shape of the rocks on the trail, tree limbs reaching for your pack, or that pair of beady eyes reflecting just beyond.

Night hiking has plenty of disadvantages. First, you simply can't see as much of what you came to see. Also, you may miss landmarks, campsites, or trail junctions. Furthermore, there is simply an increased risk of taking a spill.

Travel by night has a way of seeming slow, maybe because you can't tell where you are most of the time. When embarking on your first night hike, go somewhere with which you are already familiar. Get the feel of what it is like without bad consequences. Avoid rain and fog if you can. And make absolutely sure you have fresh batteries in your headlamp. In the final benefit-vs.-risk analysis, I will continue to use night hiking to enjoy more trails that lace the Old Dominion, especially in fall and winter.

Join the Divide Trail after FR 14. It is a steep track, climbing 700 feet in .7 mile to reach a gap, dry campsite, and trail intersection at 11.1 miles. Stay right here, joining the rolling Iron Mountain Trail (IMT). Enjoy cruising through classic pine-oak woods with potential campsites. This is arguably the most pleasant hiking of the circuit. At 13.8 miles, the IMT abruptly turns right as a faint track that continues west to US 21. Descend to an intersection, turning right onto the Dry Run Gap Trail—it parallels Dry Run and US 21, tracing the original route of US 21, now returned to seed. Look for the dynamite-blasted walls beside the trail.

Emerge at FR 14 at 15.4 miles. Head left to US 21, then turn right on the highway. Cross US 21 at 15.7 miles, then walk up FR 728/VHHT to hop West Fork Dry Run, entering a clearing and auto-accessible campsite at 16.2 miles. Just ahead, pass around a vehicle barrier and continue up a pretty vale on a wide track. Ahead, cross West Fork twice in succession and continue a gentle uptick. Wildlife clearings are in abundance ahead. Campsites can be found in the flats to your left, but you have to look hard.

By 17.8 miles, the VHHT has pulled away from West Fork Dry Run. Reach a gap at 18.3 miles. You have been here before. Make a final push up the Little Dry Run Trail, climbing almost 600 feet to return to Comers Rock Campground, completing the backpack at 19.4 miles.

Mileages

0.0 Comers Rock Campground.
1.1 Stay with Little Dry Run Trail, descending.
3.5 Sharp right with Little Dry Run Trail.
4.1 US 21, join Henley Hollow Trail.
5.6 Left on VHHT.
8.3 Dry campsite, view ahead.
10.4 Cross FR 14, water, ascend Divide Trail.
11.1 Gap, campsite, right on Iron Mountain Trail.
13.8 Sharp right on IMT near US 21, descend.
15.4 Left at US 14, then right on US 21.
15.7 Join FR 728/VHHT.
16.2 Clearing, auto-accessible campsite.
17.8 Pull away from West Fork Dry Run.
18.3 Gap, left on Little Dry Run Trail.
19.4 Comers Rock Campground.

35 • MOUNT ROGERS HIGH COUNTRY CIRCUIT

The Backpack: *The loop explores Virginia's highest elevations, making a highlight-reel hike amid meadows, spruce-fir forests, rock spires, and crashing streams. The pathways change with the landscapes, from narrow track foot trails to wider equestrian paths, from deep woods tracks to rock-strewn paths open to the sky overhead. Additionally, the circuit travels through two wildernesses and Grayson Highlands State Park, through areas busy and locales lesser traveled. A wealth of connector paths enables to alter your backpack as desired.*

The Mount Rogers High Country is a must-do experience for Virginia backpackers. This elevated land contains a maze of trails amid a score of superlatives, including Virginia's highest point, vistas that extend for miles in all directions, and wildlife highlighted by famed wild ponies. However, Mount Rogers has the harshest weather in the state as well. Be prepared for cloudy, windy, foggy, and rainy weather any time of year. In winter, conditions can be brutal.

35 MOUNT ROGERS HIGH COUNTRY CIRCUIT

Distance & configuration: 26.2-mile loop

Difficulty: Difficult due to distance

Backpacking time: 14 hours

Outstanding features: Views galore, spruce-fir forests, good campsites, wild ponies

Elevation: 3,610′ low point, 5,470′ high point

Scenery: 5

Solitude: 1

Family friendly: 2

Canine friendly: 1

Fees/permits: No fees or permits required

Best season: Late spring through mid-autumn

Maps: National Geographic #318 Mount Rogers High Country

For more info: Mount Rogers National Recreation Area, 3714 Highway 16, Marion, VA 24354, 276-783-5196, www.fs.usda.gov/gwj

Finding the trailhead: From the Little Red Caboose in Damascus City Park on US 58 in downtown Damascus, drive 11 miles east on US 58. Here, US 58 curves right. Keep straight, joining VA 603, Konnarock Road. Stay on 603 for 2.6 miles to VA 600, Whitetop Road. Turn right on VA 600 and follow it for 5.1 miles to the Elk Garden trailhead, where the AT crosses VA 600. **GPS trailhead coordinates:** N36° 38.771′, W81° 34.963′

35 Mount Rogers High Country Circuit

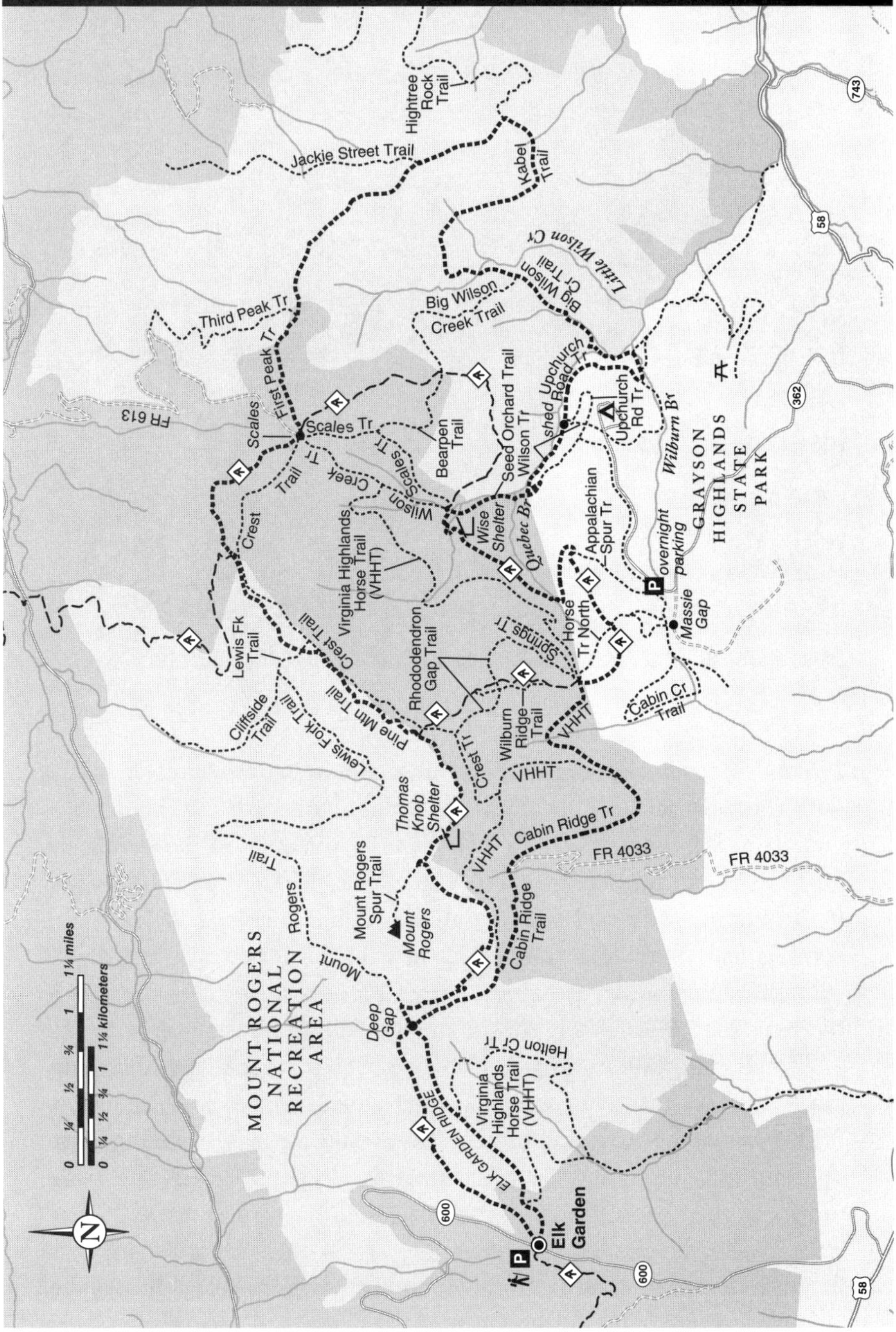

Looking back toward Scales from Stone Mountain.

That said, plenty of nice days occur at Mount Rogers. Time your trip with the weather. Also, avoid nice-weather weekends and holidays if you are seeking any modicum of solitude. This area can be very busy with day hikers and backpackers. The hike joins the Appalachian Trail (AT), starting high and rising higher in the Lewis Fork Wilderness, coming near Mount Rogers, standing at 5,729 feet. Continue through an ever-changing mosaic of habitats, from spruce-fir forests to northern hardwoods to meadows to rock plains and all mixes thereof.

After passing Mount Rogers, the backpack joins the Pine Mountain Trail, with its view-laden outcrops. You then descend to a gap known as Scales. Leave the crowds behind on the First Peak Trail, enjoying more open mountaintop views. Bisect the Little Wilson Creek Wilderness, dropping to Wilson Creek, a crashing, boulder-strewn watercourse with incredibly deep pools, simply one of the most beautiful streams in the state. Make a return to the open high country through Grayson Highlands State Park. The last part of the three- to five-day hike joins the Virginia Highlands Horse Trail, winding through more meadows

The wild ponies are a major draw in the Mount Rogers High Country.

and forests before cutting back through the Lewis Fork Wilderness and returning to the trailhead.

Campsites can be found throughout the hike. In fact, it can be argued there are too many of them in the most popular areas, such as along the AT near Thomas Knob Shelter. There is no backcountry camping within Grayson Highlands State Park, except at the Wise shelter on the AT. The loop hike does pass near the developed state park auto-accessible campground, in case you are so inclined. Water is abundant as well. Many springs and branches flow off the highlands.

Much of the loop travels along equestrian trails. They can be muddy or rocky at times, but these horse paths avail a bigger loop and more solitude. However, in some places equestrians have created unauthorized "bootleg trails." Be watchful and know that almost all legitimate trail intersections are signed. The "Mileages" section below is comprehensive and details step-by-step turns for this adventure. Read over the mileages and cobble together an adventure to suit your desires. Again, avoid nice-weather weekends and holidays if at all possible. Also, shorter loops can be undertaken. Peruse the recommended map for the possibilities. The important thing is to get up here and backpack Virginia's rooftop.

Mileages

0.0 Elk Garden, northbound on AT, views.
0.5 Gate, enter Lewis Fork Wilderness.
1.8 Spur leads right to campsites near Deep Gap.
1.9 Deep Gap, no camping in gap. Stay on AT, pass spring.
2.1 Mount Rogers Trail leaves left.
3.0 View out Brier Ridge and points south.
3.9 Mount Rogers Spur Trail leaves left; .5 mile to top of Mount Rogers.
4.1 Leave Lewis Fork Wilderness, campsites aplenty, plus Thomas Knob shelter; no fires at the shelter.
5.1 Leave AT, left on hiker-only Pine Mountain Trail, rock outcrops, views.
6.3 Pass campsites just before Lewis Fork Trail; spring ahead.
7.2 Leave Pine Mountain Trail, right on AT, southbound, descend.
8.2 Campsite below trail.
8.5 Scales; cut through corral on AT, join First Peak Trail on far side of corral, views.
8.9 Pass a spring on left in mix of woods and meadow.
9.3 Open terrain, incredible views as closed trail comes in on right.
9.5 Third Peak Trail leaves left.
10.1 Gate, enter much more wooded Little Wilson Wilderness, descend.
10.9 Jackie Street Trail leaves left, campsite just ahead.
11.2 First Peak Trail traverses First Peak, then descends.
11.7 Right on Kabel Trail as the Hightree Rock Trail goes left; path stays nearly level.
13.3 Drop sharply left off grade.
13.5 Reach Little Wilson Creek and good campsite.
13.8 Stay straight, joining Little Wilson Creek Trail on a prolonged descent.
14.3 Cut right across small tributary as bootleg trail keeps straight.
14.6 Left at Wilson Creek.
14.8 Pass campsites on left just before crossing Wilson Creek, potential ford.
15.0 Enter old homesite, reach rock cairn, stay straight along Wilburn Branch.

15.1 Straight at signed intersection, joining Upchurch Road Trail. Pass under powerline.
15.2 Hiker-only trail goes left to state park campground; pass under powerline again.
16.1 Come to boulders, storm shed; keep straight, join hiker-only Wilson Trail.
16.3 Excellent creek view from outcrop, deep pool below, bluffs ahead.
16.6 Pass a 20-foot cascade, then storm shed; switchback ahead.
16.8 Right on Seed Orchard Road Trail, easy walking.
17.0 Rock-hop Quebec Branch, pass Fraser fir seed orchard ahead.
17.4 Leave state park after crossing Wilson Creek; Scales Trail goes right.
17.5 Left on AT, southbound, bisect meadows and woods.
17.7 Pass campsite just before bridging Wilson Creek.
17.8 Wise Shelter, no backcountry tent camping in state park, ascend.
18.7 Bridge Quebec Branch, ascend.
19.2 Appalachian Spur Trail goes left near outcrop; views aplenty.
19.9 Cross Horse Trail North; stay with AT and enjoy more incredible views.
20.5 Left on Virginia Highlands Horse Trail, more views and forest.
20.9 Campsite; cross Cabin Creek.
21.6 Stay straight with Cabin Ridge Trail; wet trail sections ahead, bootleg trails.
22.8 FR 4033 leaves left; cross Middle Fork Helton Creek, climb into meadows.
23.6 Rejoin Virginia Highlands Horse Trail in open saddle; royal vistas, descend.
23.7 Reenter Lewis Fork Wilderness, steady descent.
24.4 Deep Gap, continue descending.
25.1 Helton Creek Trail leaves left.
25.8 Leave wilderness, final meadows; pass Helton Creek Spur Trail.
26.2 Elk Garden.

36 • ROWLAND CREEK FALLS LOOP

The Backpack: *Solitude seekers will enjoy this one- or two-night loop. Climb along wildflower-rich Rowland Creek past impressive Rowland Creek Falls, a scenic highlight. The hiking eases after reaching the uplands. Trace doubletrack path to meet Jerrys Creek Trail. Descend a remote valley, then finish the circuit on more doubletrack trail. Campsites are limited but scattered all along the loop, allowing backpackers to customize their daily distances.*

This loop hike offers backpackers solitude and good footing amid first-rate scenery within the federally designated 6,455-acre Seng Mountain National Scenic Area. The designation "scenic area" is an alternate to wilderness designation that still allows bicyclists to use the trails contained within. Start out on a singletrack path heading up the valley to reach 50-foot Rowland Creek Falls, a long cascade cutting through a rocky rampart. From there, the trail reaches an upland valley, once settled, that now offers a fine campsite. After rising to Hurricane Gap, join the Old 84 Trail, a foot-friendly doubletrack path that winds beneath wooded knobs. Jerrys Creek Trail takes you back down to close the loop.

Campsites are limited. Although one camp can be made before Rowland Creek, the best option is at 2.2 miles. Along the ridges, a campsite can be had at a gap between Chestnut Ridge at Round Top, as well as at the intersection of Jerrys Creek Trail and Old 84 Trail, though this camp is very near Forest Road 84. There is also a seldom-used campsite in the narrow hollow of Jerrys Creek.

Solitude is my favorite aspect of this circuit, though it is used by a few bicyclists and equestrians. You are unlikely to see anyone else, much less other backpackers, beyond Rowland Creek Falls, 1.7 miles into the hike. Moreover, the combination of singletrack and doubletrack paths eases the difficulty of the trip. It does have a 1,600-foot differentiation between high and low points, though most of the elevation change is gradual. Note: the loop does have several creek crossings, but these can be rock-hopped in times of normal flow. If the water is high or the temperatures low, you can always cross barefooted rather than wet your boots.

The hike begins by heading up FR 643, then leaving right on the Rowland Creek Trail. Cruise a wooded flat full of white pines. The valley narrows, and stone cliffs rise among lush woods. Noisy Rowland Creek flows between gravel bars and rocks. You keep rising well above

36 ROWLAND CREEK FALLS LOOP

Distance & configuration: 12.6-mile loop

Difficulty: Moderate

Backpacking time: 7 hours

Outstanding features: Rowland Creek Falls, solitude, wildflowers

Elevation: 2,590′ low point, 4,210′ high point

Scenery: 4

Solitude: 4

Family friendly: 2

Canine friendly: 3

Fees/permits: No fees or permits required

Best season: Year-round; spring for wildflowers and bold falls

Maps: National Geographic #786 Mount Rogers National Recreation Area

For more info: Mount Rogers National Recreation Area, Route 1, Box 303, Marion, VA 24354, 276-783-5196, www.fs.usda.gov/gwj

Finding the trailhead: From exit 44 on I-81 just south of Marion, take US 11 south for 2.2 miles. Just after cutting back under I-81, stay straight and join Adwolfe Road, VA 660. Follow Adwolfe Road for 1.7 miles, then turn left onto Thomas Bridge Road and follow it for 1.7 miles, then turn right onto South Fork Road. Follow South Fork Road for .4 mile, then turn left onto Stoney Battery Road. Follow Stoney Battery Road for 1.9 miles, then turn right onto Rowland Creek Lane. Follow Rowland Creek Lane for .4 mile to enter Jefferson National Forest. Keep on .1 mile to bridge Rowland Creek. Park on the left just after the road bridge crossing. **GPS trailhead coordinates:** N36° 44.128′, W81° 33.763′

the stream, then come alongside Rowland Creek Falls. Use caution on the spur path that drops to the base of the 50-foot spiller as it tumbles over stratified rock layers in white wonderment.

Continue up a perched valley where wildflowers thrive. A few more creek crossings lead you to the preferred campsite on Rowland Creek, in a formerly inhabited flat with metal relics about, as well as a closing-in clearing. The walking is easy from here while gently ascending doubletrack trail to Hurricane Gap. Join the Old 84 Trail, following what once was FR 84. The wide path weaves into moist hollows and out to dry ridges, running parallel but out of sight of current FR 84. Ups and downs are moderate.

Sometimes-rocky Jerrys Creek Trail declines to the lowlands, cutting through a narrow defile, where the stream crashes under a rhododendron screen well below the path. A small hard-to-see campsite

36 Rowland Creek Falls Loop

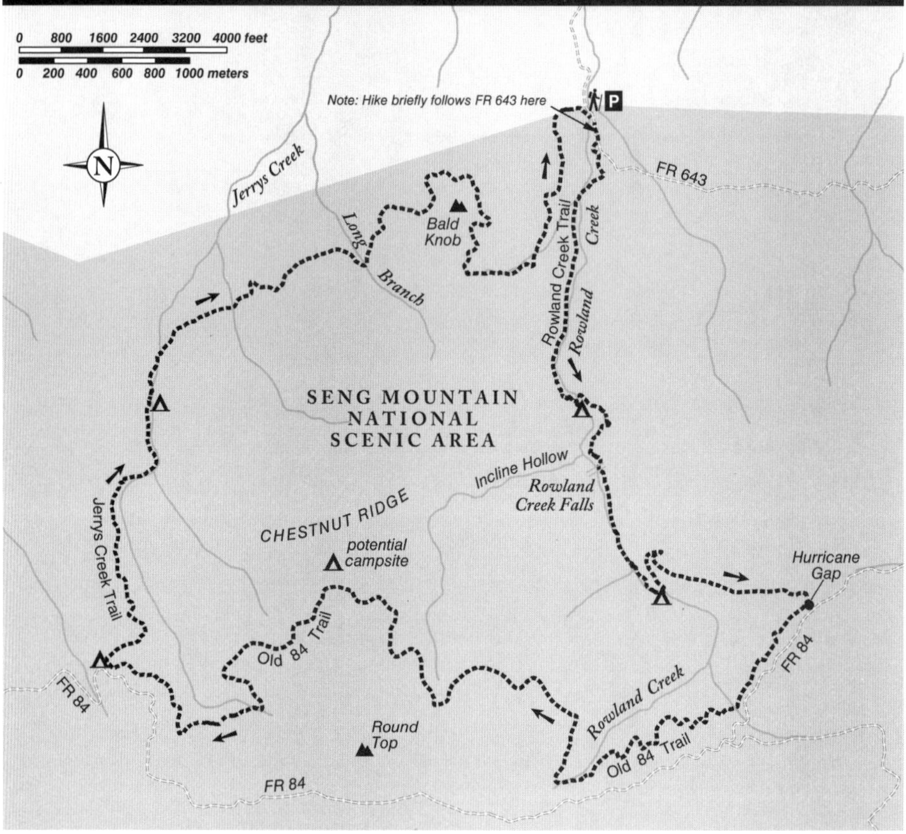

stands in a rare flat across the water at 9.1 miles and would make a good second-night camp for a two-night trip. The walking is easy after crossing Jerrys Creek. You then pick up a doubletrack path, rolling east between watersheds. The final part of the trek enters white pine woods before you emerge back at FR 643, near the national forest boundary.

Mileages

0.0 Rowland Creek parking area, FR 643.
0.1 Right on Rowland Creek Trail.
0.3 Cross Rowland Creek.
1.1 Pass a few warm-up cascades with deep pools.
1.2 Cross Rowland Creek, poor campsite; climb on a switchback.
1.7 Rowland Creek Falls, poor campsite above falls.

Jerrys Creek Trail in early April.

- 1.9 Cross Rowland Creek.
- 2.0 Cross Rowland Creek.
- 2.1 Cross Rowland Creek, now on the right-hand bank.
- 2.2 Reach preferred campsite in once-inhabited hollow. Cross Rowland Creek, join doubletrack trail.
- 3.1 Hurricane Gap. Come near FR 84. Right on Old 84 Trail.
- 3.6 Curve around headwaters of Rowland Creek.
- 4.0 Pass old wildlife clearing to your left.
- 4.8 Grassy area; unmaintained trail leaves left up to Double Top.
- 5.0 Pass old wildlife clearing.
- 6.3 Reach a potential campsite to the right, in the gap between Chestnut Ridge and Round Top.

Rowland Creek Falls flows boldly in spring.

7.9 Meet Jerrys Creek Trail and FR 84 near a clearing and campsite. Right on singletrack Jerrys Creek Trail.
8.8 Come alongside Jerrys Creek.
9.1 Small campsite across the creek.
9.3 Cross Jerrys Creek, poor campsite; join doubletrack trail.
10.3 Cross Long Branch, climb.
11.1 Reach high point near Bald Knob, descend.
12.3 Pass around pole gate.
12.6 Return to FR 643, completing the loop.

37 • VIRGINIA CREEPER LOOP

The Backpack: *This fun circuit—great for entry-level backpackers—in Mount Rogers National Recreation Area cruises up the Whitetop Laurel Creek valley on the famed Virginia Creeper Trail, the rail trail alongside which campsites are plentiful. A steady but very mild grade takes you to meet the Appalachian Trail (AT). Climb to the crest of Straight Mountain, where partial views can be had, before reaching Saunders shelter and a second night's camping option. Take the AT back to the trailhead, switchbacking downhill off Straight Mountain.*

This adventure makes an excellent two-night backpack with an easy first day. Start out on the foot-friendly Virginia Creeper Trail with its numerous campsites, ample swimming and fishing holes, and all-around excellent scenery. Backpackers can make their first day's mileage extend anywhere from .2 mile to 6 miles, depending upon arrival time and distance desires, then adjust mileages for the second day.

The second day is less flexible yet presents a completely different experience. Join the singletrack AT, winding past trickling branches to make the crest of Straight Mountain, where the rocky ridge slows travel

37 VIRGINIA CREEPER LOOP

Distance & configuration: 13.8-mile loop

Difficulty: Moderate

Backpacking time: 8.5 hours

Outstanding features: Historic rail trail, stream, trail shelter, partial views

Elevation: 2,190′ low point, 3,410′ high point

Scenery: 4

Solitude: 1

Family friendly: 3

Canine friendly: 3

Fees/permits: No fees or permits required

Best season: Early spring, summer, fall

Maps: National Geographic #786 Mount Rogers National Recreation Area

For more info: Mount Rogers National Recreation Area, Route 1, Box 303, Marion, VA 24354, 276-783-5196, www.fs.usda.gov/gwj

Finding the trailhead: From exit 19 on I-81 north of Bristol, take US 58 east to Damascus, Virginia. From the Little Red Caboose in Damascus, continue east on US 58 for 4.5 miles to the Straight Branch parking area, off US 58 to the right. **GPS trailhead coordinates:** N36° 38.645′, W81° 44.407′

37 Virginia Creeper Loop

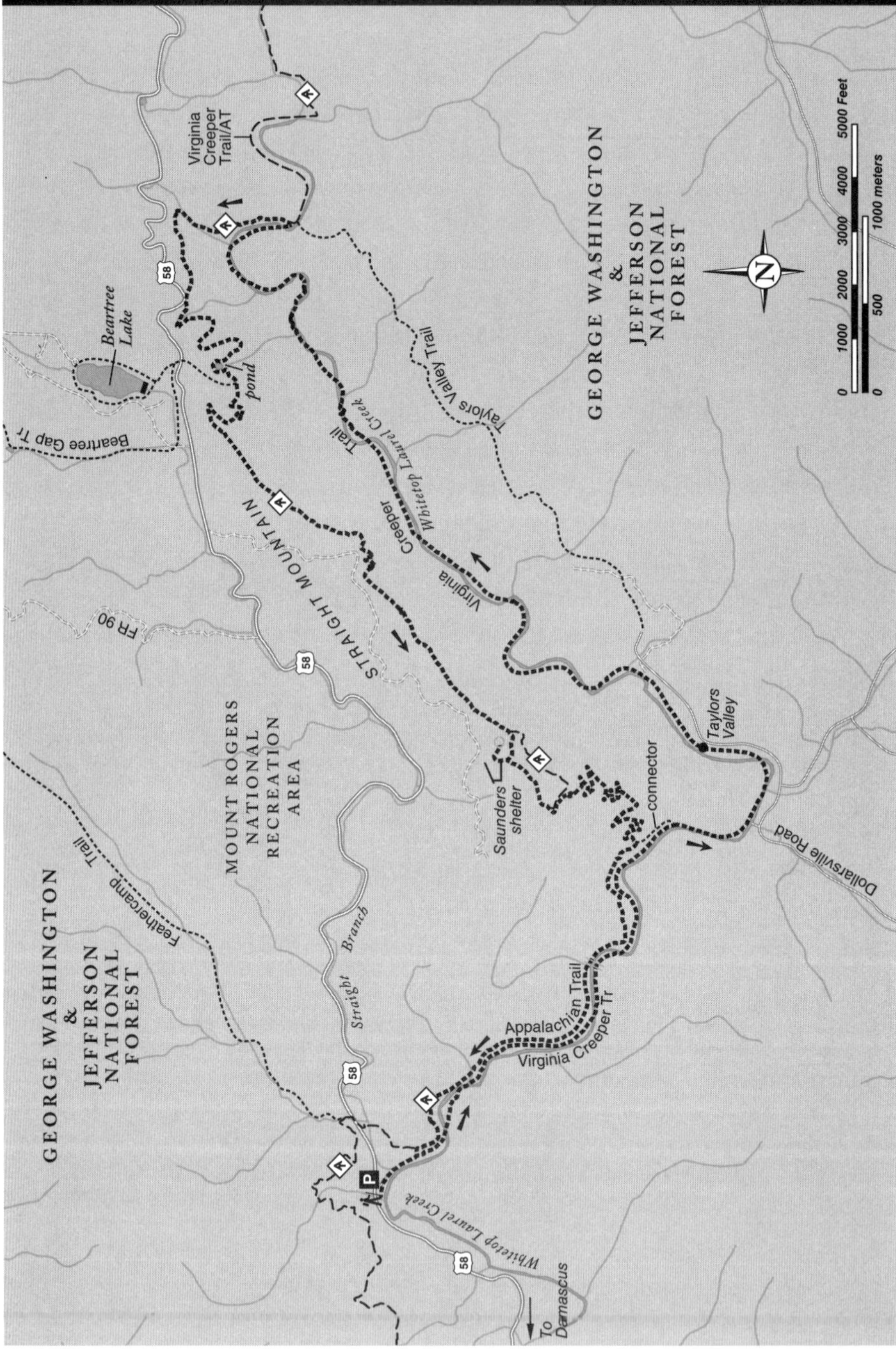

Winter is a great time to undertake the Virginia Creeper Loop.

but presents partial views of Whitetop Laurel and Mount Rogers, the highest point in the Old Dominion. The Saunders trail shelter stands on a level stretch of Straight Mountain and offers backpackers a refuge from the elements as well as quality tent sites. This is your only plausible camping option with water up here. The final day drops almost 1,000 feet off Straight Mountain, then the AT courses along a rocky hillside just above Whitetop Laurel Creek to close the loop.

Before embarking on your trip, take time to explore Damascus, America's favorite trail town. Get a meal and some ice cream and stop by iconic Mount Rogers Outfitters for last minute supplies.

Backpackers will see beauty throughout, but they will also see other hikers, backpackers, and bicyclers on the Virginia Creeper Trail—this is not a circuit for solitude seekers. The hike leaves the Straight Branch Trailhead on the Virginia Creeper Trail. A wide, pea gravel track allows you to appreciate the mountain valley scenery, dominated by Whitetop Laurel Creek. The trail, interspersed with interpretive signage, criss-crosses the watercourse using old railroad trestles that offer scenic vantages of the mountain rill often bordered with rock bluffs. These trestles on the 34-mile Virginia Creeper Trail are numbered in ascending order from Abingdon to Whitetop Station. Watch out for bicyclers pedaling down from Whitetop Station.

Good Campsites Can Make or Break a Trip

I was in the midst of an extended backpacking trip in Shenandoah National Park. I'd spent much time along the Appalachian Trail (AT), where the wind had been blowing nonstop. Furthermore, it seemed the parade of AT backpackers was as ceaseless as the wind.

I decided to seek more solitude, hoping a change of elevation would also cut down on the wind. I left the AT and dropped down to the Hughes River. The lower end of the waterway was mine. I found a fine sheltered campsite, then cast a line for brook trout. After fishing, I returned to the lovely, quiet campsite and concluded that when backpacking, an appealing camp is as important as appealing weather.

Minimally speaking, a backcountry campsite requires two things: a flat spot and accessible water. Beyond those two necessities, look for characteristics of the land that will help you deal with the situations at hand. For example, you may want an open, breezy location if the insects are troublesome. Or you may want a sheltered location if the winds are howling. You may want shade if it is hot. Or ample fallen wood for a fire if it is cold. Find surroundings that enhance your comfort in camp.

Raising the bar, begin looking for other characteristics that will make your campsite not only functionally desirable but also aesthetically appealing. Why not go for a view if you can get it? Or look over a wildflower garden? Perhaps camp within walking distance of a waterfall. Discerning backpackers will camp near such highlights, but not too close to detract from or adversely impact the overlook or waterfall.

Consider other backpackers or hikers as well. Don't camp in the middle of the trail or the absolute center of the best camp area. Don't block visitors from seeing that waterfall or overlook.

Some backpacking destinations have designated campsites that require a permit, such as Belle Isle State Park, or have specific camping rules, such as Shenandoah National Park. Other places, like national forests, are more freewheeling. Still others have designated campsites that you can stay at without a permit. Check into specific camping regulations *before* your backpacking trip.

Also consider campsite safety. Look around for widow-makers—dead standing trees that may fall during a storm. This actually happened on a backpacking trip in Alaska. My friend Scott Davis and I were camped in an aspen grove, and one of the trees fell from windthrow around dawn. Luckily the tree, while falling, hit other trees and was slowed while plunging down onto Scott's shelter. We considered ourselves very lucky.

Don't set your campsite near a stream prone to flooding. Consider an exit strategy. Will you have to ford the river to get back to civilization? If rain is forecast, hike on to another campsite where you can avoid fords. I was once stuck between stream fords one September for three days on Slickrock Creek, down in North Carolina's Nantahala National Forest, when a hurricane dropped 10 inches of rain.

Therefore, whether in terms of practicality, aesthetics, or safety, a good campsite can make or break a backcountry trip.

The wilderness scenery temporarily ends at Taylors Valley, where the Creeper wanders through a small community. After a mile, reenter the national forest and once again work up the scenic valley where more campsites are available. These sites are generally in flats near Whitetop Laurel Creek underneath a mix of hardwoods, pines, and rhododendron. The music of moving mountain water is ever present. The hillsides have closed back in on the Creeper Trail. Campsites are interspersed throughout this segment until you reach the AT, just after crossing trestle #37.

This is the end of the easy walking. You have gained around 500 feet in 6 miles. That is about to change, however; the singletrack AT has been routed up to the crest of Straight Mountain in surprisingly gentle fashion. Here you curve in and out of drainages feeding Whitetop Laurel Creek, among boulders and thickets of laurel and rhododendron. Once atop Straight Mountain, the AT courses southwesterly on a slender rocky ridgetop, heavy with oaks. Whitetop Laurel Creek rushes hundreds of feet below. Keep an eye peeled southeast for the grassy hillside of 5,500-foot Whitetop Mountain, as well as the dark mantle of Mount Rogers, Virginia's highest point at 5,729 feet.

A spur trail leads from the AT to the Saunders shelter, a three-sided, partially-open-in-the-front wood refuge, complemented with a fire ring, privy, and picnic table. A needle-carpeted pine grove and nearby grassy flat offer tent camping options. A spring is accessed via a blue-blazed trail leading northwest from the shelter.

Your final day's hike takes you off Straight Mountain using enough switchbacks to make you dizzy. However, these ease the descent and offer panoramas of Taylors Valley. Once back in the Whitetop Laurel gorge, trace the stony AT above the creek. The going is slow, but the AT ultimately meets the Creeper Trail near the trailhead. A short backtrack completes the rewarding circuit backpack.

Mileages

0.0 Straight Branch Trailhead.

0.2 Trestle over Feathercamp Creek, intersect AT; first campsite.

1.7 Pass an island on your right; island campsite accessible at lower flows.

2.0 Connector leads left to AT, potential shortcut; enter Taylors Valley.

3.1 Leave Taylors Valley; campsite on left just ahead.

3.3 Campsites.
3.6 Campsite to right of trail near two big boulders.
4.0 Campsite just after trestle #30.
4.9 Campsite to left of trail.
5.5 Cross a pair of rerouted trestles.
6.2 Cross trestle #37, last campsite on Creeper just past trestle; join AT.
7.7 Circle around a small dammed pond.
7.9 Intersect Beartree Gap Trail; keep straight on AT.
8.2 Reach the crest of Straight Mountain.
9.1 Step over a dribbling spring after descending; climb.
10.1 Take the spur trail right to Saunders shelter.
10.3 Reach the Saunders shelter.
10.5 Rejoin AT via spur; descend via switchbacks aplenty.
11.9 Connector leads left to Virginia Creeper Trail; stay with AT.
12.5 Hike just below small waterfall.
13.6 Intersect Virginia Creeper Trail.
13.8 Complete the loop.

38 • CHIEF BENGE SCOUT TRAIL

The Backpack: *The mostly downhill end-to-end backpack explores a lesser-visited parcel of Jefferson National Forest. Highlights begin at a restored observation tower with 360-degree views. Descend to Stony Creek, passing a small lake and campground. Keep in the scenic valley, then climb over a ridge, then join Little Stony Creek Valley, hiking along Bark Camp Lake. Ahead, major waterfalls await as the backpack traverses the magnificent Little Stony Creek gorge.*

The underutilized Chief Benge Scout Trail deserves more attention. The hike travels deep in two mountain creek valleys—Stony Creek and Little Stony Creek—amid rich, junglesque scenery, decidedly cooler in summer. Going high to low makes the hike much less difficult, though a slew of creek crossings add challenge and make the route a poor winter choice. Campsites are well spaced and include developed campground possibilities. Backpackers can upgrade their lodgings, overnighting at the two campgrounds along the way, each with nearby lakes.

The restored High Knob Tower—with views into five states—starts the backpack off with a bang. Then you get into mountain valleys, punctuated with campgrounds, before finally entering the Little Stony

38 CHIEF BENGE SCOUT TRAIL

Distance & configuration: 19.1-mile end-to-end

Difficulty: Moderate, mostly downhill, does have a multitude of creek crossings

Backpacking time: 9.5 hours

Outstanding features: High Knob Tower, Falls of Little Stony

Elevation: 1,520′ low point, 4,160′ high point

Scenery: 4

Solitude: 3

Family friendly: 2

Canine friendly: 3

Fees/permits: No fees or permits required

Best season: Spring through late fall

Maps: National Geographic #793 Clinch Ranger District, Jefferson National Forest

For more info: Clinch River Ranger District, Jefferson National Forest, 1700 Park Avenue SW, Norton, VA 24273, 276-679-8370, www.fs.usda.gov/gwj

Finding the trailhead: To reach Hanging Rock Trailhead, the end point, from Dungannon, take VA 72 north for 1.6 miles, then turn left into Hanging Rock Recreation Area, gated from December through March partway in. From there, resume north on VA 72 for 9 miles to Coeburn, then turn left on US 58 Alt west for 9 miles, then merge onto US 23/US 58 west toward Big Stone Gap. After 1.5 miles, take exit 1 in Norton, then head south on 12th Street/VA 619. Follow VA 619 south for 3.9 miles, then turn left on FR 238. Follow FR 238 for .5 mile, then turn right at the sign for High Knob Tower and follow that road to quickly dead-end at the High Knob Trailhead. **GPS trailhead coordinates:** High Knob: N36° 53.603′, W82° 37.711′; Hanging Rock: N36° 51.677′, W82° 26.778′

gorge, with its attractive but popular waterfalls. Other than the falls and campgrounds, solitude is yours.

After garnering views from High Knob Tower, join the Chief Benge Scout Trail, descending by switchbacks east from High Knob under a mantle of tall hardwoods and sumptuous undergrowth of stinging nettle and ferns. Reach the High Knob Recreation Area access road at 1.1 miles. The campground has drinking water and hot showers and would be a good late-arrival campsite. Stay right on the road, then split left to soon reach a picnic area. Stay left here, reenter woods, then emerge at small High Knob Lake and a historic bathhouse at 1.4 miles. The Chief Benge Trail climbs left above the lake. At 1.8 miles, stay left as a path circling the lake comes in.

38 Chief Benge Scout Trail

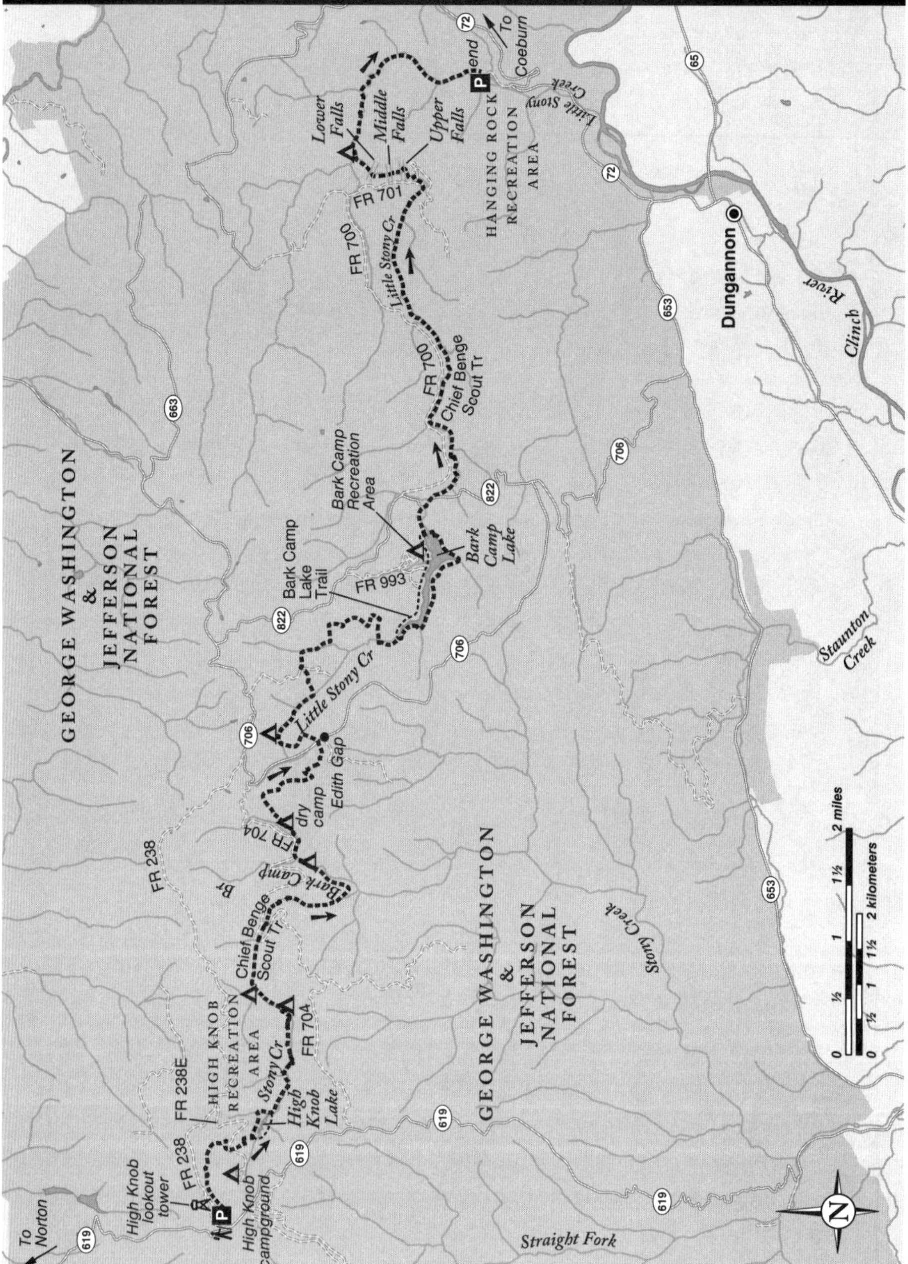

This backpack starts with an inspiring view from High Knob.

Trace now-bolder Stony Creek on a former railroad grade, ensconced in rhododendron, ferns, and a profusion of growth. Look for railroad ties. It is hard to imagine a logging rail line here, as thick as the forest is nowadays. Cross Stony Creek regularly, without benefit of bridges. In summer and fall you can hop dry-footed, save for after thunderstorms. Spring might be a wetter proposition. Walk by the first of many huge trailside boulders at 2.7 miles.

Pass by a small campsite at 3.0 miles on trail right. At 3.1 miles, hike beside a house-sized boulder, then come to a preferred campsite at 3.4 miles, set in a grove of fading hemlocks. Keep east, then reach FR 704 at 3.8 miles. Walk a few feet left over the Stony Creek culvert, then continue downstream, passing car-accessible campsites. The path turns south with more crossings of now-larger Stony Creek. At 4.6 miles, discover metal relics in a flat that may have been a logging camp.

At 5.0 miles, the trail curves left into Bark Camp Branch valley on a now-rocky path, ascending. At 5.5 miles, a difficult-to-reach camp lies across the creek. Leave the stream, gently climbing on the ridge you are now following. Top out at 6.4 miles, turning south. Watch for blazes. At 7.0 miles, head left on a gas line access road, then cross a second gas line access road in upland hardwoods of oak, sourwood, and sassafras.

Descend to reach Edith Gap and cross CR 706 at 7.5 miles. Descend more, reaching Little Stony Creek and a small campsite at 7.9 miles. Keep downstream, then turn away at 8.6 miles, bounding over a ridge to turn down Robinson Fork. The trail climbs again to make a grassy doubletrack. Follow this easy level roadbed right, then at 10.1 miles, the path turns right again, descending via footpath to reach wetlands of upper Bark Camp Lake and a trail intersection at 10.4 miles. Stay right here, still officially on the Chief Benge Scout Trail. Going left leads you to facilities of Bark Camp Lake, which includes an auto-accessible campground with hot showers, if you so desire. A long boardwalk over a wetland starts your scenic walk along the lake's south shore.

Reach the lake dam at 12.1 miles. Head left, then split right before crossing the dam spillway. Reach CR 822 at 12.4 miles; keep right, then leave the road left. You are back along Little Stony Creek from here on out. The scenery is superb and creek crossings continue. Occasional flats could be campsites using Leave No Trace principles. Ferns rise by the thousands.

At 16.2 miles, make a crossing to the left and reach FR 701. Follow the road, then cut through the Falls of Stony parking area. This area can get busy on a now well-conditioned trail. Your creek crossings are over. Come first to 30-foot Upper Falls of Stony, spilling into a big pool and rock cathedral at 16.4 miles. Bridge the creek and reach more modest Middle Falls of Stony at 16.5 miles. Curve to an observation deck and photo-worthy 20-foot Lower Falls of Stony at 16.7 miles.

The scenery stays superlative as you delve deeper into the Little Stony Gorge. Bridge Corder Branch at 17.0 miles, then reach a small, trailside campsite. Pass a cascade just downstream at a washout. Cross slick Star Branch and turn south at 17.6 miles. Bridge Little Stony Creek at 17.8 miles, then bridge it one last time at 18.6 miles. Bisect big boulders and reach trail's end at Hanging Rock Recreation Area at 19.1 miles.

Mileages

0.0 High Knob Tower parking area.
1.1 High Knob Recreation Area.
1.8 Lower end of High Knob Lake.
3.0 Small campsite.
3.4 Preferred campsite.
3.8 Cross FR 704.
5.0 Turn up Bark Camp Branch.

7.5 Cross CR 706 at Edith Gap.
10.4 Reach upper Bark Camp Lake and lake loop trail.
12.1 Leave lake at dam.
12.4 Cross CR 822.
16.2 FR 701 and parking area.
16.4 Upper Falls of Stony, then more falls.
17.0 Bridge Corder Branch, campsite just ahead.
19.1 Hanging Rock Recreation Area.

39 • PINE MOUNTAIN TRAIL

The Backpack: *This backpack straddles rugged and remote Pine Mountain, forming the border between Virginia and Kentucky. The first several miles are exclusively in Kentucky before the trip joins Virginia at Stateline Knob. Grab an astonishing view from High Rock and revel in the panoramas and intriguing geology at Mars Rock, as well as Eagle Arch. More overlooks can be found, including Twin Cliffs. In places, the trail traverses bare rock. This trek ends at Pound Gap, though long-distance backpackers can stretch their overnight adventure out another 20-plus miles, where the Pine Mountain Trail's northern terminus ends on the banks of the Russell Fork near Breaks Interstate Park. The path is well marked and maintained. Trail shelters and designated campsites enhance the end-to-end adventure.*

The Pine Mountain Trail (PMT) is the manifestation of a dream of persistent Shad Baker, who saw the rugged wildlands of Pine Mountain, much of which straddles the Virginia–Kentucky state line, as an ideal venue for a long-distance path. And it is. Eventually slated to extend 140 miles between Cumberland Gap National Historical Park and Breaks Interstate Park, the Pine Mountain Trail—a designated Kentucky State Scenic Trail—remains an expanding work in progress.

The fully completed Highland section of the PMT is the focus of this backpack, and it includes highlights aplenty, trail shelters, and a solid amount of ups and downs. The 16.7 miles is best done as a two-night trip, so you can relax and enjoy the features along the way.

Since the hike is end to end, either two cars or a hiker shuttle is required. Fortunately, the PMT governing body offers shuttles for a reasonable fee, part of which goes to maintain the pathway. Hikers are asked to schedule their shuttle at least 48 hours in advance. Please consult the Pine Mountain Trail website for the latest on hiker shuttles.

39 PINE MOUNTAIN TRAIL

Distance & configuration: 16.7-mile end-to-end

Difficulty: Moderate to difficult, does have repeated ups and downs

Backpacking time: 9 hours

Outstanding features: Eagle Arch, High Rock, Mars Rock, rock shelters, trail shelters

Elevation: 2,420′ low point, 3,274′ high point

Scenery: 5

Solitude: 4

Family friendly: 2

Canine friendly: 3

Fees/permits: No fees or permits required

Best season: Fall through spring

Maps: Pine Mountain State Scenic Trail—Highland Section, National Geographic #793 Clinch Ranger District Jefferson National Forest

For more info: Pine Mountain State Scenic Trail, www.pinemountaintrail.com

Finding the trailhead: From US 23 in Pound, Virginia, take US 23 north for 4.5 miles, passing through Pound Gap, where you can leave a shuttle car at the parking area on the southwest side of the gap near a convenience store (look for the trailhead kiosk and make sure to ask permission at the store as to where to park). To reach the US 119 trailhead, also known as the Little Shepherd Trailhead, continue north on US 23 for 1.5 miles into Kentucky, then turn left, joining US 119 south. Follow US 119 south for 11 miles to Whitesburg, Kentucky, and a traffic light. Turn left here, staying with US 119 south, and continue for 4.7 miles more to the crest of Pine Mountain and the trailhead parking area on your right. **GPS trailhead coordinates:** US 119 trailhead: N37° 4.527′, W82° 48.616′; US 23 trailhead: N37° 9.2817′, W82° 37.8866′

The PMT, marked with fluorescent yellow metal blazes, leaves US 119 as a singletrack path, then climbs to a tower access road. At .4 mile, the PMT passes around a pole gate, leaving the access road, and winds along the mountainside, then turns left, descending to reach the Flamingo trail shelter at .7 mile. The wood refuge has a two-story bunk area, capable of housing eight sleepers, and offers a covered picnic table and staging area. A fire ring, bear food storage pole, and outhouse complete the camp. Water is accessed a bit downtrail, at a concrete springbox.

The PMT continues beyond the shelter, dipping to a creeklet, then ascends to the ridgecrest and finds a communication tower at 1.0 mile. Jenkins, Kentucky, lies below. Pass a sign-in box, then a spur trail to AmeriCorps Cliff, and come to Eagle Arch, a little below the trail. The nearly straight geologic wonder stretches about 40 feet across open air.

39 Pine Mountain Trail

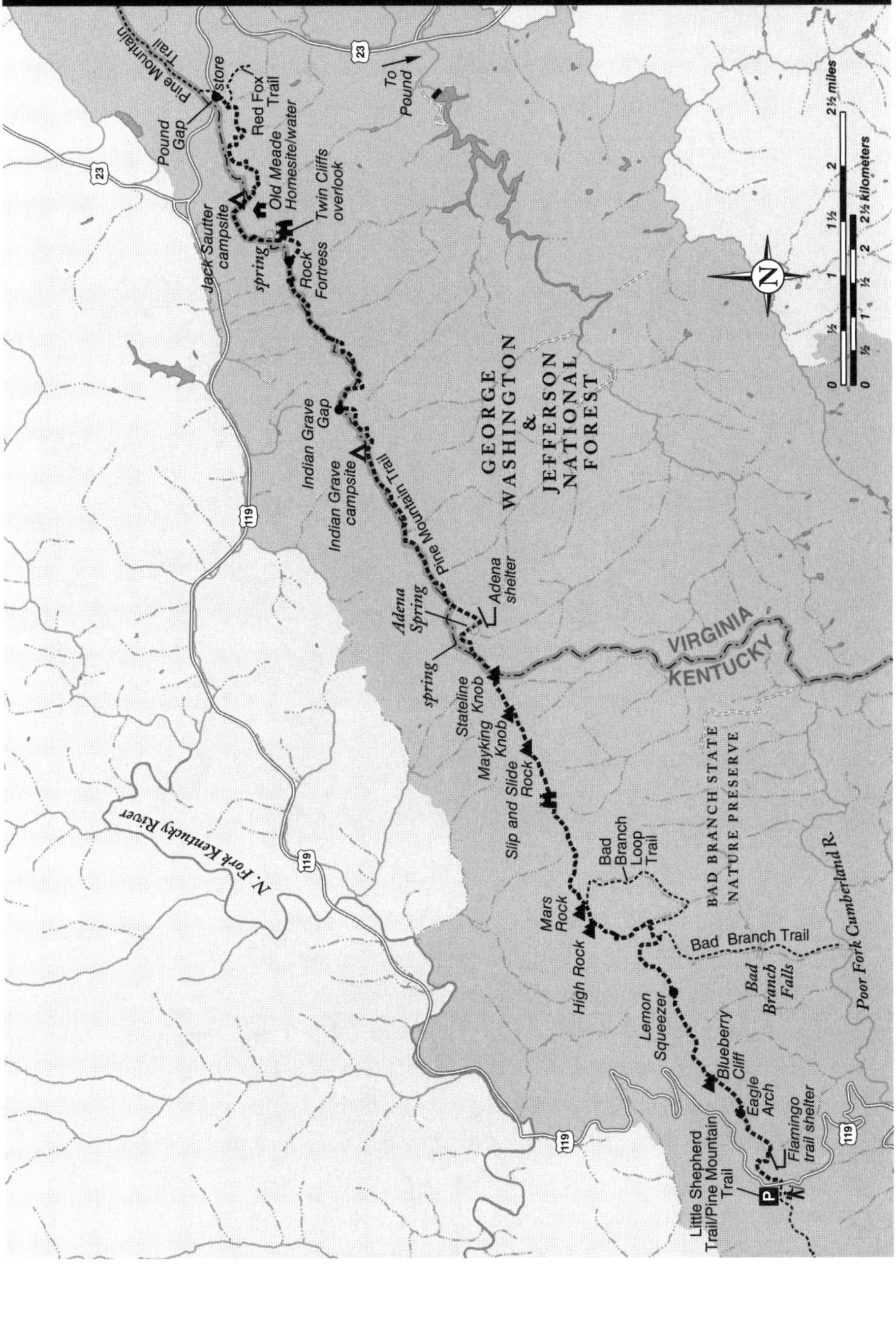

Outcrops surge from Pine Knob.

Ahead, the path borders Bad Branch Nature Preserve, where it drops past a spring, then skids atop naked rock, a common occurrence on the PMT. Drier areas feature pine, oak, and mountain laurel, while moister zones have rhododendron, magnolia, and tulip trees. Pass a spur and northerly view from Blueberry Cliff at 1.7 miles. Dip to an evergreen hollow and streambed at 2.3 miles. Regain the stony crest.

At 2.7 miles, jam through Lemon Squeezer, where massive boulders crowd the path, then pass another streamlet. The PMT surmounts a knob to meet the Bad Branch Trail at 3.7 miles. At 4.0 miles, stay left as the Bad Branch Loop Trail leaves right. Bad Branch Falls, hurtling 60 feet from a cliff, makes a worthy side trip. The PMT, however, traces an old roadbed uphill along a streamlet to reach Ran Polly Gap at 4.4 miles. Continue climbing, then wind among pines and stone before opening onto High Rock at 4.7 miles, an open-angled rock slab with eye-popping panoramas in all directions. Soak them up.

Continue past more views amid the rocks and pines. Intersect the other end of the Bad Branch Loop, then open onto Mars Rock, another angled ledge with a twist. The orange-red hue and pockmarked surface recalls the fourth planet from the sun. The views are otherworldly as well.

Continue undulating, then dip below the mountain crest at 5.3 miles, traipsing beneath a vertical cliffline. Stay with the blazes, regain the crest, and pass a grand southerly vista of Black Mountain amid stunted pines pocking a rock slab at 6.2 miles. Pass Slip and Slide Rock at 6.8 miles, then jump up to tower-topped Mayking Knob at 7.2 miles, after using iron bars to surmount a rock slope. The PMT unites with Virginia at Stateline Knob, which you reach at 7.6 miles.

The PMT dips to a spring at 8.3 miles, then climbs past Adena Spring a little before reaching the Adena shelter at 8.5 miles. This shelter is identical to the Flamingo shelter and offers obscured views into Virginia. Beyond there, the hiker-only PMT becomes doubletrack, allowing for easier footing. It rolls along and beyond a narrow gas line clearing.

At 10.7 miles, come to Indian Grave campsite, set in a small bowl atop the mountain. Just ahead a spur trail leads south down a good ways to water. Pass the actual Indian Grave Gap at 11.2 miles. The PMT rolls over wooded knobs and gaps, then climbs past signed Rock Fortress—an imposing stone monolith—at 13.7 miles. The trail is once again singletrack. At 14.1 miles, a spur leads right to the Twin Cliffs. The spur first traverses an open slab overlooking the Old Dominion, then climbs more to a panorama of the Bluegrass State.

The PMT then cuts through a break in the ridge and passes an easy-to-access spring. Reach a gap and the Jack Sautter campsite at 15.0 miles. Here, you will find designated tent sites and a .2-mile walk to a spring and the Old Meade Place, site of an ecologically significant bog.

Climb from the campsite, rolling over more knobs. Cut under a major powerline clearing at 15.7 miles, briefly joining the access road, then splitting away. Descend to meet the historic Red Fox Trail, an old road that passed through Pound Gap. Here in 1892, a family of five was murdered for money, and the crime became known as the "Killing Rock Massacre." The book, play, and movie *Trail of the Lonesome Pine* are based on the story. From this trail intersection, it is but a short distance to Pound Gap and US 23 and the end of the Highland section of the Pine Mountain Trail at 16.7 miles. Stay tuned as this path continues to expand.

Mileages

0.0 US 119.
0.7 Flamingo trail shelter.
1.1 Eagle Arch.
1.7 Blueberry Cliff.
2.7 Lemon Squeezer.
3.7 Bad Branch Trail leaves right.
4.0 Bad Branch Loop Trail leaves right, water.
4.4 Ran Polly Gap.
4.7 High Rock.
4.8 Pass other end of Bad Branch Loop Trail, Mars Rock.
6.2 View.
6.8 Slip and Slide Rock.
7.2 Mayking Knob.
7.6 Stateline Knob.
8.3 Spring.
8.4 Adena Spring.
8.5 Adena shelter.
10.7 Indian Grave campsite, spur to water.
11.2 Indian Grave Gap.
13.7 Rock Fortress.
14.1 Spur trail to Twin Cliffs, spring just ahead.
15.0 Jack Sautter campsite, .2 mile spur to Old Meade Place, water.
15.7 Powerline clearing.
16.7 Pound Gap, end of Highland section of PMT.

40 • CUMBERLAND GAP NATIONAL HISTORICAL PARK

The Backpack: *This ridgetop end-to-end two- or three-night backpack visits a host of highlights at Virginia's westernmost national park. Climb up Lewis Hollow past Skylight Cave to the Ridge Trail, which runs atop Cumberland Mountain, presenting views aplenty while trekking the state line dividing Virginia and Kentucky. See the historic Hensley Settlement, a once-isolated community, now preserved. Beyond there, visit massive Sand Cave and its waterfall, then soak in a commanding panorama from the White Rocks. Designated campsites take the guesswork out of where to camp.*

40 CUMBERLAND GAP NATIONAL HISTORICAL PARK

Distance & configuration: 20.0-mile end-to-end

Difficulty: Moderate

Backpacking time: 12 hours

Outstanding features: Views, preserved mountain community, giant rockhouse

Elevation: 1,410′ low point, 3,400′ high point

Scenery: 5

Solitude: 3

Family friendly: 2

Canine friendly: 2

Fees/permits: Backcountry permit required

Best season: Fall through spring

Maps: Cumberland Gap National Historical Park

For more info: Cumberland Gap National Historical Park, 91 Bartlett Park Road, Middlesboro, KY 40965, 606-248-2817, www.nps.gov/cuga

Finding the trailhead: From the town square in Jonesville, take US 58 west for 20.1 miles to turn right on VA 724, Sand Cave Road, in Ewing. Follow it for 1 mile to dead end at Ewing Civic Park. Leave a shuttle car here. Backtrack to US 58 and continue west on US 58 for 11.9 miles to turn right into the Thomas B. Fugate Wilderness Road area. Follow the access road .5 mile toward Wilderness Road Campground, then veer left to dead end at a picnic area. The Lewis Hollow Connector starts here. **GPS trailhead coordinates:** Ewing Park: N36° 39.167′, W83° 26.160′; Wilderness Road Picnic Area: N36° 36.570′, W83° 38.294′

Cumberland Gap is an excellent backpacking destination, so even if you cannot arrange two cars for a shuttle, consider making a one-night loop or a two- or three-night backtrack. The scenery is first rate and highlights are plentiful. Furthermore, once you are atop the main ridge, elevation changes are not strenuous. Designated campsites help with trip planning. However, a backcountry permit—obtained at the park visitor center near Middlesboro, Kentucky—is required.

The start is the toughest part of the hike. The Lewis Hollow Trail climbs 1,000 feet in the first 1.2 miles! En route, peer into the mouth of Skylight Cave and catch your breath. Once atop Cumberland Mountain, backpackers are rewarded with a view from an outcrop on the Ridge Trail. The Old Dominion and Tennessee stretch to the horizon. The wide, foot-friendly Ridge Trail undulates past Table Rock, a notable trailside geological formation, one among many stony sights.

40 Cumberland Gap National Historical Park

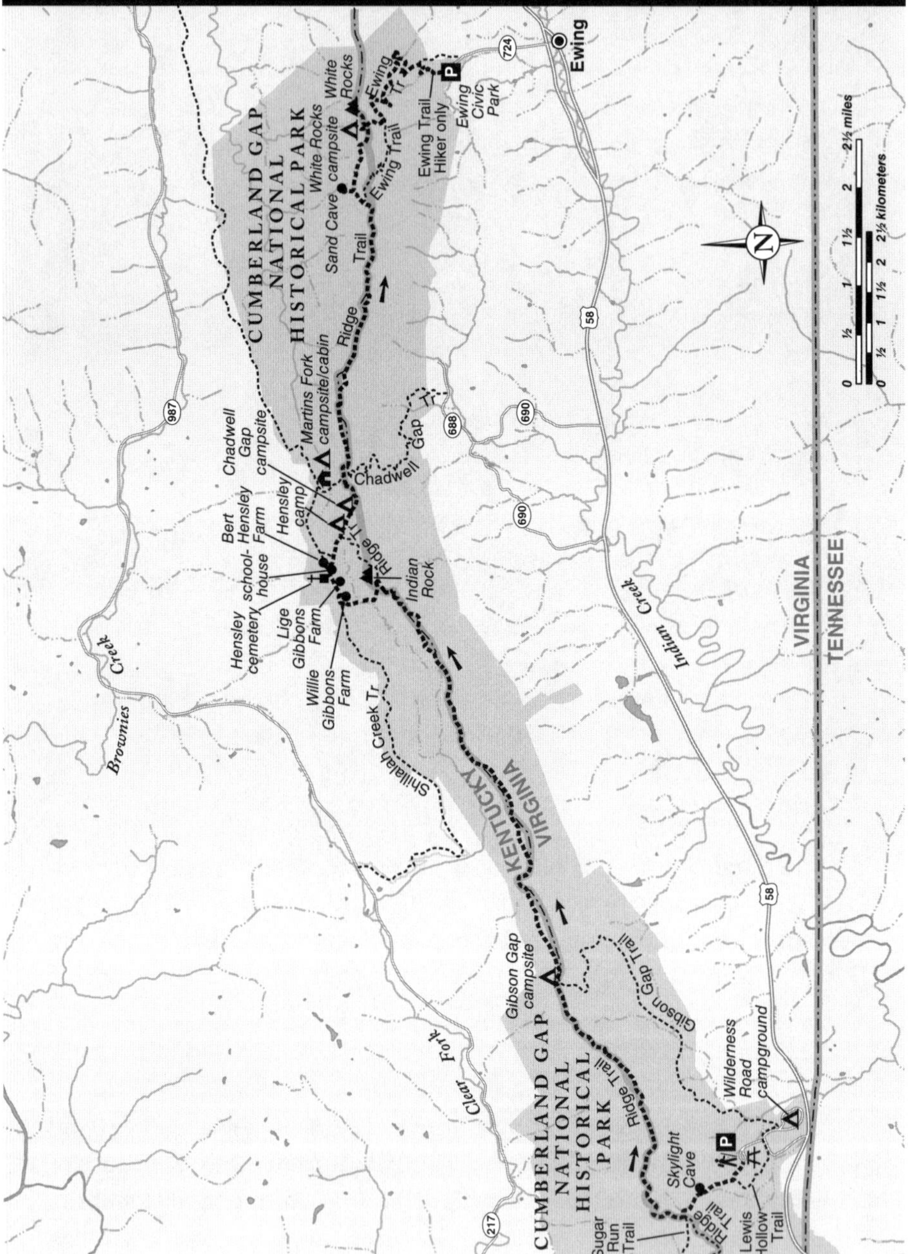

From White Rocks you can see all the way to yon Smoky Mountains.

Reach Gibson Gap backcountry campsite after 4.5 miles. The camp is next to a bluff and has a flat spot with a couple of other, lesser-used spots nearby. Water can be had from a spring leading east down a draw, under rhododendron. From here, the Gibson Gap Trail leads back to the Wilderness Road Trailhead and can be used to make a 9.9-mile, one-night loop backpack.

Your next day can be either 7 miles or 13 miles, depending on whether you want to make it a two- or three-night trip. Either way, backpackers will roll the Ridge Trail to visit Indian Rock, a rock shelter, then reach the Hensley Settlement, a preserved mountaintop community where Sherman Hensley and his descendants existed in isolation for five decades. Today, you can visit two dozen preserved structures, from homes to the schoolhouse to outbuildings, a fascinating trip back in time.

A trio of campsites is available near the Hensley Settlement. I recommend Hensley camp, a level locale mixed with pines. It avails close access to the historical area. Chadwell Gap campsite is too sloped. Martins Fork is in a cool and shady hollow near a cabin that the park rents out for overnight stays. From Hensley camp, water can be had from the upper reaches of Shillalah Creek or a spigot near the Hensley Settlement, operating in warmer times.

Following the Backpacker Gear Curve

I still remember my first backpack. It was a green Academy Broadway external frame bought from a long-defunct outlet store. It had five pockets in which to stuff gear. Neither the shoulder straps nor the hip belt had padding. Twenty bucks of hard-earned money was diverted for that pack.

Was I ever proud—and ready to tackle the woods and trails. Backpacking was new and foreign to me. I had yet to explore mountains, see bears, and fish trout streams of the Appalachian Mountains backcountry.

Now to fill those pack pockets. The first order of business was to get one of those cool survival knives with the built-in bubble compass and a hollow inside complete with fishing line, hooks, and matches. I ordered a discontinued sleeping bag from a catalog, bought a closed-cell foam sleeping pad from Walmart, then purchased some secondhand black leather combat boots at the local thrift store. A borrowed bulky blue tarp provided a musty shelter.

Thus began my journey along the backpacking gear curve. The new, make-do backpacker occupies the first stage of the gear curve. Like me, the make-do backpacker probably borrows half the equipment on his or her back and buys discount stuff for the other half. An oversized cheap tent invariably pops up at the make-do backpackers' camp. They are figuring out that with outdoor gear—like anything else—you get what you pay for. They are heading up the gear curve.

I remember when the soles came off my combat boots while trudging through snow high on Forney Ridge. String stopped the sole from flapping. After returning home, I dropped more than a few bucks on some Vasque boots.

But like anything, the new boots—or the new toy—become old. And the quest for the latest gadget continues, whether you need it or not. And that leads to the downward stage of the gear curve. Failed and forgotten equipment bought over the years joins the dusty junk menagerie lining your garage walls. You realize more stuff isn't needed to execute your outdoor adventure, but more time is. You don't use the old gear anymore because something better works for you, or the old stuff is outdated.

Or the gear may be broken. Inventory your stuff and count how many items you will never use again. Wise backpackers assess their gear needs before each situation before leaving home. Less is more. Bring the good-quality stuff that works for you and nothing else.

Perhaps you can do with less and adapt, looking outward at what you came to experience rather than inward at what you have with you. That is how I discovered many "necessities" really aren't necessary. Why spend hundreds on a gewgaw when you could use that money traveling to your dream destination to actually *do* what you love? Why spend time in the store looking at more gear, or scrolling through websites, when you can be out there on the trail? Time is the most valuable commodity on earth, my friend. And if you are like me, you want to spend as much of it as possible "out there." It really is about the experience, not what gear you use to do it.

And that is when you have completed your trip down the backpacker gear curve.

Beyond here, the Ridge Trail leads east to Sand Cave, a spectacular huge rockhouse with a deep sand base. Adjacent to the cave a stream forms a 20-foot waterfall, then flows on as a white, pebble-bottomed stream. This first-rate scenic sight is challenged only by the White Rocks, where a naked sandstone ledge presents incredible panoramas southwest, northwest, and south, where the topography reveals the ridge and valley country of southwesternmost Virginia and East Tennessee.

Unfortunately, the nearby White Rocks campsite does not match the grandeur of its namesake. The camp consists of a few level spots carved from a slope, with water down the hollow below it. However, the camp will suffice. The Ewing Trail—along with a pair of hiker-only trails—leads you off Cumberland Mountain and the hike's end.

Mileages

0.0 Wilderness Road Picnic Area Trailhead.
0.2 Join Lewis Hollow Trail.
0.6 Mouth of Skylight Cave.
1.1 Right on Ridge Trail.
1.4 Southward vista from outcrop.
3.6 Table Rock to left of trail.
4.5 Gibson Gap backcountry campsite; intersect Gibson Gap Trail.
5.0 Partial view from outcrop.
6.5 Butcher Gap.
8.2 Come within earshot of Shillalah Creek.
9.6 Left toward Indian Rock; continue toward Hensley Settlement.
10.1 Open onto Willie Gibbons Farm; veer right ahead.
10.7 Split right near Ben Hensley Farm, now a ranger house.
10.8 Pass spigot and picnic table, leave Hensley Settlement, reenter woods.
11.1 Meet Ridge Trail again; head left.
11.3 Hensley camp.
11.4 Chadwell Gap campsite spur leads left.
11.8 Spur trail leads left down to Martins Fork backcountry campsite and rental cabin.
12.0 Chadwell Gap Trail leads right.
14.9 Ewing Trail leads right.
15.1 Head left on Sand Cave spur trail; backtrack.
15.6 Rejoin Ridge Trail, eastbound.

16.3 4-way intersection; keep straight to White Rocks.
16.9 Return to 4-way intersection, descend to White Rocks campsite.
17.1 White Rocks campsite.
17.3 Return to 4-way intersection again, head south on hiker-only connector.
17.8 Left on Ewing Trail, descend via switchbacks, crisscrossing streamlets.
19.3 Right on hiker-only link to Ewing Civic Park.
20.0 Reach Ewing Civic Park, completing the backpack.

Index

Note: Bold page numbers refer to maps and photographs.

Johnny Molloy is a writer and adventurer based in Johnson City, Tennessee. His outdoor passion was ignited on a backpacking trip in Great Smoky Mountains National Park while he was attending the University of Tennessee. That first foray unleashed a love of the outdoors that led Johnny to spend over 4,000 nights backpacking, canoe camping, and tent camping over the past three decades.

Friends enjoyed his outdoor adventure stories; one even suggested he write a book. He pursued his friend's idea and soon parlayed his love of the outdoors into an occupation. The results of his efforts are over sixty-five books and guides. His writings include hiking guidebooks, camping guidebooks, paddling guidebooks, comprehensive guidebooks about a specific area, and books about true outdoor adventures throughout the eastern United States.

Though primarily involved with book publications, Johnny writes for varied magazines and websites. He continues writing and traveling extensively throughout the United States, pursuing a variety of outdoor endeavors.

A Christian, Johnny is an active member of the First Presbyterian Church in Johnson City, Tennessee, as well as a Gideon. His non-outdoor interests include reading, American history, and University of Tennessee sports. For the latest on Johnny, please visit www.johnnymolloy.com.